Arthur Ransome
under sail

Published by Sigma Leisure – an imprint of Sigma Press, Stobart House, Pontyclerc, Penybanc Road Ammanford, Carmarthenshire SA18 3HP

Originally published under the title *Nancy Blackett, Under Sail with Arthur Ransome* (Jonathan Cape 1991)

British Library Cataloguing in Publication Data

A CIP record for this book is available from the British Library

ISBN: 978-1-85058-855-9

Typesetting and Design by: Sigma Press, Ammanford, Carms

Cover photographs:
Nancy Blackett sailing past Pin Mill, May 2009 © Roger Wardale
Portrait of Arthur Ransome taken around publication of *Swallows and Amazons*

Printed by: Cromwell Press Group, Trowbridge, Wiltshire

Arthur Ransome
under sail

Roger Wardale

The Penny Whistler – Arthur Ransome on the Norfolk Broads 1938

Foreword

It was in 1996 that the *Nancy Blackett* Appeal was launched, with the simple objective of purchasing Arthur Ransome's old boat and preserving her for posterity.

However the seed of this adventure was sown three years previously, in the carpark of an ancient monument near Newbury, Berkshire. We, myself, my wife and our two daughters, were there for a TARS walk, up the aforementioned monument, Beacon Hill, and down again. We'd joined TARS – the Arthur Ransome Society – a few months earlier, after reading about it in the back of a copy of *Swallows and Amazons* (Red Fox paperback edition) that we'd bought for our elder daughter.

This purchase had rekindled my long-dormant childhood love of Ransome and once we were members of the society we quickly realised it offered exactly the sort of family-friendly outdoors activity we'd been looking for. Even though we wouldn't know anybody, and were not great joiners-in of things, this walk was conveniently close to home and we decided to give it a go.

On arrival, people were milling about, and we had no idea who, if anybody, we should be reporting ourselves to. But there was a tall, craggy man in an Arthur Ransome Club of Japan sweatshirt, who looked as if he might know what was what, so I thought it would do no harm to approach him. He turned out to be Roger Wardale, then chairman of the TARS Southern Region. He swiftly introduced us to a few other people, and we all set off up the hill in a loose gaggle, with people mingling and chatting in a most friendly way, the children soon latching onto other children. At one stage I found myself walking alongside Taqui Altounyan. We talked of nothing very significant, but my sense of connectedness with the whole world of Ransome grew at every step.

All in all, it was a most satisfactory climb, hilltop picnic and descent. At the bottom again, I discovered a little bookstall laid out in the back of an estate car. Among the titles on display was the predecessor to this present volume, then titled *Nancy Blackett, Under Sail with Arthur Ransome*, and written by this same Roger Wardale. It was a hardback, and we as a family were by nature frugal paperback-buyers, but Ted Alexander, who ran the bookstall, had little, if any, difficulty in convincing me it was a worthwhile investment. I bought it, and crashed a regional committee meeting taking place around a nearby picnic table in order to get it signed by the author.

What I can't now remember is whether I already knew, somehow, that *Nancy Blackett* was the original of the *Goblin* in *We Didn't Mean to Go to Sea*, or whether this book, which I began to devour as soon as I got home, told me. I would expect the latter, for I don't think I was well up in Ransome history at that stage, and yet I can only assume that it was an awareness of *Nancy's* significance that gave rise to a – purely transient – frisson of disappointment when I discovered that the book didn't exactly live up to the promise of the title, but wandered off into discussion of other boats. As I say, the twinge of irritation was only momentary, for of course the fact that it covers, comprehensively, all of Ransome's boats is the book's chief value. I gathered later that the decision to 'headline' *Nancy Blackett* in the title was a brainwave of the then publishers, Jonanthan Cape, to capitalise on the then-recent restoration and relaunch of the thus-eponymous boat. And good luck to them, it certainly got me hooked. It also, I'm sure, eased our later task of convincing people of the significance of *Nancy* by providing her with a provenance, and a status as a significant piece of literary heritage.

Nevertheless, I'm glad to see this revised version is sailing under the more honest and accurately descriptive colours of, simply, *Arthur Ransome Under Sail*.

In fact, I'm delighted to see it reissued at all. The original, and its paperback version went out of print most inconveniently not long after the Nancy Blackett Trust had bought *Nancy* and, so to speak, relaunched her into society. Its unavailability has been a serious loss to people, and there are plenty of them, whose interest in Ransome's boats has been awakened by a visit aboard Nancy at the various festivals and events at which she appears.

In fact, Roger' book, under whatever title, has always seemed to me to be a fundamental part of the three-legged stool of Ransome knowledge, doing for his sailing career and his boats what Hugh Brogan's biography does for his life, and Christina Hardyment's Arthur Ransome and Captain Flint's Trunk does for his locations.

Ransome was almost as prolific an owner of boats as he was of houses (in fact more so, since he actually owned his boats, whereas he mostly rented his various residences). Of course there were gaps, if you want to look at it like that, in his life where boats were either not important, or non-existent – Russia for instance, and as far as offshore cruising is concerned the long gap between the sale of *Racundra* in 1925 and the purchase of *Nancy Blackett* 10 years later. But boats, big and small, remained a touchstone throughout his adult life. If he wasn't sailing them, he was as likely as not reading or writing about them (or writing about reading about them, in his various book reviews). He actively assisted with the setting-up or running of two great nautical institutions, the Cruising Association, founded by his friend Herbert Hanson, and the splendid Mariner's Library, established by another friend, Rupert Hart-Davis. And of course, boats put in an appearance in all but one of his twelve *Swallows and Amazons* novels for children.

Some of the boats were based on his own boats, and, conversely, some of his actual boats turned up – all except for *Swallow* under assumed names – as fictional ones. There's a lot of fun to be had sorting out which is what, and this book is the ultimate guide and authority.

Of course, much has happened since the original version was published in 1991. Of the three 'skippers' to whom the book was then dedicated – Michael Rines of *Nancy Blackett*, Greg Palmer of *Peter Duck* and Christopher Barlow of *Lottie Blossom* – none remains so to speak in command. Mike Rines sold *Nancy* soon after the book was published, to another private owner, from whom we subsequently bought her, but he continues to maintain a keen and supportive interest in her welfare. Greg Palmer, rest his soul, died of a heart attack in St Petersburg. He'd sailed there in *Peter Duck*, and she lay there for a while before being brought back to England, where she was bought and restored by Julia Jones, who thus reunited herself with the 'dear old Duck' on which she had spent her childhood when the boat was owned by her parents. Of Christopher Barlow and his *Lottie Blossom*, the second of the two boats of that name owned by the Ransomes, there is no longer any trace. However, the first *Lottie*, subsequently renamed *Ragged Robin III*, is now in the ownership of a dedicated Ransome enthusiast, TARS member (and currently treasurer) Ted Evans. Both she and *Peter Duck* are based at Woodbridge, which is also *Nancy Blackett's* winter home, on the River Deben in Suffolk, one river up from the Orwell, where Pin Mill is to be found. All three regularly take part in the Woodbridge Maritime Heritage Festival every September, organised by, amongst others, Mike Rines and Ted Evans.

Meanwhile, *Coch-y-bonddhu* and *Selina King* have both been rediscovered and restored.

One poignant revision to the new edition is in the introduction. Writing of Mike Rines' 1989 dinner at the Butt and Oyster, Pin Mill, held to celebrate *Nancy Blackett's* restoration, Roger could then refer to 'most of those alive today who knew Ransome personally in his sailing heyday,' being present at the occasion.

Now, 20 years on, he writes, 'Sadly, nearly all who sailed with Ransome have passed away.'

I was privileged to meet and know some of them myself: as well as Taqui Altounyan and her sister 'Ship's baby' Brigit Sanders who became the patron of the Nancy Blackett Trust, they included Josephine Russell, who sailed *Nancy* in her teens, Helen Tew, friend of the Ransomes in their *Lottie Blossom* days, and Pin Mill yachtsman Martin Lewis who as an 11-year-old boy corresponded with him.

The links they represented with Ransome are broken and gone. But it is inevitable that people die. What remains to connect us with Ransome, in addition to his writings, are some of his possessions, the things he knew and touched and the places he lived. Among these artefacts perhaps none fulfil this function more powerfully than the boats he owned, sailed, managed, maintained, enjoyed, looked after and was looked after by. Is it fanciful to believe that in sailing *Nancy Blackett*, or *Coch-y-bonddhu* or any of the others, one might occasionally experience a rekindled flicker of the spirit of Ransome? I don't think so.

The boats live on and, given care, they need never die. As a living link, though, they need to be understood and appreciated. Roger's book represents a vital aspect of that process.

It's not uncommon, in radio interviews and the like, for people to be asked which single book has most influenced their life. The answer is usually either some great work, or a significant book from childhood, not excluding *Swallows and Amazons*. I heard such a programme a few months ago, and – as usual – it prompted me to ponder what would be my answer. I came to the conclusion that it would have to be this book. I, *Nancy Blackett* and all who sail in her and in the Trust, owe it a great deal, and I'm delighted to welcome its return.

Peter Willis
Chairman
Nancy Blackett Trust

Contents

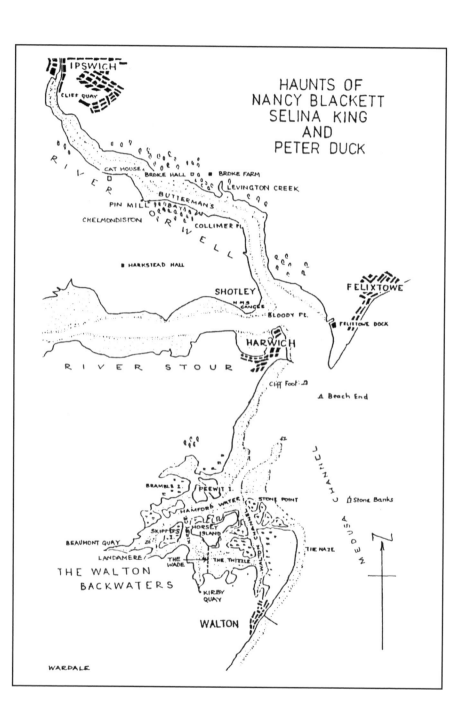

HAUNTS OF
NANCY BLACKETT
SELINA KING
AND
PETER DUCK

IPSWICH

CLIFF QUAY

RIVER

CAT HOUSE
BROKE HALL
BROKE FARM
LEVINGTON CREEK
BUTTERMAN'S
PIN MILL
BAY
CHELMONDISTON
COLLIMER Pt.
ORWELL

B HARKSTEAD HALL

SHOTLEY
HMS
GANGES
BLOODY Pt.

FELIXTOWE

FELIXTOWE DOCK

HARWICH

R I V E R   S T O U R

Cliff Foot
Beach End

CHANNEL

BRAMBLE I.
PEEWIT I.
HAMFORD WATER
STONE POINT
Stone Banks

SKIPPERS
I.
HORSEY
ISLAND

BEAUMONT QUAY
LANDAMERE
THE
WADE
THE THITTLE
THE NAZE

MEDUSA

THE WALTON
BACKWATERS
KIRBY
QUAY

WALTON

N

WARDALE

Introduction

At the beginning of *Racundra's First Cruise* Arthur Ransome declares that 'To build a house is the tired wish of a man content thenceforward with a single anchorage. The desire to build a boat is the desire of youth, unwilling yet to accept the idea of a single resting place.' That was in 1922, when he was nearly forty. More than thirty years later the desire of youth still burned in him when he built for the last time. During the years between he had sailed the beloved *Swallow* on Windermere, learnt the crafts of navigation and seamanship aboard his ketch *Racundra* in the Baltic, taken his cutter *Nancy Blackett* to Holland virtually single-handed, and led the fleet of 'Northern River Pirates' on voyages through the Norfolk Broads. After the war he had a frustrating summer with *Peter Duck* and explored the Solent harbours in *Lottie Blossom*. He was in his seventies when he made his last Channel crossing at the helm.

Ransome's *Autobiography* ends in 1932, despite its first publication some years after his death in 1967. He had completed a draft for several years more in which he had surprisingly little to say of his life afloat, and this passage is briefly summarised by his friend and literary executor Sir Rupert Hart-Davis, in a short postscript to the book. The huge collection of Ransome's papers, now mostly housed in a room specially set aside for them in the University of Leeds, is altogether more forthcoming and speaks volumes of Ransome's passion for messing about in boats.

It is only right to acknowledge that I am not the first to mine this rich vein of material. In his biography of Arthur Ransome, Hugh Brogan traced the early years in great detail, concentrating on his time as a war reporter in Russia, when he was an eye-witness to the 1917 Revolution and became acquainted with many of its leaders, including Lenin and Trotsky. He was also the first to reveal the background to the *Swallows and Amazons* and the extent to which the stories were based on real life and places that Ransome knew intimately. Then, in her jolly and well-informed book *Arthur Ransome and Captain Flint's Trunk*, Christina Hardyment explored the locations and met the people who became Ransome characters. Of course both these books touch on Ransome's own activities afloat, and no one interested in his writings or his extraordinary life should miss them. Yet sailing was not their central theme and after their publication much of Ransome's sailing life remained uncharted.

The extent of this gap was brought home to me when, as the compiler and author of two photographic books about Ransome's favourite spots — in the Lake District and East Anglia — I was invited in June 1989 to a celebration dinner at the *Butt and Oyster*, an old haunt of Ransome's in Pin Mill. Michael Rines had rescued Ransome's favourite yacht, the *Nancy Blackett*, from the elements in Scarborough and was about to relaunch her. Most of those who had known Ransome personally in his sailing heyday were also present for the occasion, and they told me a good deal more than I knew before.

Besides, Ransome kept detailed logs of his commands, and his letters and his various writings on sailing, both published and unpublished, helped to complete the picture. So it was, with permission from Ransome's literary executors and encouragement from my (and his) publisher that I decided to attempt bridging the gap. In *Nancy Blackett* I tried to tell the story of Ransome the seaman and the trusty craft he once sailed. Those who knew Ransome spoke of a large and irascible man, capable of sudden outbursts of fun or of anger. His crews found him a kind and considerate skipper, never

Hugh Brogan, Roger Wardale and Christina Hardyment celebrating *Nancy Blackett's* return at the Butt and Oyster, Pin Mill 1989

short of patience and never raising his voice. He liked explaining things that he loved to young people, and the sea was one of his great loves. All his life he made a point of reading voraciously on maritime topics and took a pride in sailing in a correct manner. He had a proper respect for the sea but was always ready to take a calculated risk if he considered it a seamanlike thing to do. The elaborate logs he kept make mention of the other vessels he met, for he enjoyed the fellowship of the sea and liked to sail in the company of friends.

Gamely Arthur Ransome sailed on into his seventy-first year when his wife Evgenia finally cried, 'Enough ... '

Twenty years have passed since Michael Rines' Celebration Dinner in the *Butt and Oyster*. In that time, nearly all those who sailed with Ransome have passed away. I feel privileged to have known them and to have heard their testimonies.

Last May I joined with other members of The Nancy Blackett Trust when we met at Pin Mill Sailing Club to mark the 20th Anniversary. Over the weekend, *Nancy Blackett* sailed back and forth along the river taking members for a sail and flying the Jolly Roger. Truly the spirit of Arthur Ransome lives on.

I hitched a lift with on one of these trips with Phil Durnsford, who is one of the Trust's accredited Skippers. As we reached down the river with a spanking good breeze, I had a chance to look around the vessel once more. There is nothing of the museum ship about *Nancy*. She is a beautifully maintained sailing cruiser that is ready at any time to sail down Channel or cross the North Sea to Holland. Apart from the necessary safety devices, she is, as nearly as it is possible to make her, just as she was when she was Arthur Ransome's much loved little ship. Looking across to Pin Mill, we agreed that apart from the increased congestion, very little had changed since the Ransomes used to sail *Nancy* through the anchorage distributing flowers to their friends. Ransome would have been delighted to see the Dutch three-masted barquentine *Oosterschelde* off Pin Mill and the barges high but 'not exactly dry' on the mud.

Since 1989, the 'fleet' of yachts and dinghies that were once sailed by Arthur Ransome has been increased by the restoration to sailing condition of his dinghies, *Coch-y-bonddhu* and *Swallow II*, and as his little ships go sailing on, there is the story to tell of their further adventures.

For this revised edition, *Arthur Ransome under Sail*, I have included additional material resulting from further research. In particular, I have been able to make use of Ransome's complete sailing log of

Nancy Blackett and also of the 'Honeymoon' cruise inland in *Racundra* which came to light among Ransome's many papers in The Brotherton Library at the University of Leeds since the first edition.

R. D. W.
March 1991, February 2010

Ukartha in the Baltic

To the children who had partially inspired, and for whom Arthur Ransome's children's classic *Swallows and Amazons* had been written, he was Ukartha — or Uncle Arthur. Their abiding memory was of a big man, tall and tending to be stout, who had beautiful hands which was particularly noticeable when he played his penny whistle, holding it with his long brown fingers. He had an infectious way of laughing and spoke in a cultured tenor voice that was gentle unless he became roused. He had worn a luxuriant, drooping walrus moustache since his youth as a struggling writer in lodgings in Edwardian South London. By the 1920s his head was as bald as that of his alter ego, Captain Flint:

And then, slowly, he came to know that the door of the study was open and that Captain Flint was standing in the doorway, Captain Flint, with a face burnt redder than ever, smiling at him and polishing a bald head with a green silk handkerchief. Captain Flint threw a felt hat on the table, brought a suitcase bright with steamer labels in from the hall, closed the door behind him and laughed.

'Well, Professor,' he said. 'What is it this time? It was astronomy when I found you in the cabin of the old houseboat. What's this? Chemistry?'

'Gold,' said Dick.

'Gold?' said Captain Flint. 'Don't you go and get interested in the wretched stuff. Gold or silver. I've sworn off both of them. Had quite enough of wasting time.

Hullo. What have you got in that test tube?'

While no retired pirate, Ransome liked to maintain a slightly raffish air to the casual formality of his dress as an English country gentleman. Plus-fours and a whole range of quaint hats were habitually worn into old age. By his mid-forties, when the four Altounyan children came into his life and he began the saga that would occupy him for almost twenty years, Ransome had already enjoyed more than his fair share of bizarre adventures. Nevertheless he remained essentially an innocent who often claimed to dislike the company of 'brats', though he always had time for youngsters who shared his enthusiasms — birdwatching, fishing and messing about in boats. Because of his short sight he had little interest in outdoor games, although he enjoyed watching cricket. He was always ready for a game of chess or billiards and his diary makes mention of games of table-tennis, squash and darts on days when he was unable to sail or fish.

Their parents, Dora and Ernest Altounyan, had been friends with Ransome since they were young, when both Arthur, and a few years later, Ernest attached themselves to her grandfather's family circle of artists and writers at Lanehead, a large house overlooking the head of Coniston Water in the Lake District. 'White Grandpa', W. G. Collingwood, (so called because of his mane of white hair) was richly talented. After a brilliant academic career, he settled by the lake where he became a painter, writer, archaeologist and mountaineer. He had found evidence of an early Viking settlement on Peel Island in Coniston, and it was there that he also first met young Arthur in the closing years of the 19th century.

For a time the boy had attended the Old College on the shore of Lake Windermere, and in 1895 experienced a great frost, when the lake was completely frozen over — a phenomenon Ransome was to enjoy again while putting the finishing touches to *Swallows and Amazons* in 1929. Until his dominating father died of tuberculosis in 1897, when Arthur was thirteen, the Ransome family spent long summer holidays at Swainson's Farm in Nibthwaite at the southern end of Coniston. One year they found the Collingwoods picnicking on nearby Peel Island. It was a less warlike encounter than the first meeting between the *Swallows and Amazons* on the renamed *Wild Cat* Island, and led to lifelong friendships. Collingwood and his wife (Ransome's 'aunt') always encouraged the young Arthur with his early attempts to become a writer — 'Not bad for a little town boy,' was Mrs Collingwood's verdict on his nature book *Pond and Stream* — and they never doubted that one day his talent would flourish.

The Collingwood's four children were about Ransome's own age. The three girls were artists and Robin became a philosopher and leading authority on Roman Britain. Although he was five years younger, it was Robin Collingwood who taught Arthur to sail. Living by the water, he had been in and out of boats from an early age, and during one holiday (while he was still at school at Rugby) he took

Arthur out in the dinghy *Swallow*, which they kept in the boathouse on the shore below Lanehead. They had the use of their neighbour's boat *Jamrach* too, and on one occasion Robin and Arthur raced the little boats to the foot of the lake and back — a distance of 11 miles. While sailing *Jamrach* some time afterwards, Ransome was called upon to demonstrate his cool head and ability to think clearly in a crisis.

Late in October, while Robin was away at university, he took *Jamrach* from her moorings at the head of the lake and beat down towards Peel Island against a light southerly wind. Suddenly the wind

Swallow and *Jamrach* (from a photograph)

dropped. A moment or so later, *Jamrach* was struck by a squall, and in the gybe which followed, the gaff-jaws were smashed and the boat was thrown on her beam ends. Ransome quickly righted her, but a strong wind was now blowing from the north and driving the wreck towards the rocks at the northern end of Peel Island. He described the scene in his *Autobiography*:

Luckily I was wearing boots with stout leather laces. I took them off under water and with the laces roughly fettled up the gaff-jaws until I could hoist a bit of sail, enough to get her moving. She cleared those jagged rocks that would certainly have holed her had we touched by about two yards, and drifted while I baled and got things more or less to rights. It was a slow job, and though the wind dropped after that freak of a squall it still held from the north, and it was black night before I could beat back to the head of the lake and put *Jamrach* on her mooring, where little *Toob*, the dinghy, was awaiting us half-full of water.

Another visitor at Lanehead was Robin Collingwood's Rugby friend, Ernest Altounyan. Ernest was the son of an Irish mother and an Armenian surgeon who ran the hospital at Aleppo in Syria, but declared that, above all, he was a poet. He was an enthusiastic sailor and always claimed that it was he who introduced Ransome to the joys of sailing while tacking down the rivers of Norfolk.

They each fell in love with Collingwood girls: Arthur proposed to Barbara, the second daughter, who eventually turned him down; Dora, the eldest, after shilly-shallying for some time also refused Arthur but they remained close friends for the rest of their lives. Dora took an equally long time to make up her mind to accept Ernest. Soon after their marriage, she gave up her attempt to gain recognition as an artist and moved to the Altounyan family home in Aleppo when Ernest qualified as a surgeon at the end of the First World War. Taqui, her eldest child, was then two, Susie only a few months old, and her mother was expecting Titty. Roger was born in 1922 and Brigit in

Dora Collingwood ('Beetle' from Stalky & Co) (Tony Colwell Collection)

Arthur Ransome ('Toad' from *The Wind in the Willows*)

1925. Having settled in Syria, the family returned every few years to visit the grandparents at Lanehead.

Meanwhile, Arthur had taken to a Bohemian life in London, working for a publisher by day and pursuing his own endeavours as a writer by night. His first real success was with a biography of Oscar Wilde, though the book landed him in court, accused of libelling Lord Alfred Douglas. Judgment went in Ransome's favour, but the misery the case brought him was shortlived compared with the suffering caused by his marriage to the tempestuous Ivy Walker. To escape he fled to Russia, where he lived in St Petersburg and translated Russian fairy tales, teaching himself the language with children's primers. The war brought a new dimension to his life. He reported the military disasters for the *Daily News* and watched the civil unrest that led to the Revolution in 1917. The gentle art of dinghy sailing must have seemed very far away.

Ransome became acquainted with the leading revolutionaries, claimed to have beaten Lenin at chess, and met his second wife

Evgenia Petrovna while she was handing out press releases in Trotsky's office. Before they could set up home in the neutral Baltic

State of Esthonia, Ransome made two perilous crossings of the opposing White Russian and Red Army lines in broad daylight in order to rescue Evgenia from beleaguered Moscow, twice cannily avoiding summary execution with clever excuses — stories he tells with great relish and a little embroidery in his *Autobiography.*

In *The Life of Arthur Ransome*, Hugh Brogan gives a brilliant and detailed account of Ransome's reporting from Russia, adding much from his papers and elsewhere that Ransome himself chose to leave out of his highly selective *Autobiography.* Always

Evgenia (Brotherton Collection))

uncommitted (some might even say naive) politically, Ransome nevertheless impressed C. P. Scott, who was editing the *Manchester Guardian*, with a little book called *Six Weeks in Russia* in which he cogently set out the reasons for his view that the Russians should be left to sort out their own troubled affairs without intervention from the West. Scott immediately retained him to write dispatches and more reflective pieces for the *Guardian*.

So when, in 1919, Ransome set up home with Evgenia in a house he found in a forest near the Esthonian capital, Reval, he continued to make occasional forays into revolutionary Russia, though he yearned for a more peaceful life near the water after seven years of turmoil. Another ten were yet to pass before he could bring together his love of sailing and fishing and his storytelling genius in *Swallows and Amazons*. During those apprenticeship years he wrote one sailing classic which is all too often forgotten today, though it remains in print as I write. The book is called *Racundra's First Cruise*, and before getting down to the untold tales which Ransome's diaries reveal of his later years afloat, I should like to spend a little time introducing it. Besides, here lies the origin of much that Nancy and John, Titty and Roger, Captain Flint and the rest were to transform into high adventure in *Swallowdale, Peter Duck* and *Winter Holiday.*

As C. Northcote Parkinson wrote: 'The world would be a poorer place indeed had he never sailed, had he never written.' To be sure, *Racundra* was not Ransome's first larger craft but she was the first, surely, in which his sailing was successful. One useful aspect of his writing, already apparent in *Racundra's First Cruise*, is the care with which he explains each point of seamanship. More admirable still is the hint of philosophy with which he explains what he did.'

One can always find a good enough reason for doing anything that one has made up one's mind to do. In this case I had a perfect one, quite apart from the fact that we did not like staying where we were, and that the jam had been so good that we had eaten all the bread and could get no more till we should come to Hapsal. There was a reason pro and a reason contra — everything, in fact, that the human mind requires when it is putting up a pretence of being logical.

For a long time there was no 'bread' for Ransome in Reval and when at last he found some it was decidedly stale and unpalatable. What Ransome wanted was a ship's lifeboat like that of E. F. Knight, one of his early mentors. Knight had picked up an old ship's lifeboat in the 1880s for a modest sum and set off on a leisurely cruise across the North Sea to Copenhagen. When his account of that voyage, *The Falcon on the Baltic*, was republished years later, Ransome wrote an introduction to the book in which he observed that 'grown up people (if those who love sailing ever grow up, which I doubt) are like children in taking particular pleasure in stories that tell of adventures that might happen, with luck, to themselves.' It was of course this very notion that in due course would bring popularity to the *Swallows* books.

Although the steamer captains who called at Reval promised to bring a lifeboat out from England, they always forgot. Having spent more than half their first summer on the Baltic coast scouring the waterfront for a boat, Ransome eventually spotted a longshoreman one day putting green paint on a narrow dinghy he had for sale. Assured by a seaman acquaintance that the boat would do for pottering about the bay, he parted with the asking price of less than £10. With no intention of remaining in Reval Bay, Ransome bought himself a pocket prismatic compass and returned home to tell

Evgenia he would collect the boat next day and sail it the 40 miles round to Lahepe Bay, just beyond the forest where they lived. Although she knew nothing of boats, Evgenia had no intention of being left behind. That meant entering her on the boat's passport as a seaman, and in the flat calm as they moved off from the pier she backwatered instead of pulling on her oar, causing the 'scoundrel' who had sold them the boat to make even more ribald remarks about her ability to row than he had already thrown at Ransome's inadequate seamanship.

The boat was rigged something like the Collingwoods' boats *Swallow* and *Jamrach*. The hull was very old and leaked, while a load of round boulders performed as ballast.

They set off with all the innocent optimism of one of Ransome's exemplars, Erling Tambs, for whose book *The Cruise of the Teddy* he also wrote an introduction:

These incredibly happy-go-lucky adventurers set sail without instruments. Well they would hardly need a sextant — (they obtained one later) until they began their ocean crossing. But they were not without a sextant only. They had no barometer. They had no light list to help them. Their charts were out of date ... They voyage as if there have been no voyagers before them. They have no prejudices at all. They do not know the meaning of the proverb, 'Second thoughts are best', because they have no second thoughts. They foresee no evil. A trouble once passed disturbs them as little as if it had never been.

Ransome started his log on July 3rd 1920 with no less expectation: 'I hoisted the sails. There came a breath of wind and slowly, slowly, — so slowly that there and then we christened her *Slug*, she moved out into the middle of the bay and we were looking at the Rock of Reval from the sea as I had so often promised that we would.'

It was a very hot day, and when the wind died again Ransome jumped overboard to get cool and failed to notice the boat drift out on a rippling breeze towards Finland. With Evgenia screaming to him to come back, he swam after her but found he was unable to climb aboard. At last, with the wind rising, he scrambled up by way of the short bowsprit. Although he tried again and again to repeat that feat he was unable to gather the strength he had found when he feared he would be left behind or hanging in the sea.

With undiminished zeal Ransome records in his log the adventure of their second day out. In very light winds they were pleased to have charted the eight and a half miles to Nargon Island where they landed and laid low, being unsure of their rights. During the war landing there had been prohibited.

Looking towards Reval, we saw a heavy black sky coining up from the east, and heard thunder. Presently the wind dropped to nothing. Then rose again suddenly from the east, and we decided to lose no time, but to run for Surop, and try to get across before the worst of the storm should reach us, as we were on a beach exposed to the east, and could see nothing but rocky coast to the west. We got aboard at 4.30, and took a course south-west for the Surop lighthouse, thinking to shelter from the storm on the western side of Cape Ninamaa. But the storm was upon us before we were two miles on this slant of six. At least not the storm but the wind. We had only a drop or two of rain, though the whole Esthonian coast east of Surop disappeared altogether, in a dark cloud threaded by lightning. The sea turned black and then white in a moment, and the wind fairly lifted our little boat along, so that we were very grateful for the good stone ballast, which our scoundrel friend had stowed in her for the voyage. She stood it beautifully. And we were sorry for a much larger boat, beating up for Reval clear in the storm, which bowed her nearly flat to the water. The wind dropped as suddenly as it rose. The storm blotted out Nargon behind us, and passed, and we sailed slowly by Surop lighthouse, recognising it from our chart, as a white round tower surrounded by trees, at about seven o'clock.
From Cape Ninamaa, we took a course west-southwest, hoping to pick up the Packerort lighthouse about thirteen miles away. But the wind fell almost to nothing. It grew dark. At midnight, sailing or rather drifting, only for a second or two at a time having any momentum on the boat, we learnt where we were, when the Packerort lighthouse glittered out, and finding ourselves on a direct line between it and the Surop, we knew that we were not out of our course. To get home, we had only to round Cape Lohusaar into Lahepe Bay. But once before, fishing for sea-devils, I had been to the mouth of that bay, and knew that isolated rocks run out from Cape Lohusaar a considerable way into the sea. If there had been much wind, we should have run on close to the Packerort, and then turned back on a south-east slant into the bay, which would have been safe enough. As it was there was not enough wind even to give one control over the boat, so there was nothing to do but to wait till dawn.

Two days later Ransome wrote to Barbara Collingwood urgently requesting her to pass on to her brother all manner of questions about sailing.

The rig of the boat is not quite the same as *Swallow* or *Jamrach's*. The Gaff? (the stick at the top of the mainsail) projected [sic] in front of the mast. The boom is as per *Swallow*. There is also a triangular foresail, ?jib, called hereabouts the cleaver.

That is something like. She is I think 18 feet long. She was built about a hundred years ago, but she practicially does not leak at all.

All her rigging is rotten. Ditto her sails, which are made from something suspiciously like old sheets. We spent the day in repairs. In the course of the repairs arose about five hundred technical questions for Robin or Ernest, and neither of these Nestors are on hand.

After all the excitement, Evgenia had lost none of her enthusiasm. She patched the sail with an old tablecloth and made a burgee. Ransome replaced some of the rotten rigging, but he was already thinking of getting something better. He had already discovered the disadvantage of open boats for cruising, and, besides, Lahepe Bay turned out to be an unsuitable place to keep *Slug*. They could reach her only by swimming and had to wade ashore carrying their belongings on their heads. The boat sank at her moorings on two occasions and her mainsail was stolen.

Ransome's next command was a bit of a joke too. He found a 16-footer with a tiny cabin in Reval harbour. She was around 6 feet in beam and drew 5 feet, thanks to an addition to her keel. They felt that she would do to take them to Baltic Port where they planned to stay for the summer. Ransome spent the £25 he had made from an

American newspaper article to buy her and approached a firm of undertakers for a box-shaped dinghy in which to get ashore from their deep-keeled ship. So unstable was this odd tender that Ransome used to say there was danger of capsize if he so much as moved his pipe from one side of his mouth to the other.

The bunks were horribly narrow, but they fitted new mattresses so that they could, if necessary, sleep aboard in greater comfort than on the *Slug's* boulders. Evgenia made some orange curtains for the cabin portholes and they fitted her out with a primus and a scattering of kitchenware.

As soon as they started sailing the new boat, which they named *Kittiwake*, they began to lose confidence in her. She was in danger of turning over even with two reefs down. They added some iron ballast, but this did little to keep her on an even keel.

On May 11th 1921 they left for Baltic Port, spending the night aboard while at anchor off Reval Yacht Club. They were woken at 6 a.m. by a couple of drunken men in a dinghy demanding vodka and wanting to sail with them to Baltic Port. Ransome went below to dress, and when he came up again the two men had vanished.

At 9 am they were drifting outside the harbour, and by 11 pm a few puffs from the south-west had got them as far as Surop. By the time it grew light at 3 am they were more than halfway between Surop and Lohusaar. Ahead Packerort was almost invisible. A swell began to make life uncomfortable, and this, together with a barometer fall of one-tenth, made Ransome think the wind would begin to pick up shortly. Around 8 am it rose strongly just as it was time to turn south, bringing increasing sea on to *Kittiwake's* quarter. The dinghy was hurled about by the waves and almost flung itself up on the counter, where it would have struck Ransome on the back like a battering ram. He shortened the painter so that it had less distance

Kittiwake (Tony Colwell Collection)

in which to build up momentum to go crashing into them, and by 9 am they had arrived at the narrow entrance to the harbour. They turned into the wind, lowered sails and made fast inside to the British steamer *Cato*, which filled half the harbour and whose skipper Ransome knew.

After going ashore to see about booking rooms at the little hotel run by the harbour master, who greeted them with cups of steaming coffee, Ransome fell asleep with his head on the table, his drink left untouched. He had been twenty-five hours at the tiller.

It was the start of a happy, lazy summer. The *Kittiwake* made a number of day excursions leaving those narrow bunks unused. They visited the nearby Roogö islands where they were surprised to find that the inhabitants greeted them in Swedish. Ransome's ability to communicate in Swedish was very limited, but he did manage to buy some eggs for their dinner from a cottager.

When the *Cato* had gone the little harbour was occupied mainly by small schooners. Nobody hurried in Baltic Port and Ransome became part of a way of life that had hardly changed for a hundred years. He made friends with the harbour master and his wife, the lighthouse keeper and skippers of the little fishing boats. It never really gets dark in Baltic Port in summer, and their favourite time of day was the late evening, when they would sit on *Kittiwake's* cabin roof listening to the accordion being played on the schooner across the water.

In mid-August the Ransomes switched their headquarters to Latvia, leaving *Kittiwake* behind. They rented rooms in the village of Kaiserwald on the shore of the Stint See Lake at Riga. Ransome soon arranged for a Lettish boatbuilder to construct a small boat so that he might fish. The little boat proved so successful that Ransome decided to see if he would build the 'dream-ship' which Otto Eggers had designed for him while they had been in Reval. Eggers, being of German origin, had lost his own boatyard in the First World War, and was unable to build it himself. In *Racundra's First Cruise* Ransome calls him 'the best designer in the Baltic, whose racing boats carried away prize after prize in the old days before the war, whose little cruisers put to sea when steamers stayed in port.' Having visited Reval and discussed the matter with Eggers, Ransome returned to Riga and the contract was signed at the end of 1921.

Racundra was built in a shed on an island near the mouth of the Dvina River. Throughout the winter Ransome made numerous journeys across the ice to watch her progress. They joined the friendly and unpretentious Riga Yacht Club which, being frequented by sailors, ice-yachtsmen and skaters, was busy all year round.

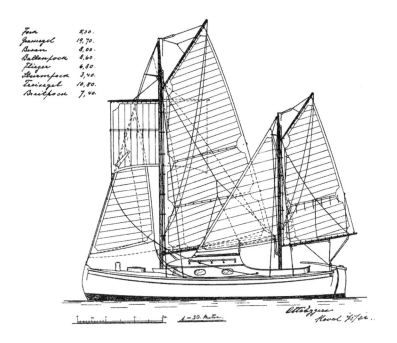

Racundra (by Eggers)

Delay followed delay. Meanwhile, Ransome had joined the Cruising Association and quickly found himself the Honorary Local Representative for Riga. For the next eighteen months he diligently sent bulletins from Riga and Reval. In April 1922 he wrote of conditions in Riga.

There were a few days thaw some weeks ago and the ice below the Dvina bridges was broken up, so that it became possible to cross the river in a ferry steamer instead of sitting in a sledge propelled by an active fellow on skates. The steamers are still running just by the town, but there is a solid block of ice at the mouth of the river, and the ice has packed above it almost to the bridges. Navigation is not expected to open for another fortnight. Winter fishing, through holes in the ice, is still going on.

The builders promised that *Racundra* would be ready in April and then on May 1st, May 15th, May 20th, and so on throughout the

summer. Finally the empty shell was launched on July 28th.
Completion was promised by August 3rd. She was not ready, and
two days later Ransome took the vessel away. The sails were setting
badly, there were no cleats and the centreboard had jammed
halfway. Somehow, under sail and power, Ransome moved
Racundra to the yacht club slip and worked on her for the next
fortnight.

The two-masted ketch was a fine example of the Scandinavian
double-ender. She was 29 feet 7 inches long with a tremendous beam
of 11 feet 4 inches. The width was balanced by her shallow draught
— 3 feet 6 inches — which was increased by 4 feet with the
centreboard lowered. She had no internal ballast but an iron keel
weighing 3 tons which was so broad that *Racundra* could sit upright
when out of the water without legs.

Ransome had given Eggers three requirements for his dream-ship.
She should be sufficiently roomy to make a comfortable home for three.
She should be capable of remaining at sea when other little boats were
running for shelter, and of being sailed single-handed if required.

Eggers designed a hull that was very strong, particularly along the
centre line. A mixture of steamed and sawn timbers measuring 2
inches by 1½ inches were spaced at 9-inch intervals, with certain of
the timbers being strengthened by iron frames. The planking itself

Racundra launched

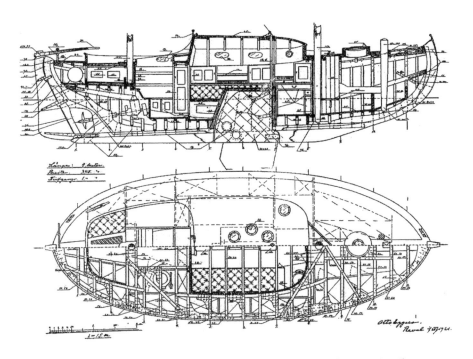

Otto Eggers' Drawings for *Racundra* showing her massive construction

was more than an inch in thickness. The result was a hull that was capable of ocean voyaging, and Ransome hoped her first passage would be to England.

Racundra was ketch-rigged to make for ease of sail-handling, yet she carried only 430 square feet of canvas. She had a staysail, mainsail, storm staysail, balloon staysail, mizzen staysail, trysail and a small squaresail which they found to be too small and never used. The mainsheet, mizzen sheet, staysail sheets and backstays were all cleated within easy reach of the helmsman. The cabin trunk was taken out beyond the steering well and mizzen mast. This allowed room for a mattress on which to lie full length beside the steering well. The well itself was self-draining and the companion could be dismantled to reveal the engine, which otherwise remained completely hidden. The engine was a 'Skandia', a Swedish hot-bulb paraffin-burning monster rated at 5 horsepower. It was only intended for use in harbour, but on their final cruise Ransome managed to reach Riga with it, after being becalmed 60 miles away.

The cabin was like a small room, almost ten feet square with full six feet headroom. The two bunks, wider than usual, left plenty of room for a 4 foot by 3 foot folding table supported by the centreboard case. Beneath, behind and above the bunks were deep cupboards. In fact there were cupboards everywhere. There was even a cupboard specially designed for Ransome's typewriter, beside the 3-foot-square writing table. The galley had space for three Primus stoves, and after the first season a Clyde cooker was fitted. On the opposite side of the companion was the WC. Ransome had a three-legged stool made for use at the writing table and this, like everything else in the cabin, stowed neatly away.

Beside the main mast was a tall cupboard for oilskins and further forward a door led into the fo'c'sle. Inside was a single bunk amd more big cupboards for stores.

Carpenters worked in the cabin during the day, and each night Ransome slept aboard, surrounded by tools and woodshavings. The centreboard had to be replaced and the rigging fashioned with whatever was available in Riga and the ship relaunched. Finally, on August 19th, Ransome discussed the carpenters and cleared up their mess, Racundra was as ready for the sea as they could make her. If they left starting any later, there would be no sailing at all that year.

Ransome's first wife had still not agreed to a divorce. This made a

return to England out of the question, and so when they left Riga on August 20th they headed instead through the islands to Reval and across to Helsingfors. For reasons of delicacy in *Racundra's First Cruise* Evgenia is referred to as the Cook:

She can take her trick at the tiller if need be, but that, for her, is holiday. All the hard work was hers. She cooked a meal. It was eaten. She washed up and, just as the dry dishes reached the rack, one or other of that hungry company would inquire whether or no the time for the next meal was drawing near. She cooked another meal. As its last remains

Evgenia (Tony Colwell Collection)

Carl Sehmel with some of the craft in his charge on the Stint See

were cleared away, as sure as fate she would catch the eye of one or other of us looking hungrily at the clock.

Whenever he went to sea with *Racundra*, Ransome had the good fortune to be able to call upon the services of Captain Sehmel, whom he found looking after the dinghies and small craft on the Stint See Lake. Sehmel was a wizened old man with a wispy grizzled beard who looked deceptively fragile. He had spent a long and varied career in sail and can be recognised easily as the dignified, down-to-earth seaman Peter Duck. Like Peter Duck, he had sailed the *Thermopylae* when she raced home with wool from Australia, and like *Peter Duck* he asked Ransome if he could ship aboard and go to sea once more before it was too late. Captain Sehmel can be seen as one of the most important influences in Ransome's life. He shaped Ransome's view of small boat cruising, just as W. G. Collingwood had encouraged Ransome's literary ambition. Ransome had taught himself navigation out of books, but he had never handled anything larger than the ill-fated *Slug*.

With Sehmel as crew, they left the Stint See and tacked through the reedy channel which linked it with the Red Dvina River. Here they fed the Customs officers on bread, butter, ham and vodka and without any further formalities were cleared for foreign parts. *Racundra* beat down the river and brought up in the Winter Harbour where Sehmel had to work on the rigging, and Evgenia, having seen how much lunch they had consumed, went ashore for more provisions. The following morning brought a good westerly wind and *Racundra* joined several coasting schooners which were leaving the harbour. The wind lasted just long enough for them to clear the moles and then dropped away entirely, leaving them wallowing in a swell which made *Racundra* roll so badly that all three of them were hard put not to be seasick. Even Ransome's rendering of 'Spanish Ladies' on his penny whistle raised only a few puffs to help them on their way.

Ransome had the little ship to himself when the others turned in at ten o'clock. Throughout the months of *Racundra*'s building he had been dreaming of just such a night. He managed a sail change without waking the others by lashing the tiller while he went forward, and then when the wind increased and blew out the light in the binnacle, he steered by the Pole Star.

At 7.30 am the island of Runö was in sight and they steered for the old wooden pier that was used for the annual visit of the steamer from the mainland. Ransome called Runö the most romantic island in northern Europe. Situated 50 miles from Latvia and almost as many from Esthonia, it had been untouched by the progress of the twentieth century. The island was divided into small farms which supported the population of 270. Men of Runö were seal hunters and each seal caught was added to the community store so that everybody benefited equally. The landing place was deserted, so they sounded the foghorn and rowed ashore. It was like landing on a desert island, just as the Swallows were to do in *Peter Duck*:

Peter Duck and the two mates came rowing in just as *Swallow's* nose touched the shore.

'Go on, Bill,' said Titty, as she felt the scrunch of the keel on the sand. 'It's really desert. You're the first to put your foot on it.'

Bill splashed overboard with the painter and pulled *Swallow* a foot or two up the beach.

'What did you say this bay was to be called, sir?' he asked with a grin. 'Bill's Landing,' said Captain Flint.

'Pleased and proud to welcome you,' said Bill.

The forest reached down to the beach and through the tall pines came the lighthouse keeper who had heard the foghorn and hurried to welcome them as everyone else was on the other side of the island, busy with the harvest. The lighthouse keeper warned them that the wind would soon be changing and advised them not to remain at anchor once it did. They stayed on the island just long enough to visit the lighthouse and returned to the ship.

A good south-west wind drove them 40 miles to Paternoster at the eastern end of the island of Qesel. By now they had discovered that the compass could not be relied upon, and it was with some relief that Ransome sighted the Paternoster light just where he thought it should be.

Racundra logged 6 knots as they drove through the Moon Sound. The sun shone, the wind blew stronger and stronger and suddenly there was a crack overhead and the gaff-jaws broke. Eggers had planned an iron saddle for the main gaff-jaws, but the builder, in order to save money, had made wooden ones which split. The jaws had been jammed in place against the mast by a halyard and seemed likely to stay there as long as they held the same course. By this time they were off the island of Worms and Ransome decided to try for Roogowik or Baltic Port that they could reach while it was still daylight.

They turned south for Roogowik and Sehmel brought the mainsail down, but it was soon evident that under staysail and mizzen alone they could not beat up the deep bay to Roogowik. Here Sehmel and Ransome had their only quarrel. Sehmel wanted to go as close to the harbour mouth as possible, but Ransome, who knew the coast had many outlying rocks, decided to run for open sea. The wind had blown out the sidelights and binnacle light, yet Ransome was happy alone at the tiller. In *Racundra's First Cruise* he wrote:

On the face of it, misery. Yet there was no misery about it. While in that narrow bay I had been much afraid, but here, in the open sea, things were better. Besides, we were doing the thing which I had myself urged as the right thing to do. It was my own thing, this careering business out here in the dark, and I had the joy of possession. I was still afraid, of course, but I knew where I was, and knew what I had to avoid. I had to prevent *Racundra* from being blown too far out to sea, to prevent her from working sideways to Nargon island, and to make headway if possible towards the shallow bay on this side of Surop, without going on the rocks off the near point of it and without getting into the bay until it was light enough to see what we were about.

Fifteen years later, in another little ship on a different sea, John Walker felt much the same: —

If anybody could have seen his face in the faint glimmer from the compass window, he would have seen that there was a grin on it. John was alone in the dark with his ship, and everybody else was asleep. He, for that night, was the Master of the *Goblin*, and even the lurches of the cockpit beneath him as the *Goblin* rushed through the dark filled him with a serious kind of joy. He and the *Goblin* together. On and on. On and on.

Racundra stood up wonderfully well to the buffeting and Ransome, not usually given to bursting into song, began to shout out his favourite songs and sea shanties. Evgenia responded magnificently and produced hot coffee and sandwiches during the night and porridge in the morning. When it was light enough to see, Sehmel replaced the broken jaws with stout rope. With the mainsail now playing its full part, they had an exhilarating and wet sail through the storm until they came to Reval bay and saw, through the rain, the spires of Reval town. They tied up alongside the yacht club mole and made all tidy on deck while Evgenia prepared a celebration supper.

Racundra remained in Reval for five days while Eggers examined her to see what sort of mess the Riga builders had made of his dreamship. The gaff-jaws were replaced and Eggers agreed to make a new horse and some gratings for the seats in the steering well. Battens were put in the sails, but they were unable to find blocks the right size, so they decided to carry on with the makeshift ones until they could find replacements in Helsingfors. Evgenia remained in Reval while a friend, on his way to attend a ball in celebration of the visit of the British fleet, took passage aboard *Racundra*. Their friend was in such a tearing hurry to be off that he towed *Racundra* out of the harbour with the dinghy. Then, exhausted by his exertions, took to his bunk where he remained until within sight of Helsingfors. They arrived off the Aransgrund light-vessel at midnight, when Ransome decided to take a pilot rather than try to enter a strange harbour in the dark. After some frantic signalling, the pilot dressed and came aboard and explained that they had sighted *Racundra* just before nightfall, and had taken her for a smuggler. It was the last boat they expected to call for a pilot.

With the pilot at the helm, Ransome thought it safe to lie on his bunk for a minute or two. He woke three hours later to the sound of the anchor going down, having been at the tiller for twenty-eight hours of the preceding thirty-two. *Racundra* was moored by the Nylands Yacht Club, south of the bustling main harbour, where Sehmel went ashore for the only time during the cruise, and he and Ransome bought stores and fittings for Racundra. While they were there, Ransome arranged for a compass adjuster to go aboard and raw up a table of deviations after 'swinging the ship'. They left at 1.15 pm and beat out against a strong south-east md. It was a bright, cold day which pleased Sehmel who did not like sailing blind in fog. The night was cold and clear, and Ransome and Sehmel took turns in steering. It was a long, hard beat to Reval, but at dawn they could see the masts of the schooners anchored in the roadstead ahead. They anchored off the yacht club, warmed themselves with hot rum and water, and slept.

During their twenty-four hours in Reval, Eggers fitted the new horse and gratings and Evgenia came aboard for the return to Riga. They left at 6.20 am with a light south-east wind, but it soon died completely. Evgenia demanded that they start the engine. Neither Ransome nor Sehmel were familiar with the ways of engines and they failed. Evgenia then asked them to throw it overboard and was not in the least placated when they explained that it was valuable ballast. They crept on to Baltic Port, arriving at 1.30 in the morning.

The following night was spent at Spithamn, rather than risk the unlit Worms/Nukke Channel at night. Ransome by now felt sufficiently confident as a navigator to try in daylight the direct passage through the Channel, though his Baltic Pilot warned those without local knowledge to avoid it. Local vessels never attempted the narrow, winding channel against the wind, but Ransome had set his heart on going ahead as planned, in spite of the strong southerly wind, the following day. He knew that as the wind increased so would the current, but after a careful look through binoculars he saw it was not yet very strong.

They set off again with Sehmel at the tiller and Ransome forward to keep a look-out for shallows. The wind increased in strength, and so it was in the conditions which suited her best that *Racundra* made short tacks backwards and forwards in an exhilarating race against wind and current. Apart from one moment when the centreboard touched, the whole remarkable passage went without incident. Finally they rounded up by Hapsal Pier and dried out. 'A gorgeous day,' Ransome wrote in the log.

The rest of the voyage was, to say the least, turbulent, though their spirits remained high. As ever, the Cook remained busy. 'We saw her throughout the day in a cloud of cooking,' Ransome wrote, 'and the steersman at night, looking down the companion, saw always busy hands cleaning obstinate aluminium, and who rested on his bunk heard, as he turned in comfortable sleep, the clink of crockery and the splash of washing up. The Primuses roared continually, like the blast furnaces of northern England. And we, relentless and without shame, called continually for food.'

The master and owner of *Racundra* (from a photograph)

After crossing to the island of Dago, where they sheltered for five days from the strong southerly winds, *Racundra* took advantage of a light westerly until it backed south again and strengthened, forcing them into a sheltered anchorage on the island of Moon. The motion in the gale that blew all night made cooking impossible. Cold bacon, tinned herring and beer must have seemed cheerless fare after the Cook's pampering. They made a dash for the new harbour at Werder, in a brief respite in the equinoctial gale, and when they ran out of food and tobacco the lonely lighthouse keeper came to their rescue with milk, butter, potatoes and home-grown tobacco leaves.

On September 25th the barometer was steady for the first time in a fortnight and the wind had veered to north-west. It was enough to encourage Ransome to have a try for Riga. As the day progressed it became clear they were moving much too fast and would arrive in the Dvina River in darkness, where currents would be waiting to sweep *Racundra* on to the shoals. They reefed and under almost bare poles raced in, with Ransome and Sehmel taking turns to steer. The dawn showed Ransome a furious line of breakers smashing against the moles and shore. They crossed the bar almost without realising it and came to the mouth of the river where Customs officers wrapped up a tired Ransome in red tape. Eventually they allowed *Racundra* to proceed with Customs men aboard until she was finally cleared as she entered the Stint See.

It was the end of leisurely pursuits for a time. *Racundra* was laid up and left in the safe keeping of Captain Sehmel. The *Manchester Guardian* sent Ransome on two missions to Moscow in four months, during the second of which Lenin died and he reported the funeral for the paper. While he was away the Ransome home burnt down. Fortunately Evgenia managed to escape, but they lost almost

The Ancient Mariner

everything they had. There was a more promising outcome to his visit in December to London, where he met his first wife Ivy who finally agreed to a divorce. There was another report to the Cruising Association the following spring, based on *Racundra's* wanderings.

Sailing Directions? The Baltic Pilot (Parts I and II) while pessimistic in the extreme is indispensable for information about the larger ports. It has, however, a horrid habit of remarking about all the more interesting channels and harbours for small draught vessels: 'As this should not be attempted without local knowledge, no directions are given.'

Charts? English and German Admiralty charts are best in a general way, though neither have been able to keep pace with the changes made by the war. These waters used to be Russian, and none of the small countries, Finland, Esthonia or Latvia, can afford the cost of a hydrographic department on the old scale. The Finns, however, have issued a number of delightfully printed and coloured charts of their coast, and the Esthonians have produced charts of the Islands which should certainly be obtained by anyone cruising in this direction as they mark harbours and many land and sea marks which have not yet been recorded elsewhere. These can be obtained from the Harbourmaster, Sadama Kontor, Reval, Esthonia.

Language? To be at home everywhere, one would need Finnish, Lettish, Esthonian and Swedish. One can get on quite well with Russian or German, and in the larger ports there is usually someone about with a good lot of English words acquired on British ships. In the larger ports. Riga, Reval, Helsingfors, one can buy all necessary food supplies, but not always such things as blocks, shackles, etc. Of the three, Helsingfors is best but not perfect. At Abo, further west along the Finnish coast, almost everything can be obtained. Away from the larger ports, milk, eggs, butter and potatoes can usually be bought, though here the language difficulty becomes real.

At a number of places on my autumn cruise last year I found islanders who, for patriotic reasons, or else from necessity, refused absolutely to talk any language but their own Esthonian. Tobacco is the very devil to get. English tobacco is almost unobtainable, and, when you do find a stray tin of it, it is priced as if it were the Elixir of Life. Local tobacco, except in Helsingfors is horrid except for the actual smoker, and only just tolerable by him for want of something else. Even local tobacco is sometimes not to be had. For some time I had to do with raw leaves given me by one of the lighthouse keepers and dried over the cabin lamp.

Fishing? On some of the banks a stout fish like a cod is to be caught on a weighted spinner jerked up and down in four to six fathoms of water.

Among the islands and off most of the harbours you can catch small fish called killos, like sprats. I caught a lot on fly, but when hungry went after them with a worm on a very small hook, one minute shot and a very light quill float thrown out to lie flat along the water. You give it a pull now and again to prevent it from hanging straight down, and strike at the first stab of the float. These little fish swim in shoals and take the bait in a petulant manner, ejecting it immediately, so that there is some sport in catching them, they make good soup and a really admirable fry. The water is not very salt and in many inlets perch and pike are to be caught in the usual ways. There are also small flat fish. There are any quantity of revoltingly oily sea duck.

Clubs are extremely hospitable to all members of recognised clubs. In Helsingfors the best moorings are those of the Nylands Club in the southern corner of the Southern Harbour. In Reval, the two clubs, the Estland and the Reval, have their buildings on an island mole in the harbour. There are mooring buoys for visiting yachts, and immediately after their arrival they are warped into places by the mole by the Yacht Club boatmen. In Riga, the visiting yacht must stop in the mouth of the river for examination. This, for a small boat, is often almost impossible, and it is best to anchor in the Winter Harbour for clearance, thereafter proceeding up the river, either to the Nyland Club, which is immediately opposite the town, or through the Muhlgraben, to the Stint Lake, where the Riga Club has an excellent private harbour. On leaving, yachts can clear either in the Muhlgraben, or in the town, but must hand over their tickets of leave to the officials at the mouth of the river. It is well to be very careful in declaration here. An unlucky yacht with a crew of German students was held up for some days owing to the accident of an unopened parcel handed on board just as they were leaving Germany and not entered in the stores list, turning out to contain a few bottles of schnapps.

While in England, Ransome showed his sailing log to W. G. Collingwood, who told him, 'You've got a book ready-made.' Taking heart from this response, Ransome returned to Riga for Christmas and made a determined start on *Racundra's First Cruise.*

The book and journalism kept Ransome busy until July, when he managed to get free from his desk and made *Racundra* ready for sea again. He recorded that they had an additional member of the crew:

Racundra this year ships a fourth member of the crew; a grass snake from Moscow over a yard long with a passion for frogs, and the name of Oureberes. He takes his name from *The Worm Oureberes*, a romance by

E.R. Eddison — a childhood friend. 'Oureberes travels in a huge jam-jar, crawls hither and thither on deck and over the cabin table and is happiest curled round and round the bottom of the teapot. The rest of the crew is unchanged except that it is a year older than it was, by calendar reckoning, but agrees unanimously that it feels more than a year younger after its pleasant adventure last year. The crew consists, accordingly, of the Cook, the Ancient Mariner, Oureberes and the Master.

Carl Sehmel confided to his daughter that Oureberes abandoned the teapot at night in favour of Evgenia's ample breasts.

They left on the morning of July 18th. At the Customs House they collected their ticket of leave from the same old scoundrel who had made things so difficult the previous year. That evening they saw a waterspout which Ransome sketched in the log. After they passed the island of Runo, Ransome recorded:

Anvil clouds. Clouds like scattered torn out handfuls of white hair. Pillar clouds upright out of the sea. Clouds like jagged swords. Pillar clouds collected into clouds like ferocious beasts.

By ten o'clock the following morning they were 100 miles out from Riga. They ran through the narrow channel in the Rohukulla Reef and

From Ransome's Log

anchored in the little sheltered harbour. From there it was a grand passage north through the Nukke Channel, and soon reached Reval. Their holiday cruise came to an abrupt end after only a week when a telegram brought the news that Ransome's wife might at last be willing to consider a divorce, and he hastened to England to consult his lawyer.

It was not until August 21st that they were able to sail once more, and having abandoned all hope of reaching St Petersburg that year, sailed for for Helsingfors instead. After a short stay they set off for a cruise among the Finnish islands. On one of the islands there was a large population of frogs, and there they marooned Oureberes. After a week of pleasant sailing they returned to Reval, but a series of southerly gales decided them against returning to Riga. It was already quite late in the year for Baltic sailing. They arranged to lay *Racundra* up at Reval for the winter in the Esthonian Government dockyard, but the yacht was barely ready for the winter, however, when urgent messages from the *Manchester Guardian* once more took Ransome off to Russia.

Back in England the following spring to attempt to bring the divorce saga to a conclusion, Ransome applied for membership of the prestigious Royal Cruising Club, and such was the success of *Racundra's First Cruise* that he was proposed by the Commodore himself.

In April 1924 Ransome's divorce came through, just before they were due to go to Reval to prepare *Racundra* for more voyaging. At last Arthur Ransome and Evgenia Petrovna Shelepina could be married. Their affection for one another was enduring, though at times each found the other's eccentricities and quirks of character testing. Hugh Brogan believes that it says m u c h f o r t h e i r marriage that 'Arthur was free to paint such a f r a n k, i f s l i g h t, sketch of her' in his book. To Brogan she is 'companionable, c o u r a g e o u s, l o n g - s u f f e r i n g, w a r m - h e a r t e d and rather warm-tempered too', rather than simply the 'dervish of pots and pans' caricature as *Racundra's* 'Cook'. 'Of t h e t h r e e o f u s,' Ransome wrote, 'the Cook, without doubt, was the one who worked her passage.'

They were married at the British Consulate on May 8th, and Arthur's mother wrote warmly to Evgenia, welcoming her into the family. They were to manage a 'working holiday' cruise in August, before returning to England, as Ransome explained in the 80-page typescript giving a day by day, fish by fish account of the trip, presumably intended for possible publication:

Racundra is for me a floating study, not merely a holiday boat, and cruising has always to give way before the more serious needs of earning bread and butter with a little jam.

They had decided on a leisurely honeymoon cruise up the River Bolderaa (now called the Lieupe) from Riga to Mitau (Jelgrava) and back — a round trip of nearly 100 miles. Their departure was delayed when the engine stopped within sight of Sehmel who had gone to see them off. Ransome had forgotten to open the cock of the lubricator. They set off down the Dvina River as if they were heading for the open sea once more, but near its mouth they turned to port up the Bolderaa. The lower reaches of the river formed a broad and busy highway, and *Racundra* motored upstream, threading her way carefully between passenger steamers and cargo vessels that had little or no regard for the convenience of yachts and were liable to sail with 'four barges tandem.' On the third morning they woke to find the cabin floorboards under water and the pump rusted solid. While Ransome struggled to free the pump, the water continued to rise. Eventually, he was able to pump *Racundra* dry and track down the cause of the leak to a loose nut on the propeller tube. This was quickly tightened, and all was well again. Later that day Ransome noted:

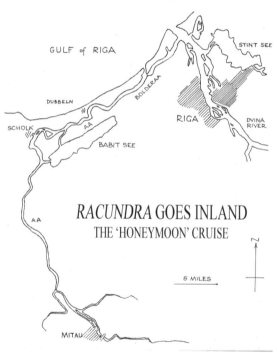

This stretch of the river above Dubbelm is one of the loveliest on the river, The left bank is broken; here and there are broad water meadows with grazing cattle and the forest behind them with little wooden houses tucked under the trees. The right bank in places has been under-cut and carved by the spring floods and the outrush of ice after the winter into low sandy cliffs.

For a month, Ransome detailed their uneventful progress with notes that were eventually published in 2002. It was a gentle and lighthearted cruise; although in his *Autobiography* he confessed that they lived mostly on eggs and the fish they caught.

> Hickory, dickory dock,
> *Racundra* came to Scholk
> She found it was harder
> To fill up her larder
> By fishing than shopping at Scholk.

There were some idyllic moments;

We chose a gap in the reeds on the east side and pulled the dinghy ashore onto a flat gravelly area already set up for camping with the remains of a fireplace and a log seat. Above us was the 'cliff' actually no more than a sandy escarpment. The cook set to work on supper while I put up the tent on the edge of the pine forest at the top of the cliff. We had no light. Our torch batteries had failed, and we had found none in the shops. No matter. It was a clear night, the moon was rising and we had a good camp fire. We ate chicken and drank champagne.

Racundra (by Ransome)

From time to time the outside world crowded in, and Ransome had to settle down to articles for the *Manchester Guardian*. For the most part they kept in deep water, but there were times when *Racundra* nosed her way into 'narrow winding romantic and claustrophobic maze of shallow channels winding between enormously tall and strong reeds for what feels like thousands of square miles.'

'Which way do we go?' said Roger. 'It divides in two.'
The Mastodon stopped rowing, and his boat ran instantly aground.
Just ahead of them the ditch turned into two ditches, one twisting to the
right, the other to the left. Both seemed about the same size.
'Right I think,' said the Mastodon. 'But it's a long time since I've been
through.'

They never missed an opportunity to fish, and Ransome
carefully itemised their successes and failures in his diary: 'Fished all
day in N. wind like a fool with the natural result,' and 'Fished for perch
with a small bleak caught by the Cook. She caught a good one. I missed
two.' In the typescript he observed: —

Perch are the most capricious fish. I got up on their behalf at four in
the morning and fished in one good-looking place after another until the
foghorn called me to breakfast on *Racundra*. I did not have a single bite.
Yet after breakfast as the Cook was not ready to start, I took the dinghy
out again, and between eleven and two o'clock caught a magnificent lot
of them, hardly a fish under the half a pound and the best of them well
over a pound.

Years later, the fisherman of the *Death and Glory* would experience
a similarly fruitless morning.

As is often the way in fishing, getting up early was a waste of time that
might have been spent in bed. Pete began fishing soon after seven. It was
a still day without a breath of wind, and until the sun grew hot you might
have thought that there was not a fish in the river.

They reached Miteau on 16th August and arrived to a fanfare of
trumpets and the sound of marching feet, and on going ashore
discovered that a local regiment of militia were celebrating their
'birthday'. Ransome went ashore and shopped in the ' jolly' open air
market. He returned laden with stores and a 'magnificent nutmeg
grater'.
The following day the river was closed for a swimming festival, but
on 18th August they left civilisation behind and turned downstream.
It had been a successful visit, marred only by their failure to buy ice
creams.

'What is civilisation?' asked Bridget.
'Ices,' said Roger, 'and all that sort of thing.'

Four days later Evgenia threatened mutiny, as Ransome recalled in a handwritten note:

The Cook says there is no point in living in *Racundra*, that only children are glad to live in a ship, that there is nothing to see, nothing to write about, and that she's sick of living in a small cabin, that I grow worse with age, and that proper authors live at home and write books out of their heads.

Having said her piece, the Cook remained aboard until 4th September when they discovered a stowaway. How the mouse was able to climb aboard, since *Racundra* had never touched shore since they started, or how long it had enjoyed their hospitality they never discovered.

The cruise has ended or is on the point of death. I am alone in *Racundra*, or rather not quite alone. I am alone with a mouse, which has sent the whole six foot three of the Cook, undaunted hitherto by anything but calms in headlong flight to Riga ... The Cook has gone, and I am left a hero to face the raging lion in a mouse's skin.

The following day Ransome scoured the nearby town of Dubbelm from end to end in a fruitless search for a mousetrap. At this point of their cruise, the typescript comes to an end. From entries in Ransome's diary and his log, it is possible to complete the story: Evgenia returned that evening, complete with mousetraps, ashamed of her flight, and agreed to return to Miteau once the mouse had been caught. They left Miteau on 9th September and were back in Riga in time for lunch the following day.

Quite recently, Brian Hammett who published Ransome's log of their 'Honeymoon' journey up river, was able to retrace the voyage. He found that things had hardly changed in the intervening 80 years. The lower reaches are still full of commercial traffic, but up river the journey was as idyllic as in Ransome's day and the fishermen on the banks were just as plentiful.

Racundra was laid up, and on 14th November they sailed for England. In April 1925, the Ransomes settled in the Lake District, where it became impractical to keep *Racundra*. The cost was simply too high, and with regret (though he had to admit the boat was horribly slow) Ransome advertised her for sale at £300 in the *Yachting Monthly*. The yachting writer K. Adlard Coles, then twenty-four and recently married, saw the notice and was attracted by the thought of the cruise he could make returning the boat to England. Having produced one cruise book already, he looked forward to another. He wrote on May 21st, asking Ransome for more details. The letter was sent to Ransome in Riga and it pursued him to England but was sent back again to Riga before finally it caught up with him Ransome replied on June 21st, describing the construction and detailing the equipment. Coles was very interested offering £150 in cash and £100 guaranteed. (The sum of £250 in 1925 was the equivalent today, in 2009, of something in the region of £13,000 —scarcely a high price for such a boat) — Ransome accepted, and letters and telegrams went to and fro almost daily for the next ten days. Eventually Coles made a new offer: he would pay £220 in cash. This Ransome also accepted, though it led to a misunderstanding. He assumed that Coles meant £220 in cash and a further £30 guaranteed. To avoid a bitter row, Ransome proposed to waive the £30 if Coles would agree to rename *Racundra* and not use the name anywhere in print. The deal was done. Ransome answered requests from Coles for information and help in full. Captain Sehmel (or 'The Ancient Mariner' as he was called in *Racundra's First Cruise*) was to do what he could to prepare the boat for its new owner.

The Ancient will rig and get *Racundra* ready for sea in a very few days AFTER your arrival. It is quite useless to tell him to do anything before you arrive as he simply won't do it. He will ship with you for the passage to England if he likes you, not otherwise. He is called Captain Sehmel by me. Other people address him less respectfully and get less out of him. He is an extremely charming old man, and makes himself very useful. You would have to come to some agreement with him about payment, privately, so as to avoid having articles made etc. Of course, you would have to send him home at the end of the trip ... You will get no navigational assistance from him. He is incapable of reading a chart and though a first-rate rigger and admirable seaman, is a very old man. I never let him stand a night watch alone. You would have to pay him a pound or two a week, and naturally [you] would not discharge an old man in a foreign port without sending him home to the dinghies and little boats by looking after which he keeps alive.

Sehmel was as helpful to Coles as Ransome said he would be, although he was unable to ship with him to England.

Ransome had not used the engine during the first cruise, but he advised Coles that it was extremely simple to operate. Coles christened the engine 'The Smelly Monster' and used it infrequently and with difficulty. Ransome also passed on some helpful advice about dealing with the Customs.

You anchor, ready for sea, in the Club harbour and the Customs Officials will come from the Customs House at your request and make a pretence of looking over the ship. You give them a drink of the local spirit (vodka) in the cabin and a ham sandwich (this is important) whereupon they stamp your passports and give you a paper ticket which you have to give up at the mouth of the river to a ruffian who will wave at you from a small pier close by the big lighthouse on the port hand going down. Having handed over their ticket, you are free.

In the event Coles merely went to the harbour police who stamped the passports and telephoned the Customs office and Ransome's ruffian, and told them to let *Racundra* leave without formalities.

Sehmel, who felt about *Racundra* much as Ransome, went with her to the harbour mouth and stood waving until she was almost out of sight.

Coles soon found that it would be necessary to sail by day and night if they were to make any progress tow England because *Racundra* needed a fresh breeze to reach even 3 knots. Coles considered her 'woefully under-canvassed and in due course was to have her gaff rig replaced with Bermudan, though this would make her no longer the single-handed sailing boat Ransome had always wanted. As it was, Coles and his wife had to keep her close-hauled for the crossing against heavy seas. It was a difficult passage for *Annette II* (as she was renamed) and a very tiring one for her new skipper. Once home, Coles wrote to Ransome brief news of the cruise and to thank him for the opportunity of acquiring such an excellent little ship. He enclosed a cheque for £10, as a concession towards the disputed £30 but it was never paid into Ransome's account.

A few short months later Coles had the nerve to offer *Annette II* to Ransome for £350! Ransome could neither afford to buy her nor, probably wanted her back. Coles soon disposed of the yacht elsewhere, whereupon she regained her former name.

Swallows and Amazons

SWALLOWS AND AMAZONS FOR EVER!

Ransome was well established in a remote cottage, Low Ludderburn south of Bowness-on-Windermere by the time the Altounyan family returned to Coniston for the summer of 1928. He continued to write for the *Manchester Guardian* — among other things articles with titles as unlikely as 'Dust' and 'Winding up the Clock' — and he had become a close friend of the editor, C. P. Scott, who from time to time sent him on missions abroad, to places as far flung as Egypt and China. Much closer to his heart were his weekly fishing essays, some of which were published in 1929 under the title of *Rod and Line.* 'So completely does fishing occupy a man', Ransome wrote, 'that if a good angler had murdered one of those people who prate about patience and were allowed to spend his last day at the river instead of the condemned cell, he would forget the rope.'

One of the pleasures of Low Ludderburn was the chance to fish again the rivers of his youth. Down in the valley at Barkbooth lived their neighbours, the Kelsall family. Colonel Kelsall shared Ransome's passion for fishing and his son Desmond, still a keen fisherman, remembers his first sea trout, caught nearby in the River Winster. It was small, fresh run and bright silver, weighing no more than half a pound. Having hooked and landed his fish (more by good fortune than by judgment) Desmond rushed home to tell his father. That done, he ran all across the valley to show Mr Ransome, who shared the small boy's delight and made as much fuss of the fish as if it weighed 8 pounds rather than 8 ounces. On another occasion Ransome went to endless trouble to teach Desmond how to catch trout with a worm when the Winster was in flood, where the trout would lie, how to present the bait and above all how to hook them. The fish were small (a quarter-pounder was a good one) but this in no way diminished Ransome's enthusiasm.

Low Ludderburn (from a photograph)

Ransome never claimed to be a good fisherman (although he undoubtedly was) or that he had ever caught any big fish; rather that he was one who thoroughly enjoyed fishing. He shares that enjoyment in *Rod and Line*, which is full of gentle humour. While Jonathan Cape, his publisher, was eager for another book of such essays, soon Ransome was occupied — with *Swallows and Amazons*.

At that time Ernest Altounyan, now settled in Syria, kept a leaky sailing boat called *Beetle II* on a nearby lake. This boat, named after one of the old Collingwood boats at Coniston, was quite unsuitable, however, as a vessel in which to begin to teach his young family to sail. When they returned to England for the summer of 1928, he decided that two dinghies would be needed for his four eldest children to learn seamanship on Coniston Water. Hugh Brogan tells us that it was agreed between Ransome and Altounyan to share the cost of the boats equally and that when the Altounyans returned to Syria one of the dinghies would become Ransome's. Altounyan hurried to Barrow-in-Furness to secure the boats while the rest of the family were busy unpacking and settling into Bank Ground Farm, where they were staying, just below the Collingwood family home of Lanehead.

Titty, Susie, Roger and Taqui Altounyan at Coniston 1928 (from a photograph)

He bought two heavy sea-going dinghies with standing lugsails, built for sailing in the shallow waters of Morecambe Bay. Certainly the boats were not new, but opinions differ as to their age. Taqui's cousin Tadeus believed they had been little used. He was several years older than Taqui, who remembered being envious that he was allowed to sail when there were white horses on the lake while the youngsters were not. Altounyan paid £15 apiece for the sturdy little craft.

The boats were put on to the back of a lorry and delivered to Lanehead, where they were taken down the field to the boathouse. One they named *Swallow* after their old sailing boat, and the other they called *Mavis*, Titty's real name, though the family never used it. The nickname — from the story of Titty Mouse and Tatty Mouse — was used by family and friends throughout her life. Taqui was then eleven, Susie nine, Titty eight and Roger six. Brigit, not yet three when they arrived in England, merely waved goodbye to her brother and sisters when they went boating, just as Vicky (a short-lived name-change which the Altounyans disliked) does in *Swallows and*

Amazons. The dinghies were both 13 feet long and rigged in a similar manner. Their parents were away for much of the rather wet summer of 1928, and the children were too young to do very much on their own. When they could, they spent their days trying to sail in circles near the boathouse, and occasionally Ransome came across from Low Ludderburn and would show them how to catch perch in the shallows. *Mavis* was 'crewed' by Taqui and Roger, and *Swallow* by Susan and Titty. The best expeditions were those when the family took sandwiches and a kettle to Peel Island, four miles to the south. Sailing correctly was a matter of some importance. There were not many boats on Coniston and everyone knew each other. Friends and acquaintances were judged by the way they handled their boats. The young Altounyans were always expected to observe high standards. Until they were able to swim they were never allowed to stand up in the boats, and this made moving about on board an awkward business. Before consent was given for taking out a boat alone they each had to jump into the middle of the lake fully clothed.

The children really began to sail *Mavis* five years later, during the long summer holidays that they spent at Lanehead after they had returned to England to go to school. Occasionally somebody would stay overnight on Peel Island. They never put up a tent, but rigged up a sail as shelter, just as their parents and the young Arthur had done years before.

Built specially to navigate the treacherous and changing sands of the Kent Estuary near Arneside, where she was built by William Crossfield, the *Swallow* is described in detail by Ransome at the beginning of *Swallows and Amazons*:

Most sailing-dinghies have centre-boards, plates which can be let down through their keels, to make them sail better against the wind. *Swallow* had none, but she had a rather deeper keel than most small boats. She was between thirteen and fourteen feet long, and fairly broad. Her mast lay in her, and beside it, neatly rolled up, were boom, yard, and sail, and a pair of short oars. Her name, *Swallow*, was painted on her stern.

Susan had got the sail ready. On the yard there was a strop (which is really a loop), that hooked on a hook on one side of an iron ring called the traveller, because it moved up and down the mast. The halyard ran from the traveller up to the top of the mast, through a sheave (which is a hole with a little wheel in it), and then down again. John hooked the strop on the traveller and hauled away on the halyard. Up went the brown sail until the traveller was nearly at the top of the mast. Then John made the halyard

fast on the cleats, which were simply pegs, underneath the thwart which
served to hold the mast up.

When Ernest Altounyans was taking his children in *Swallow*, the
halyard led from the traveller to the masthead and was taken forward
of the mast thwart before being made fast to the centre thwart with a
slippery hitch. Squalls — common on Coniston Water sweeping over
the lake without warning — would leave the children wondering from
which direction the next gust would come, and the *Swallow's* halyard
enabled them to lower sail immediately. The boats were also made
safer by wooden pegs fitted underneath the transom knees behind
which the sheet led. Those knees made ideal seats for fishing. Titty,
in particular, loved those tranquil days she spent sitting on *Mavis* with
her legs dangling above the water, as she watched her float. Part of
the stern bench was removable to give access to the store for tackle
and lines, jam jars, bailer, rowlocks, oilskins and rags.

Captain John puts up a spirited defence of *Swallow* and her deep
keel, and then in the race at the end of *Swallowdale* he cleverly defeats
Amazon by exploiting the difference between the two boats.

Close ahead of them was *Amazon*, now almost at the point, and Nancy
was wishing she had held on a little longer before trying to head for the
river. She, too, remembered the shallows, and was thinking of the centreboard deep below the keel of her ship. There was no doubt about it. She
would have to make one more short board out into the lake to be able to
clear the shallows and get into the river.

'They're going about again,' shouted Roger.

Just and only just *Amazon* cleared *Swallow* as she headed out once
more.

'You'll be running aground,' shouted Peggy, as *Swallow* held on her
way.

'I can see the bottom,' shouted Roger.

'Now then, Susan,' said John.

'Hold tight, Roger,' said Susan.

Just as *Swallow* came over the shallows at the point, Susan and John
threw all their weight over on her lee side and brought her gunwale so
low that a few drops lapped across it. This, of course, lifted her keel. The
wind had dropped to next to nothing, and so, on her beam ends, *Swallow*
slid across the shallows and into the river.

'Deep water,' said Susan, and in a moment John had flung his weight
back to windward and *Swallow* rose again to an even keel, just in time to
meet a little puff that carried her up the river to the Beckfoot boathouse.

The same puff caught the *Amazon*, but that last short board out into the lake had lost her twenty yards and more, and *Swallow* slipped past the boathouse a full two lengths ahead of her.
    'Well done, little ship,' cried Titty. 'Well done!'

In real life *Swallow* became the young Altounyan's favourite. There was no heavy centreboard for them to struggle with, and she was a most attractive craft with her brown sail and brown and white painted hull. Susie much preferred *Swallow* and thought *Mavis* rather a tub. When the summer was over, and the Altounyans would soon be returning to Syria, they decided, with a characteristically generous gesture, that Uncle Arthur should have *Swallow* while they kept *Mavis* for themselves. *Mavis* had been built by McIlroy's of Piel Island near Barrow, as a tender to a larger vessel. McIlroy's ran the ferry between Piel Island, Roa Island and the mainland and they may have engaged in boatbuilding as a sideline during the winter months. *Mavis* was

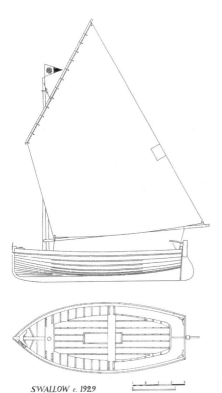

SWALLOW c. 1929

called *Pansy* in those days and took part in local races off the coast. She was a narrower vessel than *Swallow*, and the heavy iron centreboard had to be hauled up by means of a folding handle leading up through the centreboard case. In recent years Roger Altounyan had an old brown sail, but when they were young they used a larger white sail in summer. Taqui remembered the thrill of excitement as she jumped aboard and felt the boat sink and shiver beneath her feet.
    The artist John Berry, a friend of Ransome and Altounyan in their old age, sailed *Mavis* and found her a delight to handle after sailing modern racing dinghies. An alternative view was expressed by Richard Pierce, a naval architect who had built his business on the design and manufacture of Lakeland sailing dinghies:

My one and only experience of sailing *Mavis* was unforgettable. She was unique in my experience. Most boats have a few quirks and flaws. *Mavis*, in my opinion, is without saving grace, The dinghy is so slim-bowed her stability does not increase as she heels ... I thought the boat was a killer.

Although Pierce did not know it at the time, *Mavis* had indeed capsized with loss of life during World War Two in a Coniston squall. In spite of her faults, the Altounyans (with the possible exception of Susie) loved her like a member of the family.

Ransome took *Swallow* to Windermere and continued to sail her until Christmas that year. Before returning to Syria in January, Altounyan and two children called on Ransome and presented him, for his birthday on the 18th, with a pair of slippers bought in Aleppo.

In his letters to Syria in the months that followed, Ransome hinted that he was writing another book and that it would be a suitable subject for Dora's illustrations. When a parcel containing a very early unillustrated copy of *Swallows and Amazons* arrived in Aleppo in July

Mr Sumner Sen and his son John attending to their camp fire beside Coniston Water (Sumner Estate)

1930, the Altounyans did not find the title of the book particularly revealing. But once the children opened it and found three of their names, they soon saw that the *Swallows* referred, not to birds, but to the crew of their favourite dinghy. The dedication made it clear that the book was for them, in exchange for the slippers which had pleased him so. The family believed that Taqui had been turned into a boy, John Walker, to make the story feasible commercially, and she even signed some letters to Uncle Arthur 'Captain John' — though it has to be said that her personality was quite unlike his. Hugh Brogan floats the not altogether convincing notion that John is the boy Ransome himself passionately 'wanted to be', and that choosing his first wife's maiden name of Walker would somehow magically reconnect him with his estranged daughter Tabitha, who had sold all his precious books after he divorced her mother. But it is all in the realm of conjecture, for Ransome leaves no clues to the matter.

I did find some evidence, however, of Ransome's early planning, slipped among the pages of *Nancy Blackett's* log book. There were a

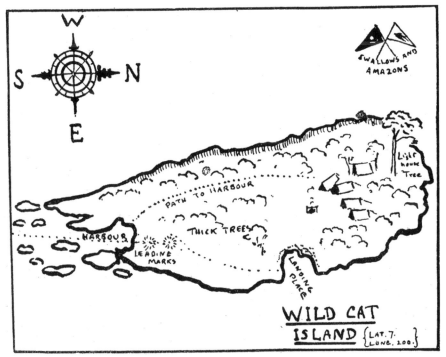

Wild Cat Island (from *Swallowdale*)

couple of pencilled sketch maps, one of which was obviously Wild Cat Island, and a list of chapter headings. The *Swallows* are listed as Dick, Susan, Titty and Roger with a young sister Vic aged one and a half who 'does not count'. The *Amazons* are Jane and Mary who have a young brother Tom aged three.

It has recently come to light that Ransome knew a family called Sumnor, generations of whom camped on the shore of Coniston Water for weeks at a time, over a period of 60 years, dating from before the First World War. The camp site was close to the western shore of the lake, not far from Peel Island and their days in camp were mostly spent sailing and fishing. Among the five children were John (aged 12 in 1929), Nancy (aged ten) and Margaret (known as Peggy, aged five)! All Ransome ever said about the origin of the *Amazon* pirates was that they 'had sprung to life one day when, sailing on Coniston, I had seen two girls playing on the lake shore.' It is tempting to wonder if these were Nancy and Peggy Sumnor. One other page from Ransome's notebook found its way into *Nancy Blackett's* log and contains a further list of characters. Dick has given way to John, and Jane and

Captain Flint's Houseboat (from *Winter Holiday*)

Mary have become Nancy and Peggy. The notion that Ransome used names from the two families for his Walkers and Blacketts is an attractively simple one.

Swallows and Amazons was written in the converted barn at Low Ludderburn with a glorious view across the Winster valley to Yorkshire. Desmond and Dick Kelsall were allowed to overhear the author at work. From time to time Ransome descended to Barkbooth and read aloud passages to the boys in order to test their reaction. When the book was published, the Kelsalls received one of the first copies, suitably inscribed.

The setting of *Swallows and Amazons* is the Altounyan's own familiar lake country, although Ransome created a fictitious landscape by blending features of Windermere and Coniston. The *Swallows* (or the Walker family) stay at Holly Howe, the very farmhouse where the Altounyan children stayed in 1928, above a field sloping down to the lake with the *Swallow* and *Mavis* waiting in the boathouse. Bank Ground Farm, to use its real name, is now a very comfortable guest house where some of the scenes for the *Swallows and Amazons* film were shot, and it became our base when Claire Kendall-Price and I took part in the series *On the Trail of Swallows and Amazons* for BBC Radio 4.

The Walkers camp on the island that was the Altounyan's favourite picnic place, just as it had been for the Collingwoods and Ransomes before them. There has been some debate as to the identity of the 'real' Wild Cat Island, but the Altounyans had no doubt it was Peel Island, nor had Ransome's mentor, W. G. Collingwood writing in *The Lake Counties* in 1932. Ransome, himself mentioned Blake Holme on Windermere. Was this a red herring? Wild Cat Island, like so much in that enchanted landscape, cannot be pinned down to a single place; all the literary explorer can hope for, is to identify the places most likely to have been the chief pieces that make up Ransome's jig-saw puzzle countryside.

To add to the fun, Captain Flint, who lives on a houseboat in the next bay, was none other than Uncle Arthur himself. The houseboat reminded the Altounyans of the steamboat *Gondola*, which used to run from the pier opposite Lanehead. In recent years a restored *Gondola* has been conveying holidaymakers to a pier halfway down Coniston Water close to Brantwood, Ruskin's house, which is now open to the public. Captain Flint's houseboat, however, seems more like *Esperance* on Windermere, which (unlike today) once had its mast where Ransome drew it for *Winter Holiday*, and, at the time, that he was writing, was without its funnel and moored near Bowness where it was used as a houseboat.

Esperance (model for Captain Flint's Houseboat) in Rayrigg Bay,
WIndermere 1952

Esperance was built on the River Clyde in 1869. She was
constructed of the finest iron for the Furness iron magnate Harry
Schneider, who had just acquired Belsfield, the Victorian mansion on
rising ground above Bowness Bay. Each morning the butler, carrying
breakfast on a silver tray, led his master down the path to the private
pier where *Esperance* was waiting. Breakfast was served in the gold
and ivory saloon while they glided silently down the lake to Lakeside
where Mr Schneider's personal train was waiting to take him to his
office in Barrow.

The 65-foot vessel was steam powered and was one of the first
craft to be fitted with twin screws. She remained in Schneider's
possession until his death in 1887, after which she passed into the
keeping of a Mr Logan, who owned the Ferry Hotel. He used her partly
to promote the hotel and also to transport his foxhounds to meets.
Between the wars the Scott family owned her, after the boiler and
engine had been removed from the hull and they used her as a
houseboat. They moored her near Ramp Holme, south of 'Rio' and
'Long Island', close to where Ransome placed her in *Swallows and
Amazons*.

After sinking at her moorings shortly after the outbreak of war, she remained on the bed of the lake until T. C. Pattison, a local steamboat enthusiast, succeeded in raising the hull a year or so later. His son, G. H. Pattison, restored the hull, fitted petrol engines and added a false funnel. He sent Ransome a postcard when the work was completed, inviting him to go and inspect her. When Pattison's collection of steamboats became the nucleus of the Windermere Steamboat Museum, *Esperance* was moved from her mooring in Rayrigg Bay to shore so that the public could view her at close quarters.

In Ransome's story, Captain Flint's houseboat sports a shiny brass cannon and a green parrot when the *Swallows* first go to investigate it, and that is enough to persuade Titty that the ship belongs to a retired pirate. Soon afterwards their peaceful island camp is invaded by two *Amazon* pirates in red caps sailing a centreboard dinghy, whose Uncle Jim turns out to be the houseboat's resident. The *Amazons* live in a house beside the mouth of a river similar to that which can be seen across the water from Peel Island. When the rival crews go to war, *Swallow* sails up the river to a pool covered with water-lilies, recognisable as Allen Tarn on the River Crake just below the foot of Coniston Water. During the night of the war, Titty — who is left to guard Wild Cat Island — hears burglars burying 'treasure' on nearby Cormorant Island (that Ransome claimed was Silverholme

CAPTAIN FLINT WALKS THE PLANK

Walking the Plank
(from *Swallows and Amazons*)

on Windermere, with its own legend of a buried hoard — although he directed the BBC film makers to an islet on Coniston) and she and Roger succeed in finding the buried trunk, which in fact belongs to the retired pirate on the houseboat. But the treasure turns out to be no more than the manuscript of the book that Captain Flint has been writing all summer. Grateful for its recovery, he arranges a party aboard the houseboat for the *Swallows and Amazons*, and even falls in with their demands that he walk the plank.

Suzannah Hamilton as Susan and Simon West as John in a still from the
1974 film of Swallows and Amazons

It was all greatly entertaining and the Altounyans were delighted, enjoying especially all the private jokes, as Arthur Ransome had hoped they would. Before breakfast the following morning Dora wrote to thank him:

> *Swallows and Amazons* arrived yesterday at 1 pm and it is now 6 am and there have been very few hours of those 18 when it was not being read by somebody. I didn't ask Ernest what time it was when he came to bed — I myself read it till 11, and got to within 7 chapters of the end. Well, all I want to say is that we all like it enormously. Now I see why you think I could have illustrated it! How I wish I could!!

Ernest Altounyan was perhaps taking Ransome's 'game' a little too seriously, when he wrote a couple of days later.

> What I most especially like and marvel at is your extraordinarily accurate characterization of the kids. Each is just right — as far as I know them — and each got a really good look in, and though Titty is the

heroine, yet all the others get a really good share. You've made me to bulge with paternal pride, and I kept saying to myself as I read — damn fine sporting kids and then realising that they were mine! ... But the book. I was really excited by it and rushed along its pages breathlessly and revelled in the waters of Windermere. Captain Flint is a very good you.

I am personally quite content to go down to posterity as the author of the famous Duffer telegram.

Letters from Taqui and Susie also said how much they liked the book, and Titty wrote from their summer house in Souookolook: 'It is absolutely lovely and very exciting. I wish we had such lovely adventures as the Walkers had.'

All the family joined in the game, and Ernest began some of his letters with 'Dear Captain Flint ...' Everyone accepted Ransome's explanation that Taqui had been turned into a boy, but it seems more likely that John Walker was a replacement. Susan they thought perhaps 'a little too good' to be Susie Altounyan, who was only nine the summer they spent at Coniston and never bothered much if Titty and Roger were getting their shoes wet. She believed that Susan owes more to Evgenia, who was always concerned about the welfare of her young friends. Ransome nevertheless used the structure of the Altounyan family to create the ideal family he never had. Eighty years on, it would be wrong to identify the individual Altounyan children too closely with the *Swallows* — as Titty herself told me a few years ago. 'Titty Walker wasn't and couldn't be me'.

Meanwhile, Ransome was working on a sequel. While *Swallows and Amazons* is a celebration of childhood, of holidays and imaginative play, in which the lake becomes childhood's vision of the world, *Swallowdale* is a celebration of the Lake District, in which the landscape and its inhabitants are much more strongly drawn.

Titty said nothing. She was looking all round the low-beamed farm kitchen. There was a grandfather clock in the corner with a moon showing in a circle at the top, and a wreath of flowers all round the clock face. Then there was a curled hunting horn on the black chimney-shelf, and above that, on pegs jutting out from the wall, an old gun, and a very long coach horn, nearly as long as a man. There were white lace curtains to the low windows, and in the deep window-seats there were fuchsias in pots, and big spotted shells. Each shell had its own thick knitted mat, and the pots were in saucers, and each saucer had its knitted mat, just as if it were a spotted shell. Titty looked back to the chimney-shelf to see if the curly hunting horn was standing on a knitted mat. But it was too high

Ransome's Swallowdale

for her to see. Close beside it on the chimney-shelf were some pewter mugs, and china candlesticks, and a copper kettle that Titty thought would be just the thing to please Susan.

Desmond Kelsall, who had enjoyed *Swallows and Amazons*, told Ransome that in the next book John should become over-confident and put *Swallow* on the rocks. At that, Ransome let out a great guffaw of laughter and said that was exactly what he was thinking of but had got no further. In the end, Ransome decided that while waiting for their ship to be repaired the *Swallows* should camp in a little secret valley near the western shore of the lake. The Kelsall boys were treated to readings of the work in progress while Evgenia prepared a huge feast. When signatures were needed for the Ship's Papers, they obliged by signing 'John' and 'Roger'. The claw print of Titty's parrot was also required, and the boys arranged for their own bird to leave a sooty mark when it perched on a piece of paper wrapped round a broom handle.

Over the years Ransome enthusiasts have tramped many a mile looking for possible secret valleys, pushing through the bracken and following becks between the rocky outcrops that are to be found in the Beacon Fell area. It is grand country, but they have been on a wild goose chase, misled perhaps by a map of the area found in the Ransome papers and published a few years ago. Others claim to have discovered Swallowdale near Windermere or at Miterdale — even in Yorkshire!.

In some respects Miterdale is not a bad guess. It looks sufficiently like Ransome's drawing of Swallowdale to have made me wonder if this remote valley could be his inspiration. I am not convinced. To begin with, the first three Lakeland books are so firmly rooted in Ransome's childhood holidays at Nibthwaite, that Miterdale, away by Wast Water beyond two ranges of hills, seems unlikely for geographical reasons alone. And this despite his mother staying within easy hiking distance to the south of it. More significant, Miterdale lacks a lower waterfall, which Ransome so exactly describes. It is also too large. The little valley Ransome drew is no more than 60

Waterfall at the entrance to Swallowdale   Clifford Webb's drawing of the entrance
to Swallowdale

feet across between the rocky walls. No, Miterdale seems no more than a tantalising coincidence when just across the lake from Nibthwaite there is a waterfall leading to another secret valley.

The best clues to the site of Ransome's principal inspiration for *Swallowdale* are to be found in Clifford Webb's drawings for the early editions of the book. Webb also produced drawings for early editions of *Swallows and Amazons*, and to help him get the feel of lakeland scenery Ransome took him afloat in *Swallow*. But Webb was no sailor, and when Ransome landed him at Bowness so that he could catch the train from Windermere, Webb made such a mess of the pierhead jump that *Swallow* was badly bumped. He was never forgiven. I find it hard to believe Ransome would have trudged with such a man the many tough miles beyond Coniston to show him Miterdale. But did Webb even get to see the little valley close to Coniston Water? His drawings of *Swallowdale* do not look very much like those Ransome made some years later, yet it is Webb's drawing of the waterfall that so exactly resembles the one you can find if you follow the beck just as Titty and Roger did up from a semi-Horseshoe Cove.

Again Webb's drawing of the north headland of Horseshoe Cove is a help in identifying the bay on the western side of Coniston Water from which to start. Having climbed up beside the waterfall, you will find yourself in a secret valley with grand look-out places from which to see over the lake towards Peel Island and across the fells to The Old Man of Coniston.

Swallowdale was as well received in Syria as *Swallows and Amazons*, and in November 1931 Taqui Altounyan wrote in appreciation: '*Swallowdale* is EVEN BETTER than *S's and A's* and you needn't have been so pessimistic about it. However tiresome the Great Aunt might have been to the *Amazons*, Taqui found her 'amusing to read about' and she felt sure no Walker aunt would be such a beast as the G. A. Titty's attempts to do justice with a wax image also went down well, but the abiding impression left by the book was clearly the role of its author. 'I don't care what you say, we all think Captain Flint is exactly like you — is you in fact.'

Ransome himself was not so satisfied with the book, he told his mother, and Clifford Webb's drawings pleased him even less. Both he and the Altounyan children would have liked Dora to illustrate the books. Her notebook of flowers, family and friends, and the Syrian scenes she painted, only served to remind them of what might have been if she had been less occupied with raising her family and helping to educate them. Dora herself was less critical of Clifford Webb:

I don't think the illustrations are so awfully bad as you seem to think. Of course he hasn't the smallest idea what mountains are, to him they have no more form than bits of crumpled paper. But other things I think he's done jolly well. He's got the right angle of rocks at Peel Island and the bit of shore in *Loading Firewood* is quite good. Holly Howe has quite the look of Bank Ground, though wrong in almost every detail. Altogether, I don't think that on the whole I could have done them much better and they illustrate the story pretty adequately, don't you think? Don't go and think that I mean to insult the book by saying that the pictures are good enough for it. No, what I mean is, that the things in which the illustrations fall short are the things nobody knows about except us, the secret japes and details that your general public doesn't know anything about. Of course the kind of illustrations that you IMAGINE I could have made (though I myself am perfectly sure I never could have done them) would have made a 'perfect book' more perfect still, and I do most awfully wish I could have done it.

Early in the New Year the Ransomes set off on the long sea voyage to visit Aleppo — partly in response to requests from the parents to go and see what the Altounyan children were like now and partly as a result of Altounyan's confidence that he could do something to alleviate Ransome's stomach troubles. For some years Ransome had been suffering from a duodenal ulcer, brought on very largely by worry. His recovery had been a slow business, helped by strictly avoiding aluminium cooking utensils. Now he felt it worthwhile to take a chance and see if the Aleppo hospital could hasten his cure. When Dora replied to say how pleased they were, she enclosed £20 with a request that he bring with him a clinker-built dinghy with a centreboard and one sail.

At the end of January the Altounyans drove across the plain of Antioch, over the mountains and down the coast to Alexandretta (now in Turkey) where they met the steamer bringing the Ransomes on the last stage of their journey. Ransome had not failed them. He was accompanied by a large wooden packing case containing the precious dinghy. The case was taken to the farm by the Anouk Lake and the new dinghy launched there. She slid out into the blue water between beds of water-lilies, and they named her *Peter Duck* after the new book Ransome was just starting.

The hospital which the Altounyans — father and son — ran was in the jewish quarter of Aleppo and the three generations shared the tall house opposite. Only in the summer did the children move into their bungalow at Souookolook in the cool of the mountains 70 miles to the

north. In her memoir, *Chimes from a Wooden Bell*, Taqui describes the
routine during the two months of the Ransomes' stay:

Arthur settled down to work in Dora's studio at the top of the house.
At lunch time each day, he would
come slowly down the stairs. We
met him at the bottom: 'How many
pages?' He would silently hold up
different numbers of fingers and
always repeated the refrain, 'Aunt
Genia thinks them AWFUL.' After
lunch he would read them to us
and we did all we could to cheer
him up. In the afternoons we
played tennis, not very well, and
Uncle Arthur would play to us on
his penny whistle. We all grew very
fond of them both. Then suddenly
it was all over. We children had no
idea why they left in such a hurry.

Sums, aboard the Wild Cat
(from *Peter Duck*)

Taqui remembered something
being said about Aunt Genia's
concern that the Altounyans'
aluminium pans were not good
for Arthur's ulcer, but it seems an
unlikely excuse when you think
that he visited his doctor friend in part for medical help with his
stomach troubles. No doubt there had been a quarrel of some sort,
though the surviving correspondence draws a veil over exactly what
started it. Underlying, though not necessarily the immediate cause of
the row, was Ransome's opinion that it was high time the children
went to school in England. In Taqui's view 'It almost seems as if a fight
had developed for possession of the children.' Dora, recovering from
what Titty had said was a bout of malaria, was upset by the suggestion
that they were not being responsible parents; Ernest was angry and
resentful. 'Genia probably took a hand in the argument' — Taqui
continues — 'which must have gone on after we were all in bed with
Arthur and Dora looking miserable and not enjoying it at all. Genia
and Ernest were both people who had to get their own way and,
probably, Genia felt forced to "sweep out" when she was defeated.' At
all events, with Ransome's internal problems growing more severe,

and his knowledge that they always improved at sea, they set sail from Cyprus aboard the *Scottish Prince*.

It was a melancholy homecoming in April. While Ransome had been away his great friend Ted Scott, the newly-crowned editor of the *Manchester Guardian*, had died in a boating accident on Windermere. Ransome had introduced Scott and his son to sailing and for a while felt responsible for his friend's death.

At the same time, Low Ludderburn had been burgled, so the Ransomes stayed at Barkbooth with the Kelsalls for a week. While they were there, Ransome finished off the illustrations with the aid of Desmond and Dick and other young neighbours, Joan and Peggy Hudson. Using anything they could find round the outhouses for props, the children posed for what he called 'Hollywoods', or stills from which he could draw scenes for *Peter Duck*. These were purely working aids and Ransome never showed the photographs to the children. On makeshift bunks Peggy and Joan posed for the drawing of Titty and Susan in their cabin. All the children joined in at the capstan contrived by Colonel Kelsall and climbed ladders doing duty as ratlines.

For a while the exchange of letters between Ransome and Altounyan was acrimonious and sad. They bandied such terms as 'psychological bilge' and 'savages', while Dora wrote: 'I don't know what to say about sending the children to school. It is such a terrible uprooting for one thing, and I hate to think of it. But we are thinking...' Though Ernest, 'never one to sulk', attempted reconciliation in a moving letter which Taqui suspects was received at Low Ludderburn with derision as 'mere sentimental twaddle', the relationship was never the same again.

As it happened, the Altounyan children had only that one summer of 1932 in which to sail their little boat, *Peter Duck*, before their parents agreed with Ransome and sent the four eldest to boarding school in Windermere. In the Christmas holidays, after the children had been staying at low Ludderburn for a few days, the Ransomes suggested that they should adopt thirteen year old Titty, as they had no children of their own. Ernest's reaction can be imagined, but Dora made Ransome a present of the portrait that she had painted of Titty, by way of compensation.

It is tempting to see a hint of jealousy behind the whole sorry business. The two men had each fallen for the Collingwood daughters when they were young and, in Taqui's words, 'There were more tangled threads in Ernest's friendship with Arthur than we were aware of — some of them never got sorted out!' Evgenia, too, could be uncommonly possessive of Arthur and his growing reputation, and in later life she did her level best to exclude any unwelcome outside influence from his past. Why else would she withhold his *Autobiography* from publication until her death, which followed some years after his in 1967? In that year she took to remonstrating with four of the Altounyan children for what she saw as monstrously false claims on their part that they had been models for the *Swallows*. She wrote to Taqui objecting to such claims appearing in Ernest Altounyan's obituary in *The Times* and to a feature in the *Observer* in 1965, for which, she surmised, Taqui had been responsible. It had 'made Uncle Arthur angry' when he was ill, Evgenia insisted, 'but he could not protest without hurting your mother.' She also had complaints about Roger's and Brigit's behaviour, but 'Titty's performance (in a television inter-view) was the last straw.' Her letter to Titty spoke of 'a show in very bad taste' and proposed printing a disclaimer in the paperback editions that were about to be published, which was hurtful and not a little insulting. It led only to a sad farewell.

It is a strange outburst when seen in the light of Ransome's open 'letter to a friend', written in 1930 and found among his papers at Leeds, just a few phrases from which reveal his original thoughts. 'The slippers, I say, were given to me by the Walkers just before they went away to Syria ... to do the thing properly I should have to put the Walkers in the story as well as their boat ... Meanwhile the Walkers away out there in Syria had found a sheet of water and got a boat sent out to them and were sailing themselves ... after that, of course, I ought to have thought that there was no need to go on writing *Swallows and Amazons*. But I could not stop ...'

Peter Duck was actually planned before *Swallowdale* and is supposed to have been a story the *Swallows and Amazons* made up to amuse themselves one winter on board a wherry in Norfolk. They give themselves a conventional treasure-seeking adventure on a Caribbean island, the most memorable feature being the introduction of Ransome's Baltic sailing companion Captain Sehmel, alias *Peter Duck*. The quiet, sober Cape Horn seaman is a corrective to the romantic, unworldly Captain Flint and his child crew and a fitting tribute to the bearded old salt who had rigged *Racundra*. It is *Peter Duck* who first suspects that the dastardly Black Jake and his ship the *Viper* will follow them wherever they go, convinced that the *Wild Cat* is bound for Crab Island and the treasure:

John looked round. Away there in the dark were a red and green light close together. As he watched them, the red light disappeared. The green light was left alone. John glanced down at the compass, and when he looked back again the green light was showing on the port quarter.

'Sailing vessel, that's certain,' said Peter Duck. 'And I'm just a-wondering if that ain't the *Viper*. One green light's much like another, and you can't tell t'other from which — but seems to me that vessel's got her eye on us. She's not steering a course. See! There's her port light, red again. Now it might very easy be that Black Jake was holding of her wheel. Well, skipper's set a course, and it's not for us to change it, but I doubt he wouldn't mind us finding out if that vessel ain't following us and not shaping no course of her own. Just you let me have the wheel.'

Peter Duck spun the wheel and suddenly headed the *Wild Cat* in, as if for the lights of Folkestone.

'You tell me what lights she shows us.'

'Red and green,' said John.

'Heading down Channel same as us.

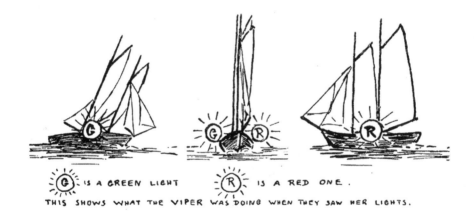

THIS SHOWS WHAT THE *VIPER* WAS DOING WHEN THEY SAW HER LIGHTS.

'Now then?'

'Green light's gone,' said John.

'I thought so,' said Peter Duck. 'She's headed in to see what we're going to do in Folkestone.'

Once more he spun the wheel and put the *Wild Cat* back on her course. 'Aye,' he said, 'and now he'll show his green and come after us again.' As he spoke the green light shone out again beside the red, the red disappeared, and the other vessel was once more heading down Channel.

'The *Viper* sure enough,' said Peter Duck. 'Plain as talking that was.'

The other new character is the red-haired Bill, whom Ransome thought 'rather a lark'. Rescued from a dinghy adrift in the fog, Bill feels the need to establish himself with the *Swallows and Amazons* aboard the *Wild Cat*. He chews tobacco, but it is his grisly cure for seasickness that has a devastating effect. Don't hold it in if you want to feel better — that's Bill's advice.

'Well, you want a bit of string,' said Bill. 'Then you ties the string to the biggest bit of bacon fat you can swallow. Then you swallows it, keeping a hold on the other end of the string. Then you ...'
There was a noise of scuffling up the ladder and out of the forehatch. Roger, with a face the colour of old mousetrap cheese, came bolting out of the fo'c'sle, was brought up sharp by a lurch of the vessel, grabbed at the bulkhead, came -skidding through the alleyway into the saloon, dodged Captain Flint, struggled round the table, flung himself at the companion steps and climbed desperately.
The voice of Bill came again from the fo'c'sle, in tones of mild surprise. 'Well,' he said, 'if they won't wait to be told'.

Peter Duck was published in October 1932 to excellent reviews. Hugh Walpole, writing in the *Observer* newspaper, said it was 'so well written that you don't realise it is written at all'. Shortly afterwards, when Ransome's doctor advised him to give up journalism altogether, he left the *Manchester Guardian* with few regrets and settled to its successor. 'Books are all right.' he told his mother with relief.

Sadly, this proved to be far from the case, and he went through agony with his winter story. To us the story reads so easily and fluently that one can scarcely imagine it giving him any trouble at all. Yet it gave him sleepless nights, and the pain was exacerbated by the fact that, in February 1933, he fell and broke his ankle a few yards down the hill from his front door. Then his old stomach trouble erupted as he struggled through the summer, with his publisher clammering for the book in time to make it Cape's big Christmas children's book.

For *Winter Holiday* he looked back to his childhood just as he had in *Swallows and Amazons*, this time to his prep school days in Windermere when the boys were allowed to enjoy the delights of the frozen lake during the great frost of 1895.

It was thought at the time that up to 20,000 people were on the ice. The freeze lasted for six weeks and each day trainloads of visitors from Manchester and Liverpool pulled into Windermere Station.

Bowness Bay photographed by Arthur Ransome during the big freeze of 1929

People skated, walked or cycled on the ice, ate, drank and danced to the two bands which played in Bowness Bay. In 1929 Windermere froze again with an estimated 50,000 enjoying glorious sunshine. This time the music of gramophone, barrel organs and the wireless, as well as musicians, echoed across the ice. Sporting motorists took their cars on the ice and performed spins and skids. Ice yachts which had raced in 1895 were brought on to the ice again, but a skating race had to be abandoned when the crowds along the course found the ice cracking beneath their feet.

In *Winter Holiday* Nancy decides that the *Swallows and Amazons* should become Arctic explorers. Ransome had met the Norwegian explorer Nansen, his childhood hero, while he was in Riga, and so Captain Flint's houseboat becomes Nansen's *Fram* and the headquarters of the expedition. Ransome introduced two new characters, and it is through their eyes we see the winter landscape.

'Everything was white, and somehow still. Everything was holding its breath. The field stretching down to the lake was like a brilliant white

counterpane without a crinkle in it. The yew trees close by the farm house were laden with snow. The lower branches of the old fir were pressed right down to the ground by the weight of snow they were carrying. The island was a white island, except where the rocks rose straight up out of the still water.'

The newcomers, brother and sister, discover the others living in an igloo and fall in with Captain Nancy's plan to direct an expedition across the ice to the North Pole, which she does, undaunted, from her sickbed when she is forced to retire with mumps. Hugh Brogan suggests that Dick and Dorothea Callum are projections of Ransome's own character. To begin with their father, like Ransome's, is an academic, though in place of history, Professor Callum's subject is archaeology. 'Dick', Brogan writes, 'is the young Rugbeian Arthur, bespectacled, with a strong scientific bent, deaf and blind to everything except the matter in hand. His triumph in the story is also a triumph of the author's wish-fulfilment.' Then if Dorothea, the budding writer, is not quite Titty's match in intuition, 'she has plenty of insight into people and situations; but what sets her apart from all the others, including Titty, is her concern with language. She alone constantly tries to find the right phrase or word.' What if her storytelling does tend to move forward in headlong leaps of purple prose? It is, as Brogan observes, 'something to have any style at all at the age of eleven.' And Ransome unfolds with utmost delicacy Dorothea's striving to realise her vocation.

At first the *Swallows and Amazons* are inclined to be condescending towards the naive newcomers, despite being impressed by Dick's knowledge of astronomy and the signalling to Mars.

Close behind her came the four whom Dorothea put down in her mind as the elders, though she did not think that Peggy could be very much older than she was herself. She could not help hearing what they were talking about.

'Shiver my timbers, but why not?'
'An astronomer might be quite useful.'
'But what's she going to do?'
'We'll soon know if they're any good.'

This was dreadful, and Dorothea hurried out of earshot — along the frozen track.

The tables are turned, however, when it comes to skating. Experts in signalling and sailing though these Arctic explorers appear to be, they aren't — as Dorothea fears — the masters of everything else as well.

Dick had never a thought of the others who might be watching. The moment his skates were on he pushed himself off from his clump of heather, rose to standing height as he slid away, and was off.
The Arctic explorers stared, open-mouthed.
'But he can skate,' said Titty.
'Like anything,' said Roger.
'Why didn't you tell us?' said Nancy. 'Of course, you ought to be in the Polar expedition. Not one of us can skate like that.'
'Golly!' said Peggy. 'He can do it either way.'
Dorothea was now almost afraid they would think that Dick was showing off. But anybody could see that he had forgotten all about them and was simply skating for himself. He went flying up the little tarn, spun suddenly round and flew backwards, spun round once more, and came flying back to Dorothea.
'Come along, Dot,' he said. 'This is lots better than doing it indoors.'

Once the lake is frozen over the explorers see an ice yacht. Dick and Dorothea have never sailed themselves and could not be expected to understand what 'the sight of that white wing gliding past the dark trees' means to the crews of *Swallow* and *Amazon*. As the sail sweeps up to the shore Captain John is heard to say, scarcely above a whisper, 'She'll be going about. But how can she?' The explorers fix up a sail of sorts on the Beckfoot sledge and, sitting astride it, let the wind take them.

A loud word of command rang out.
'Shove your port legs down ... hard!'
Five boots met the ice. The sledge swerved violently to the left, came broadside on to the wind, skidded sideways with a sharp screech from the iron runners beneath it, and turned over with a loud crash as its mast slammed down on the ice. Skates, knapsacks, and explorers seemed to be almost everywhere.

After the D's have joined the North Polar Expedition they are given their instructions for the day, by means of square and triangular shapes hung on the wall of Holly Howe Farm. This was the system in use between Low Ludderburn and Barkbooth for the exchange of fishing intelligence with Colonel Kelsall. There was no telephone in the Winster valley so the signs could be used to summon help for Ransome in any emergency. Kelsall added a cross to the square and triangle and the two men would rattle their signals up and down the wall as messages became more complex. The two wives were discouraged from social chat and were restricted to sending messages such as 'come to tea', to which there were only two possible answers. Desmond and Dick posed for more 'Hollywoods' with their wooden sledge. Ransome used to hold parties for the young Kelsalls and others in the barn where he did his writing. There he played sea shanties on his accordion while the children sang or joined in on their penny whistles. The West Indian tales of Anansi the spider-man were great favourites with the children, for Ransome used his whole body when telling stories. He brought the characters to life and was clearly having as much fun as they were. Ransome was always ready to join in with whatever his young friends were engaged upon. Dick Kelsall remembers flying a model aeroplane from the yard at Barkbooth when Ransome arrived in his car. He was as excited as the boys and wound the elastic up as far as he dared and released the plane. It climbed away to a great height and then, helped by a following breeze, flew right away and landed in a large oak. With a great cheer, Ransome pushed the boys into the back of the Trojan car and they chugged up the hill in pursuit. It was this spontaneous enthusiasm and willingness to join in which endeared him to all the youngsters he knew. They in turn provided him with the youthful company he seemed to need to assist in the creative process. They found Evgenia a striking figure — large and jolly, with a thick accent and a habit of calling out for 'Ar-tur!'

There were other young visitors at Low Ludderburn that year. At weekends Ransome would take his car and collect Taqui, Susie and Titty Altounyan from their school in Windermere. In the barn beside the cottage they listened to the latest chapters until he was quite exhausted. Then Evgenia would call them down to generous helpings in the tiny dining room beneath the gaze of a stuffed pike that fascinated the girls. Susie told me, 'On fine days we'd go fishing or sailing; we were always on our best behaviour for fear of being compared with tripperish tourists! Uncle Arthur was very changeable, bubbling over with mirthful laughter if all went well, or growling and cursing if someone displeased him in any way. Aunt Genia had a warm deep voice. She was a keen gardener and I remember the neat rows of brown and yellow pansies round the house. They always remind me of her to this day. To my everlasting regret our paths never crossed after I was seventeen. They could be such fun!'

It is easy to understand why Ransome admitted 'a sort of tenderness' for *Winter Holiday* because, apart from the charming evocation of frozen Windermere, it brings together for the first time all his warmth and humour.

There followed a gap, for it was not until 1935 that Ransome began his next Lakes book. His diary for February 17th reads: 'Gnossies to tea. Oscar full of help about the mining.' On March 2nd Ransome started work on *Pigeon Post*.

Some years after turning Ransome down, Barbara Coilingwood married Oscar Gnosspelius, and at that time they were living at Lanehead. In 1928 Gnosspelius had started to mine for copper, high on the flanks of Coniston Old Man. He kept it going for a few years, but it failed to yield any appreciable return and in 1933 he put John (Willie) Shaw, the old miner who had been working for him, into quarrying slate at Horse Crag, Tilberthwaite, below Wetherlam. On March 27th Ransome recorded: 'Went up behind Tilberthwaite with Gnossie. Saw several old workings and a suitable bit of country for my story.'

The *Swallows*, *Amazons* and D's engage in some gold-prospecting in the fells after Slater Bob, an old miner, tells them that gold had once been found on High Topps. In reality, High Topps is based on the dangerous area of mine shafts at the head of Tilberthwaite Gill.

'Well, what do you think of it?' said Nancy, waving her arm as if she had somehow conjured the whole of High Topps into existence.

Titty at first could hardly speak. That last run to the rock after the long climb from the valley had left her altogether out of breath. Spots swam before her eyes, but in spite of them she knew she was looking at a Klondyke, an Alaska, better than anything she had dreamed when they were talking of the goldfields in the camp at Beckfoot.

High Topps is too far from Beckfoot for the prospectors to commute daily, so Mrs Blackett agrees to them finding a camp site on condition that a daily pigeon brings a message from the parched wilderness of that long hot summer. A mysterious stranger in a squashy hat is also exploring High Topps, and Ransome is able to make one of his best stories out of the slenderest of notions — jumping to conclusions. 'He's looking at a compass,' Nancy almost shouted. 'Won't you believe now? Go on. Take the telescope and see for yourself. Giminy. He's in the very middle of prospecting.' And so he is — but not for their gold.

Before they can start the serious business of mining gold, however, a good water supply has to be found. But how? The story of their experiments with a divining rod shows Ransome at the very top of his form.

It is Nancy who first latches on to Dick's story of a dowser visiting his school with nothing more than a forked hazel stick. Before long she has her troops lined up as dusk begins to fall; one of them must be able to do it. Of course, nothing would be better than for the Captain herself to produce the goods in minutes, but when the stick refuses to budge, the others are marshalled in turn to try. Dorothea, desperate to be the one despite Dick's scepticism about such an unscientific method, hands over to Roger. No one falls for his larking about. The others having failed, it is Titty's turn.

'Half a minute,' said Captain Nancy eagerly. 'Didn't it give a sort of jerk just now?'

Titty, frightened of what is happening to her, looks round miserably as the fork dips and dips again. Suddenly it springs out of her hand, as if nothing can stop it, and Titty bolts up into the woods, shaking with sobs.

It could be said that Arthur Ransome kept all his best scenes for his favourite character. But that was only practice by the water pump in Tyson's yard: how were they to try again where the water was really needed, up on the fells, unless the able-seaman overcame her fears? With no one watching her, perhaps she could just bring herself to try again. Titty 'found herself breathing very fast . .

She left the platform and went in among the trees, looking in the dim light for Dick's green rushes. She found a tuft of them. Still nothing happened.

'It's all right,' she said to herself. 'You can't do it. It was only accident the other night. Nothing to be afraid of anyway. And you've tried. So it isn't your fault.'

And then she nearly dropped the twig. There it was, that tickling. Faint. Not like that other night at Tyson's. But the same thing. The twig was trying to move.

For a long time she stood where she was, somehow not daring to stir. Then she took a step or two, and the stick was as dead as ever.

'This is silly,' she said, and stepped back to the place where she had been and felt the stick press against the balls of her thumbs just as it had before.

'Well, it can't bite you,' said Titty, and made herself walk to and fro, in and out among the bushes and low trees at the edge of the wood . . The twig was pulling harder and harder. She wanted to throw it down, but, somehow, by herself, she was not as frightened of it as she had been when, all unexpectedly, she had felt it for the first time. No one was watching her now, for one thing. She had won her battle the moment she had brought herself to hold the twig again. Now, already, she was almost eagerly feeling the pulling of the twig. When it weakened she moved back until she felt it strengthen. Then again she walked on. It was like looking for something hidden, while someone, who knew where it was, called out hot or cold as she moved nearer to or further from the hiding place.

Suddenly, as she came nearer the Great Wall, the twisting of the twig became more violent. Here was a shallow dip in the ground between two rocks, and, yes, there was another tuft of those rushes in the bottom of it. She walked in between the rocks and it was just as it had been in the farmyard at Tyson's. The stick seemed to leap in her hands. The ends of it pressed against her thumbs, while the point of the fork dipped towards the ground, bending the branches, twisting her hands round with them, and at last almost springing out of her fingers.

'It's here,' said Titty. 'I've found it.' She had no longer any doubts. Dick was wrong. This was nothing of her imagining. No imagining could make the hazel twig twist her hands until they hurt. She was no longer afraid. This was a secret between her and the twig. Whatever the reason might be, the thing worked.

In June, Gnosspelius took Ransome to Swallow Scar near Wetherlam. 'Very jolly up there above the screes,' the diary says. He was shown how to pan for gold and to use a blowpipe. It was all grist to the mill. Predictably perhaps, Nancy does more than her fair share of the crushing — thud, thud, thud — with pestle and mortar, to keep the panners supplied. It is Dick, the man of science and precision, who develops his skill with the blowpipe into an ingenious charcoal smelting furnace. 'His cheeks were blown out to hold as much air as he could and let him keep up a steady blast through the pipe even while he was breathing in through his nose. The flame made a hissing noise. Again the charcoal round the hole turned red, then glowing white. The little pile of gold dust darkened ... the glowing drop moved in the hole, driven round it by the jet of candle-flame.' All the while, they must be on their guard against 'claim jumpers'. Scouts report back constantly on the movements of Squashy Hat. 'Walking? Was he going somewhere or just mooching about?' Nancy expects all the details.

Gnosspelius himself appeared as Squashy Hat (he did indeed wear a large hat) and Willie Shaw was portrayed as the old miner, Slater Bob.

Horse Crag Level served as Slater Bob's mine. Even the tunnel through to High Topps once existed, but it was a much more complicated and dangerous affair than the one into which Titty, Roger and the D's stumbled. Young Janet Gnosspelius posed for the drawing of Nancy with the pestle and mortar and Dick Kelsall rose to Ransome's challenge to construct a device so that homing pigeons might ring bells. Ransome carefully drew his invention.

But *Pigeon Post* had to wait until the following year before completion, as Ransome was much too busy with his latest acquisition — the 7-ton cutter *Nancy Blackett.*

Jibbooms and Bobstays

SIGNAL FOR A PILOT

Once Ransome took possession of *Swallow*, he sank an old motor car engine in Bowness Bay with a hook attached to a little wooden buoy with *Swallow's* name on. One of the boatmen, George Walker, who had his boatshed close to the Windermere ferry (the boatyard is still in the family today), looked after her, and Ransome paid him £5 a year to keep her baled out during the summer and to see that she was taken out of the water and stored under cover during the winter. Just before leaving for Syria, Ransome had applied for membership of the Cruising Association (his membership having apparently lapsed), giving as his 'yacht' the sailing dinghy *Swallow* with a length of 13 feet.

Ransome and Evgenia missed very badly their happy Baltic voyaging so, from time to time, they sailed larger craft on the Norfolk Broads. Their first boat, called *Welcome*, was about 17 feet long, una-rigged with a gaff sail and the mast stepped close to the bows. She drew very little water and Ransome claimed she could make her way in a ditch. In her the Ransomes thoroughly explored the Broads above Yarmouth. They made a point of sailing in the spring when, in those days, motor cruisers were lying unused or waiting for summer. They enjoyed the Broadland birdlife, looking for bearded tits and admiring the spectacle of the harriers over Hickling and Horsey. At that time they regularly heard the booming of the bittern and occasionally spotted one flying over the marshes. Ransome photographed a great crested grebe on its nest as he sailed by, and watched from a few yards away a pair of grebes giving their young swimming lessons. In notes for his *Autobiography* he recalls:

I had known the Broads in the far away past when, in an ancient wherry, I had gone fishing for pike there in the late autumn after all the pleasure craft of those days had been pulled out to winter into their sheds. I had no idea what it would be like to hire a small yacht. But I knew that

Arthur Ransome sailing *Swallow* in Bowness Bay

supposing anything were to go wrong with me it would not really matter. That, of course, is why the Broads make so admirable a training ground for the inexperienced. If in difficulties the anxious mariner can always run the nose of his boat into the reeds, consult a book, learn what he is doing wrong, and start again. Again and again I have watched a couple of young people pushed off from Wroxham where they had hired their boat, after a few sailing instructions from a boatman. I have seen them making mistake after mistake, tacking earnestly with a following wind, desperately trying to sail straight into the wind with the boom amidships, sending their halyards in a hurrah's nest to the top of the mast when they lowered sail, making every possible mistake, and taking several hours to get a few hundred yards down the river before tying up, exhausted, for the night. I have seen those same young people twenty-four hours later, quite possibly sailing with a taut topping lift, almost certainly most brutally misusing the tiller, but all the same getting along with smiling confidence. And at the end of the week I have seen them come sailing back to give up their boat with a skill picked up by watching others, round up and come alongside as to the manner born, stow their sails, coil their ropes, and affectionately swab down the decks of the little ship that, though they are just about to hand her over, they have come to think of as their own.

One year they had taken Ted Scott, and his son Dick. Scott, then editor of the *Manchester Guardian,* had been over-working for years and it had taken all Ransome's power of persuasion to drag his friend away on holiday. What joy it was for him to see Ted and Dick provisioning their boat at the big store in Wroxham with all 'the eagerness of children let loose with unlimited money in a toyshop'. One morning, while sailing past the Ransome boat, Ted Scott explained their delay in getting under way —

'not without a wicked glee' — with a tale of Dick tumbling overboard. That evening they listened to Dick's exultant story of his father going overboard too. 'I went in only up to my middle, but Daddy went in up to his ears.'

The Ransomes' favourite boats were the *Fairway* class of yachts, which they hired from Jack Powles of Wroxham. The *Fairways* were 24 feet long with gaff rig and had three berths in two cabins, with the cooking done in the well under an awning.

They had a similar programme each year. Starting from Wroxham, they visited every corner of the northern Broads during the first week — Horning, Ludham, Barton Broad, Stalham, South Walsham, Potter Heigham, Horsey, Hickling and Acle — and then would go down with the tide to reach Yarmouth at low water. They worked through the bridges and sailed across Breydon Water, spending the next week going to Oulton Broad and on to Beccles, doubling back to Reedham and then up the River Yare to Norwich. 'Some of our happiest memories', Ransome wrote, 'are of slipping along in the dusk, using the best of the tide to bring us to a distant staithe when, in northern waters, we should long ago have been tied up and cooking supper.' Then it would be back through Yarmouth again and up the River Bure with the rising tide to spend the third week pottering round the easy waterways of the north. 'Going there as often as we did, we came to know the Broads extremely well and to feel very much at home there. In the sixteenth century one of my ancestors was a miller at North Walsham, and he may have helped me to feel no stranger.'

In 1933, for the first time since their sailing days in the Baltic, Ransome began to think that some day he might again have a seagoing boat of his own — if *Winter Holiday*, which he had just completed, should prove a success. In late September Ransome hired a nearly new three-berth *Delight* class Broads motor cruiser for a fishing trip, and with him went Charles and Margaret Renold whom he had met through Ted Scott. Margaret was

The Ransomes on the Broards
(Tony Colwell Collection)

Norfolk Broads Delight Cruiser — Margaret looks at her watch
(by Arthur Ransome)

the sort of person with whom he could discuss plots; she was to play a crucial part in the construction of both *Coot Club* and *The Big Six*. Charles caught Ransome's love of fishing and was equally at home with a fly rod as he was coarse fishing with a float. Ransome felt unwell at the start of the trip, but he thought it was no more than the usual duodenal trouble that a few days of sea air would put right.

They collected the cruiser from Herbert Woods boatyard in Potter Heigham, complete with a sailing dinghy for Ransome to use when he tired of fishing. After stopping briefly, they moored for their first night in Kendal Dyke. Next morning Ransome sailed off in the dinghy to fetch milk, leaving the others aboard to fish. On the return he was not quite satisfied with the set of the sail and gave it an extra hard pull. He tells the story in an unpublished part of the *Autobiography*:

It was as if some villain had stabbed me in the vitals. I collapsed in the bottom of the boat and could not get up. Luckily the wind was light, though a head wind for my return. However it was a kindly little dinghy, and lying in the bottom of her, in the position that seemed best to ease the horrible pain, I sailed her up the river. Lying flat, I could not see much, and steered with a finger on the tiller above my head. Whenever I saw reeds over the gunwale I put her about, and in this way managed to take her back to Kendal Dyke and to the cruiser.

Somehow Renold managed to help the 17-stone Ransome out of the dinghy and into the centre cockpit of the cruiser. Renold then took the

cruiser right through to Wroxham, although it was dark when they arrived
— and sailing after dusk is not allowed in Broadland. Ransome knew the
Wroxham doctor who called Blaxland, the surgeon. He diagnosed acute
appendicitis, whipped Ransome into Norwich, and operated straight away.
Three weeks later Ransome was sitting in an armchair on the lawn of the
King's Head in Wroxham, swathed in blankets, while Evgenia and he
watched their floats in the river. He sent a wryly amusing letter to the
Renolds:

They let me up several days ago, walking round my bed, holding
myself together. Then yesterday they let me have a bath.
Today I have been in the garden. Tomorrow the King's Head.

In the middle of November they sailed in the steamship *Southern Coast*
from London Docks to Falmouth. Herbert Hanson, the long-serving
Honorary Secretary of the Cruising Association, found rooms for them in
St Mawes. Hanson compiled the *Cruising Association Handbook* that
carried the Latin verse and cautionary drawing which Ransome later
borrowed for *Missee Lee*. The Ransomes stayed in St Mawes for two
months, recuperating, and for a while they considered buying an old
Thames barge and making it their home. One of the boats they were
particularly taken with was the *Deerfoot*, a 45-foot Falmouth 'Stone' barge,
which Hanson was having converted to an auxiliary ketch and which later
was owned by 'Bosun' Walker. He was a master mariner, who spent his
winters moored in Horning Reach on the Norfolk Broads and his summers
cruising on the East Coast, with occasional crossings to Holland.

Having successfully introduced Renold to fishing, Ransome persuaded
his friend to have Crossfield (who made *Swallow*) build a dinghy for him

so that he could teach him to sail on Windermere the following summer. After seeing work in progress on the new boat, Ransome wrote:

She is all but finished planking and we have to report that you are in very great luck. How the devil they do it, I do not know, but they have got hold of the most beautiful spruce for the planking and a really lovely bit of wood for the keel and stem and covering board. I think you have got a real bargain in her and we are both full of envy.

The boat was called *Coch-y-bonddhu*, after a favourite fishing fly. Renold sailed *Cocky* a little, but he preferred to fish, and in the end he presented her to Ransome.

Meanwhile *Coot Club* was completed and in May 1934 they hired a *Fairway* from Wroxham and had a gentle three weeks following the route of *Teasel* so that he could take photographs from which the illustrations could be drawn. In the book Ransome gives a fascinating and accurate picture of Broadland at that time.

Never in all their lives had Dick and Dorothea seen so many boats. Mrs. Barrable had taken them shopping at a store that seemed to sell every possible thing for the insides and outsides of sailors. She had taken them to lunch at an inn where everybody was talking about boats at the top of his voice. And now they had gone down to the river to look for the Horning boatman with his motor launch. The huge flags of the boatletters were flying from their tall flag-staffs. Little flags, copies of the big ones, were fluttering at the mastheads of the hired yachts. There were boats everywhere, and boats of all kinds, from the big black wherry with her gaily painted mast, loading at the old granary by Wroxham bridge, and meant for nothing but hard work, to the punts of the boatmen going to and fro, and the motor-cruisers filling up with petrol, and the hundreds of big and little sailing yachts tied to the quays, or moored in rows, two and three deep, in the dykes and artificial harbours beside the main river.

In *Coot Club* a crowd of pleasure-seeking Hullabaloos chase Tom Dudgeon, the Horning doctor's son, around the Broads because he has cast off their cruiser after they had refused to move from a coot's nest with eggs about to hatch. Tom, as well as doing his best to avoid capture, is teaching Dick and Dorothea to sail. Eventually the Hullabaloos wreck their powerful cruiser by ramming a post on Breydon Water. Tom's allies, the three boatbuilders' sons in their *Death and Glory*, save them from drowning by taking their helpless quarry off the wreck. The conflict between young Tom Dudgeon, the local boy, and the Hullabaloos is essentially one between the old traditional way of life and its values and the new wave of holidaymakers. The 1930s were a time of change for the Broads. In little more than a decade the sailing wherry would be gone from rivers becoming increasingly polluted.

For several years the Ransomes considered leaving Low Ludderburn. Although it had the advantage of a magnificent workroom in the converted barn adjacent to the house, there was no electricity or proper water supply. Early in 1935 they began house-hunting on the edge of the Lake District south of Kendal, convenient for those rivers Ransome loved to fish. They almost bought the Old Vicarage at Old Hutton, but at auction it fetched more than Ransome felt he could afford. 'A very sad affair as Genia would have liked to live there.' They would probably have gone on looking in that area had not a chance sea voyage with a friend given Ransome a reminder of his *Racundra* days. His friend owned a modern 5-ton cutter and on the passage from Barrow to Fleetwood Ransome steered in both directions. 'Very jolly to be doing it again after ten years,' he wrote in his diary.

At the end of a month debating whether to move to the East Coast and buy a boat in which they could cruise or remain in the north and enjoy the fishing, the attractions of the East Coast won, and Evgenia began studying the map. Eventually she chose the Shotley peninsula, and down they went to find a home. There was nothing at all suitable, so they looked round Ipswich, Felixstowe and Levington. On July 25th they saw Broke Farm at Levington and decided to rent it. At the beginning of August he worked steadily on *Pigeon Post* and then stopped. There would be no new Ransome for Christmas 1935.

Broke Farm was originally the home farm of Broke Hall. In those days it was a plain red brick house with cowsheds and dairy on one side and a row of cottages on the other. From Ransome's upstairs workroom he could see Levington Creek, Harwich Harbour and the open sea. There were steamers passing to and from Ipswich, and the Danish butter boat as well as the mail steamers between Harwich and the Hook. Near at hand there were always smacks dredging for oysters.

One of Ransome's Royal Cruising Club friends, William Mc. C. Meek, found Ransome a 7-ton cutter, which had just been put up for sale, lying at Poole. Ransome travelled to the South Coast on Sunday September 8th and after making a token show of haggling, bought her on the spot for the asking price of £525 — £100 more than she had fetched two years earlier. The boat had been built by David Hillyard's Littlehampton boatyard in the spring of 1931 for Seymour Tuely, a retired solicitor, who called her *Spindnft.* In January 1933 she was bought from him by Paget Bowyer with the money he received for his twenty-first birthday. Bowyer

Broke Farmhouse

was an engineering student and he changed the boat's name to *Electron*, a word which had recently come into use and sounded thoroughly modern. Originally *Electron's* sails had been tanned, and the mainsail had hoops with a wire running from top to bottom of the mast to support the sail above the cross-trees. By the time Ransome acquired her, she had new white canvas sails and the mast hoops had been replaced by a track. The hull was constructed of pitch-pine, copper-fastened on oak frames. The cabin coamings and deck fittings were of mahogany, and the little ship had the added luxury of decks laid with planks that followed the curve of the hull instead of straight planks covered with canvas.

Ransome disliked the name *Electron*. He changed it again, to *Nancy Blackett*, saying that if it had not been for the colourful *Nancy* and her adventures he could never have afforded to buy her.

Nancy climbed over the bulwarks between two of the cannon, found a hold for her feet, then another, and dropped down into her own old ship. 'Jibbooms and bobstays, what a beastly mess,' she said. 'Lucky we wedged the bailer under the stern sheets.'
She began scooping out the water.

Although it was late in the season, Ransome decided to sail *Nancy* round to Pin Mill. His friend Hanson found him a crew, Peter Tilbury, strong enough to do the heavy work of hauling and young enough to cheerfully leave the navigation to Ransome.

Having bought 30 fathoms of new grass warp, they spent the first night at anchor off Brownsea Island, rather than sail on a Friday. The following morning they sailed for the Wight. It was almost Ransome's first taste of sailing off the coasts of England, and in some ways he could not have had a worse introduction. At the same time, as both the boat and he came through it all with flying colours, he could hardly have had a better. They had just left the shelter of Poole Harbour when the gale started. He nearly lost *Nancy* that first day, meeting the full force of the ebb out of the Needles and, in the wild water there, being swept almost on the Shingles. Ransome recorded his first passage in the log:

Saturday 14th September. 9.50.

Approx 4 hours late for the tide, sailed from moorings under trysail and reefed staysail. Wind SW force 4. Billy at work.

10.55 Bar buoy abeam. Streamed log. Course E by S. Shut off Billy.

Got a wet stern with a little sea that slapped up near the bar. After that fine sail to the Needles, land intermittently visible, but visibility not too good. Needles well on port bow.

Dinghy unexpectedly charged our transom and started its top plank. I had put the grass warp in the dinghy and Tilbury hooked it overboard

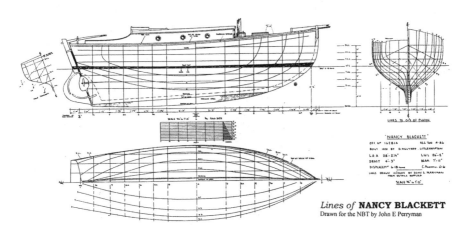

Lines of **NANCY BLACKETT**
Drawn for the NBT by John E Perryman

Nancy Blackett's Lines taken off by John Perryman

with the boathook. Dinghy then behaved, but we were going at such a lick through the water that the warp cut through the seas instead of riding them and looked most odd, coming out of them as stiff as a bar of iron. This helped a good deal in the bad water, and we got aboard only a few seas that came up on the quarter.

Met violent tide streaming out. Started Billy who was off at once. And with strong wind, and Billy, just able to stem the tide which leebowed us across from the Needles to the North passage, so that we found the Shingles uncovering on our starboard. We passed close to Hurst Fort, just making a little on the tide, came across to the fort on the other side, and at last got into Yarmouth at 3.55. Tilbury getting the trysail down by going up the mast just as we got in by the quay. Billy took us to a mooring buoy, and the local authority moored us stem and stern, and told us that the coastguard on the Needles had telephoned to Yarmouth to tell them to be ready to come out for us with the lifeboat. We expressed suitable surprise, and made a very rough wet stow before settling down to hog. On the trip across the best we could do was two thermos flasks of hot tomato soup, which was grand at the moment we got it.

Ransome meant to leave *Nancy* in Yarmouth while he went up to London to sign the lease on Broke Farm. The unpublished part of his *Autobiography* gives this account:

Part of the sea wall was washed away. A houseboat was thrown up on the road, and of four small boats moored close to us, only the tops of the masts of three were visible next morning. Frantic SOS knocking in the dark told of a man overboard. The boarding boat, taking men from the quay to the lifeboat only twenty yards away, was swamped at once, and the man was drowned in the harbour. A big motor boat had come in at dusk and moored between the same two buoys as ourselves and my young man and I spent most of the night naked, using up mattresses and coils of rope to protect our topsides from those of the cruiser, and in the morning the harbour master, looking from the quay, thought that we had sunk, because he could see nothing but the spray flying high over the top of us. It was not until late the next day that the Lymington Ferry was able to cross to Lymington.

Eventually Ransome completed his business in town and, while the gale eased, they took *Nancy* into the shelter of Haslar Creek, Portchester. Here Ransome's naval cousin, Godfrey Ransome, came down to admire the staunch little ship and entertain them with stories of shooting the Yangtse rapids.

They sailed again on September 23rd, taking the Looe Channel off Selsey Bill which Ransome had not been through before. They were rather confused by the 'extraordinary fairground of Brighton lights', and it was eleven at night, with the tide against them, before they arrived off Newhaven. 'I have never yet seen Newhaven in daylight,' he wrote, 'but it is an easy harbour in the dark. I went in and my young man had a sleep. At three in the morning my alarm clock went, and a very unwilling young man, rubbing the sleep from his eyes, cast off our mooring ropes and we were off again.' They cleared Beachy Head, passed by the Royal Sovereign light-vessel and were soon 'going like a train past Dungeness, reaching Dover at ten minutes past two in the afternoon, very wet and very cold.' A gale blew up as they struggled into Granville Dock and lay at peace beside a barge.

The weather did not improve, as expected, on the way to Ramsgate, where they decided to go right on through to Pin Mill. Ransome was anxious to get back to Windermere for the move. Under trysail they took the Edinburgh Channel and arrived at the Barrow Deep just as darkness fell. 'With the dark came rain and wind', wrote Ransome, 'so thick that we could not see the Barrow lightship while still close to it.'

Nancy's compass — an installation of a previous owner — was lit by electricity alone, and when the current failed they were left 'bucketing along in the dark', able to see the compass only by flashing a pocket torch.

Nancy Blackett

Ransome had worked out a course for the Sunk lightship and set his heart on reaching the estuary into Harwich in daylight. The rain lifted and visibility cleared, but he resisted the short cut through the Medusa Channel and kept on course to the Sunk, and from there to the Cork lightship. 'We hung about miserably, having the utmost difficulty in wearing *Nancy* round (she would not stay). I hasten to add that nothing was wrong with her but bad trim ... presently I had her so well balanced that she would sail by herself without attention while I sat working in cabin or cockpit.'

In the log he wrote:

And thence WNW to Cork LV which we had difficulty in making owing to strong ebb. Found it impossible to go about, headsails being too much for our reefed main, so wore her, and kept going to and fro, making nowt until the tide slackened, and soon after dawn we were able to make up from the Cork in one tack to the first of the fairway buoys, with another tack the second, and at last, as the light strengthened, to the platters and round into Harwich, and so to Shotley and up to Pin Mill where we moored, picking up a buoy at 9.10 am. Their only damage, beyond scratches to paint and varnish, was the destruction of the dinghy, the remains of which were still tethered astern.

Ransome summed up the whole experience, 'It had been very uncomfortable, but at least it had shown me that Meek had found me a wonderful little boat.' In spite of his resolution to return to Low Ludderburn, he did not want to leave his little ship and he remained aboard for a few days before Evgenia sent an SOS and he had to go north and prepare for the move. A fortnight later, on October 21st, they began settling into Broke Farm and a week after that Ransome sent a progress report to Taqui Altounyan, then living in Cambridge studymg for Oxford entrance:

Nancy Blackett is still afloat and getting into trim, but there seems a lot to do. It will be a fortnight at least before I can lay her up, because I am having a little coal fireplace put in, a tiny stove for people to bark their shins on, which will be in the forecabin ... I very much want you to see her before we put her to bed.

I have been at work in her all day, finishing off the dreadful bad splices left by previous owners. She is beautifully dry, but the Turkey carpet is all over fluff from bad rope ends. You'd better come along and do some brushing.

Nancy's first visitors were Ransome's publisher friend Wren Howard and his family. Wren Howard was Jonathan Cape's partner who had the unenviable task of jollying Ransome along in his frequent bouts of depression in order that his current book might arrive not too desperately behind schedule. They were followed a couple of days later by Hanson and Meek, who came to welcome the new 'Master and Owner'.

By the time Taqui arrived at Levington on November 9th, bringing with her Meriol Trevor (a friend from the Perse School), Ransome had the sails tanned but the stove was not fitted until 1937. Meriol Trevor had been a *Swallows and Amazons* fan from the beginning, and was in the same form as Susie Altounyan, who stayed with her family during the term. Meriol told me 'Susie was not at all like Mate Susan (rather to my relief). She maintained that Mate Susan was more like Genia — and when I met her, I could just see it, though Genia was a much more formidable lady than Mate Susan would have become! Ransome seemed to me then exactly how I imagined Captain Flint to be, although he always repudiated the identification. Unable to sail in Cambridge, we turned ourselves into the crew of an imaginary boat called *Albatross* and used to go out for long walks and picnics, on pretend adventures, wearing pirate caps made out of my brother's football stockings!'

The Master and owner of *Nancy Blackett*

Even on their mooring Meriol Trevor found the motion in *Nancy's* cabin too much for her and she sat in the cockpit in the rain. They managed a couple of short trips by motor in between bouts of bad weather, and that completed *Nancy's* season. Not at all put off by that experience, Meriol Trevor and Susie Altounyan returned to spend a weekend aboard at the time of the Abdication crisis, and Meriol remembered that Ransome, 'who was very pro-Edward, kept buying papers and swearing over them'. By that time he was full of his 'seabook' and he read them the Woolworth plate episode. 'He also asked us if we would be frightened if we found ourselves at sea. Of course we silly teenagers said, 'No', which justifiably irritated him, as we certainly would have been.'

Nancy was put on a mud berth and Ransome removed her gear to Broke Farm. Every now and then he went aboard and, in spite of finding the deck leaking, always felt better for the visit. *Coch-y-bonddhu* was brought from the north and kept in Levington Creek beside an old sluice. Whenever the tide served he was able to sail across to *Nancy*, or to Pin Mill.

In January a diary entry says simply: 'Planned *We Didn't Mean to Go to Sea.*' He wrote to Wren Howard, ' During the last four days I have seen, grabbed, clutched at and pinioned a really gorgeous idea for another book ... *Swallows* only ... no *Nancy* or Peggy or Captain Flint ... but a GORGEOUS idea with a first-class climax inevitable and handed out on a plate ... lovely new angle of technical approach and everything else I could wish'. The following month he wrote 26 pages of his 'seabook'. Just as his earlier boats had been put into print, he was ready to do the same for the *Nancy Blackett*. She had four berths and would make an ideal command for John Walker who could take the *Swallows* to adventures on the East Coast. The origin of the voyage itself may have been the occasion when Jim Clay and his elder brother took charge of the 6-ton yawl *Firefly* on a family cruise to Holland. Their father Henry Clay (later knighted) was an old friend from the *Manchester Guardian* who frequently used the Pin Mill anchorage.

In the book, *Nancy* is faithfully and accurately portrayed under the pseudonym *Goblin* — even to Ransome's Royal Cruising Club burgee — (presumably Jim Brading's uncle was a member). The fidelity stopped short of giving *Nancy's* official number — 162814, not 16856 which Jim Brading quotes to the Harwich harbour master. But Ransome could go no further with the new book just then, because he still had a lot of work to do to complete *Pigeon Post*, and Wren Howard was urging him to complete the illustrations for *Swallows and Amazons* and *Swallowdale*.

On Hanson's advice, Ransome ordered a tiny pram dinghy for boarding *Nancy* from a Bembridge boatyard, for *Cocky* was a heavy boat to row. It was delivered by train and road to Pin Mill, where Ransome collected it. 'Very easy rowing, though inclined to throw up spray in any

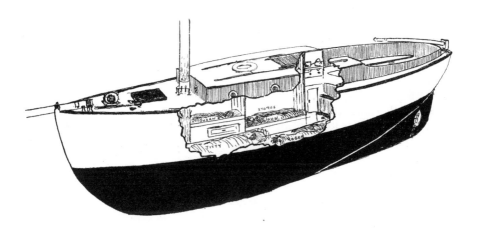

The *Goblin* (from *We Didn't Mean to Go to Sea*)

ripple.' The tiny boat was christened *Queen Mary*, and when both Ransomes were embarked there was precious little freeboard!

As Easter approached he was still completing the first draft of *Pigeon Post*. Then came an orgy of fitting out. King's, the Pin Mill boatbuilders, gave *Nancy* some new cross-trees, and Ransome for some reason — perhaps to make it easier to hoist the mainsail returned to mast hoops instead of the neater and more convenient track. Pin Mill was, in the 1930s, still very much a workaday place with a few yachts. There were always barges up for repair on the hard, and Ransome came to know all the skippers, which added to the pleasure of meeting them at sea. With no crane at Pin Mill, the bargemen were always in demand at the start and end of the season when they used their huge sprits as derricks for stepping or taking out the masts of the yachts.

One very cold day, early in April, Ransome took *Nancy* down to Felixstowe Dock and brought up alongside a collier. The collier's crew took the ropes. No sooner were they made fast than a big black kettle was lowered down the side to *Nancy*. 'Reckon you're three parts froze,' a voice from above called down. 'You'll be wanting a cup of tea.' In the *Autobiography* he observes: 'It is only one of the many kindnesses shown by fishermen, barge sailormen and other professional sailors who, recognising that the sea makes no distinction between professional and amateur, treat us who merely play about in boats as members of their own brother-hood, on sole condition that we shall take our sailing seriously, as they perforce take theirs.'

Ransome hoped to make the first cruise of the season a good one, and try for Lowestoft. A hard, cold, north-east wind made that impossible, so he sailed 2 miles down the river and anchored off Collimer Point for the night. Evgenia seldom sailed aboard *Nancy*, thinking she was altogether too cramped. Ransome wrote to Taqui Altounyan:

> Aunt Genia says she is not going to have anything to do with her, except PERHAPS between May 15th and July 15th. I think however that in decent weather I ought to be able to manage her with a couple of A.B.'s. Anyhow we'll try. But they must be proof against seasickness.

Evgenia did not quite keep to her word, but she had taken against *Nancy* from the start, because the little Taylor paraffin stove to starboard of the companionway and little white earthenware 'housemaid's' basin to port into which water had to be poured, gave little scope for the Cook of *Racundra* to show her mettle. She sailed aboard *Nancy* in early May, when they went down to the Outer Ridge buoy and back. It must have been more successful than either expected, for afterwards they feasted at the Butt and Oyster, where Evgenia drank rum and Ransome 'pop'. He made several short trips with a man called Woodard during May, although most of the month was spent revising *Pigeon Post*. Then, in spite of his recurring duodenal trouble, he planned something much more adventurous. He did not feel that he could start seriously on *We Didn't Mean to Go to Sea* until he had made sure of his facts by following the *Goblin's* tracks across the North Sea.

Evgenia at the helm of *Nancy Blackett*

On May 31st *Nancy* was anchored off Shotley, 'I had a bad go of duodenal with the usual snorting headache, felt very sick but was not and went to sleep for a few hours which more or less did the trick'. The following morning he put out for Holland. His crew, Herbert Smith, was a man with little or no experience at sea. The wind was variable and they had to beat against it from Felixtowe to Landguard. Ransome felt that *Nancy* was comfortable under full main and jib and was utterly disgusted when his crew urged him to give up the crossing and make for Brightlingsea. Ransome held on, but the man was still fretting about turning back when they reached the Sunk LV. 'His attitude and lack of faith made me feel pretty beastly,' Ransome wrote in his diary. Smith then retired to his bunk while Ransome held on, meeting the train ferry closely followed by the Flushing-Harwich mail boat. *Nancy* reached the Galloper LV around 7.30 and Ransome enquired what sort of night they were expecting. 'Light westerlies,' was the reply. Smith came on deck and said, 'If she was mine' I'd put about now. We ought to be making for the coast Yarmouth or Lowestoft way. He retired below once more when Ransome made it clear that he had every intention of going on. Ransome steered until his crew finally relieved him after ten hours at the tiller at 10.30. At 2.30 am Ransome took over once more, ignoring the crew's plea to turn south for Ostend. The *Queen Mary* was swamped by a cross wave from a steamer, but Ransome called his crew from his bunk, and together they hauled the little craft up to the transom and emptied her. At 8 am they sighted the West Kapelle LV, but now the wind headed them and they motored up the Deurloo Channel in bright sunshine with thunder clouds approaching from the Belgian coast. They were soaked through by the time they reached Flushing lock at 1.30, In the log, Ransome recorded, 'Lots of crabs and jelly fish in the lock. Moored to post on port hand in the canal. V comfortable berth, barring small boys who in the end behaved all right.' They had sailed and motored 93 miles, with Ransome 'pretty tired after steering nineteen hours out of twenty-five, only pausing to go below and feed the crew'.

The little *Goblin* was swooping along under the steep grey wall of a stone pier. A Dutch boy in wide blue trousers shouted from the top of the jetty and waved. The pilot solomnly lifted a huge hand and dropped it again. They passed a beacon on the end of the breakwater. The pilot was hauling on the end of the mainsheet. Jibing. John wanted to go and help, but it was over too quickly. A huge open space of smooth water opened before them. The *Goblin* was on an even keel. Away to the left of the breakwater were the gates of a lock and a couple of steam ferryboats. The high breakwater shut off the wind. There was an almost startling peace.

Meanwhile, his family were naturally concerned about his first sea crossing for more than ten years. His mother confided to his sister, Joyce, ' I am wondering so much how Arthur and his friend are getting on. I think they were leaving Harwich for Flushing Friday night or early Saturday morning — the boat looks so much too small and Arthur so much too big for this venture.' They need not have been so bothered, for if any vindication were needed of Ransome's navigation and seamanship, or of *Nancy's* qualities, then this voyage surely provides it.

The following day they had planned to start back, but with Ransome suffering from the after effects of his long passage, they motored up the canal, passing an Estonian steamer *Narwi* whose crew were astonished to hear him hail them in Russian, 'Long live the Estonians.' Their old berth was occupied, so they tied up near a pilot steamer,

Ransome recorded his stay in Flushing in the log.

June 4. had to shift from Pilot Vessel No 7. E.de Smit, Pilot (apprentice) on foredeck very kind, in making our shift easy. Got back to our old place when we adapted an excellent old motor tyre on one of the piles to soften our lie, hanging our own fenders on piles fore and aft. V. comfortable, but a bit blackening from tyre on the topsides.

June 5 Strong Nly wind. Cooking and washing up as usual. Mate before going off for for his walk enquired, 'What are your plans for meals?' I told him and off he goes, coming back to feed and then off he goes again. He has told the Pilot that he is a professional seaman from sailing ships.

June 6. Strong Nly-NWly winds. Got some good rope and made ready for start tonight, but again bad forecast and heavy sea outside. Mate caught out lying to the Pilot.

Ransome was quite convinced that Herbert Smith, his mate, had done only day and coastal sailing, and after five days in Flushing sent him home. ('Paid his fare and thankful to be rid of him.') Ransome made friends with the helpful pilot, and he found a young Dutchman happy to crew for him for £1 a day and his return fare. On the seventh day in harbour they left on the afternoon tide. With evening came a change of wind, and as Ransome felt he would rather not spend the night beating against it, they altered course for

All but O.B
(from *We Didn't Mean to Go to Sea*)

Zeebrugge, which they reached around 9.30 pm.

Downed sails and steamed slowly up the channel to the inner harbour where we hunted about for a place to lie. Nothing doing in the main harbour and we were warned off anchoring in it by local boatmen who urged mooring alongside a boat in the SE corner. Went off to have a look and found said boat already aground! So took our five feet, off elsewhere, and had a peep in the fishing basin which seemed like a well-packet sardine tin, so, in the end, went out again to the lightbuoy at the end of the mud, and then, using the leading lights on the Mole, came along the Mole to its inner end, getting horrid glimpses of mud every now and then, and anchored in four fathom, just beyond the last pair of lights. Decent quiet night with wind piping up outside and overhead.

My Dutch mate said, 'Well I've never been in Zeebrugge before, and I don't think I've missed much.' Hotted up a tin of Army Rations and French beans and then had stewed peaches, and turned in very content with new crew.

Meeting the sailing ship
(from *We Didn't Mean to Go to Sea*)

Ransome's photograph of *Pommern* towing out of Ipswich

At first light the following morning they discovered that they had anchored just off the mailboat's berth, and after a solid breakfast decided to leave before the mailboat should arrive, rather than look for another mooring elsewhere. They motored out in the hope of finding some wind outside. It was very misty along the coast and they decided to give up and make sure of a good night's sleep in Ostend. Leaving just before mid-day next morning they found they could lay a course for the Sunk LV. The wind dropped at dusk and they motored on. Soon after midnight, 'Wind suddenly came from the SW pretty hard, and she would have gone a lot faster if we had re-hoisted the mainsail, but the Dutchman was sleeping peacefully, and there was no violent hurry, and I was enjoying myself and knew that the change of motion would wake him, even if I did not call him to help. So we went lazily on ...'

With the morning came mist and very poor visibility. They were close to the Cork LV before they saw its ghostly form.

Then we saw a lovelier sight, the four masted barque *Pommern* being towed out. I was was lucky to get three photographs of her in the mist from close to, and by giving short exposure and wide aperture, got good ones, from which, except that the nearby coast does not show at all, one would not guess that there was any fog.

They anchored off Shotley pier soon after 8 am Ransome put the Dutchman ashore so that he could catch the mailboat, and, after being cleared by Customs, continued up the river singlehanded. At Pin Mill Miss Wiles helped him to moor and she went aboard to tidy up below, just as the *Swallows* helped Jim Brading:

'I say, just look down,' said Titty.
They looked down into the cabin of the little ship, at blue mattresses on bunks on either side, at a little table with a chart tied down to it with string, at a roll of blankets in one of the bunks, at a foghorn in another, and at a heap of dirty plates and cups and spoons in a little white sink opposite the tiny galley, where a saucepan of water was simmering on one of the two burners of a little cooking stove.
'Look here,' said Susan. 'Hadn't we better get on with those ropes. We oughtn't to be here at all really. We're going to be late for supper ...'
One by one they disentangled the ropes from the mass on the floor of the cockpit, coiled each one separately and laid it on a seat. Meanwhile John and the skipper were busy on the foredeck, closing the hatch, coiling the buoy rope, throwing overboard handfuls of green seaweed, dipping the mop over the side, sousing water on the deck and sweeping the mud from the mooring chain away and out of the scuppers. In about ten minutes nobody could have guessed that the *Goblin* had only just come in from the sea.

Miss Wiles (no one at Pin Mill ever called her anything else) was a redoubtable young woman. She had already won trophies for cruises in her yacht *Coquette* and she thought nothing of climbing aloft to sort out Ransome's rigging for him. Such was the spirit of fellowship that existed.

Ransome always kept a good look out for visiting boats, either from *Nancy*, or with a spyglass from the room at the top of Broke Farm. One day, when he was fishing from *Nancy*, he saw a tiny gaff-rigged yacht bring up close by. On board were P. G. Rouse and his wife. The two men had not seen each other for forty years; not since they were contemporaries at Rugby. Rouse and his wife were invited back to Broke Farm for tea and then supper, and when the time came for them to return to *Mermaid* they found the boat aground and out of reach on the mud. Even if they had been able to get to her, they would have spent a most uncomfortable night, for usually they slept on the bottom-boards. When the boat heeled over as the tide receded, one or other of them would have ended up lying in the bilgewater.

By August Bank Holiday the revision of *Pigeon Post* was completed and ready for Evgenia's inspection. Ransome had learnt by bitter experience that it was safer to be out the way while she studied any typescript. 'Rouse and I had a couple of really gorgeous sails,' Ransome wrote cheerfully to his mother.

... Spent the night anchored in a creek called the Pyefleet behind Mersea Island ... That night was pretty wild and blowly [sic] and next day it blew as you know very hard, and we were in two minds about what to do. In the end we took in three reefs in the mainsail, and put on my little storm jib, and tried what it was like. It was pretty well submarinish down to the Bar buoy, and we got very wet indeed but then, when we came round the Bar buoy and were able to bring the seas on our quarter, things were easier, and we had the best run I've had since coming home to Riga in the gale back in 1922. With the storm sails she was quite happy, and fairly flew, big waves picking her up, and she riding the top of them in a

George Russell

The Busk Family aboard
Lapwing

Josephine Russell at the
helm of *Nancy Blackett*

flurry of white foam until they passed her and she slipped down to be picked up by the next. It really was gorgeous. We did not see any other yachts on the whole passage, just one steamship and two barges, which looked very fine indeed. The three of us, the two big Thames barges and my little *Nancy* all came storming round the Naze together, and we got good shelter down at Shotley at the mouth of the river, where we lay all night, coming back to Pin Mill yesterday.

The new anchor is a huge success. I can carry it about the decks in one hand, and yet it held us perfectly each night, in the strongest tides of the month, and very hard winds which shifted a good deal, so that it would have not been surprising if she had dragged even with an ordinary anchor. Total distance sailed just above 80 miles.

Rouse is a charming companion, and a very handy, quick sailor, by many long chalks the best crew I have ever had aboard her.

What sort of a person was Philip Rouse to have found favour with Ransome? He was the cousin of Ransome's Rugby mentor, Dr W. H. D. Rouse and by profession, was a naval architect who had been interested in the construction of boats since, as a boy, he had built himself a dinghy and a sand-yacht. He was modest and unassuming, but in his quiet way he was a fine seaman who, if the occasion demanded, could be very determined. These qualities had to make a pleasant contrast to the critical and opinionated Evgenia.

During the summer months there were always friends coming in for a day or two before going on elsewhere. There was Herbert Hanson in *Ianthe*, and his friend Davey in *Jenny Wren* from Brightlingsea. There was 'Bosun' Walker, whose *Deerfoot* they saw being rebuilt at Falmouth, and one day, as he was returning to

Levington, Ransome saw two children running along the shore to meet him and help him land. George and Josephine Russell were fans of his books, yet they had no idea whom they were helping. They soon found out. The Russells had taken Broke Hall and were practically neighbours. Ransome thought they were very nice children who would be likely to make a good crew in a short time — which they certainly were during the holidays. In the winter they joined him in the attic of Broke Farm, or aboard *Nancy*, scraping and varnishing blocks, painting lanterns, greasing rigging and so on, while Ransome entertained them with stories and his penny whistle.

Josephine Russell remembered what a good and patient teacher he was, and how he had the gift of making ordinary things interesting. When out driving the car, he would hoot once if he were turning right and twice if turning left, as if his car were a motor cruiser.

There was also the Young family from Maldon who sailed past him in a Blackwater smack flying the skull and crossbones and firing guns by way of salute. Ransome was so taken with this display that he invited them all to tea the following day. Another time, while crossing to Pin Mill in *Cocky*, he noticed some children who were having great fun capsizing their dinghy. Attracted by their laughter, he made some enquiries when he was ashore. 'Oh, it's only the Busks,' he was told, and it was not long before he had made their acquaintance.

Young people doing things always attracted Ransome. Major and Mrs Busk lived at the Grange, up the lane leading to Pin Mill, and sailed the 9-ton cutter *Lapwing* as a family boat. Their children — John, Gillian and Michael — were devoted Ransome enthusiasts, and they sailed their dinghy *Wizard*. Busk was a shy man who, like Ransome, was wary of anyone he didn't know. The two soon became firm friends and remained so for the rest of their lives.

At the beginning of September Rouse sailed *Mermaid* around from Walton without a dinghy and arrived earlier than expected. A local worthy helped them moor to a small can buoy to windward of *Nancy*. While they were lowering sail, *Mermaid* began to drag and drifted quickly down on *Nancy*. They let go of the dinghy mooring and manhandled *Mermaid* alongside, then astern, and made fast. When Ransome arrived after lunch, Rouse borrowed the *Queen Mary* and went to replace the mooring. Suddenly both boats began to drag *Nancy's* mooring. Mrs Rouse and ten-year-old Clive fended off the bowsprit of the yacht astern, while Ransome started his engine. With *Mermaid* in tow, he circled round and picked up Rouse and the dinghy, and then put *Mermaid* on *Nancy's* mooring. Circling again and again, Ransome picked up the Rouses one at a time. Clive was the first to scramble aboard.

Ransome promoted him to mate and put him at the tiller while he went below to attend to the engine. Although Clive tried very hard to do exactly what Ransome had told him and steer in a circle, *Nancy* left the deep water and, with the tide ebbing, was approaching the mud. Fortunately they did not touch, and soon they were all aboard and motoring down against the wind. With the engine beginning to labour, they anchored off Shotley so that Mrs Rouse and Clive could return home via Ipswich.

Next day the wind was still strong, but Ransome and Rouse took down two reefs and had a grand sail around to Hamford Water and their favourite anchorage in Kirby Creek. Just north of Felixstowe they sighted two waterspouts like the one he had seen in the Baltic. Ransome always enjoyed the passage to Hamford Water. After the Beach End buoy there was the Pye End buoy to pick up, then the channel between the invisible shallows, aiming for a distant clump of trees. Finally, the entrance to Hamford Water opened up. They shared one very comfortable night in Kirby Creek 'with a single persistent pleasant curlew', before returning to Pin Mill.

In October, Herbert Hanson invited Ransome to join him aboard his 7-ton cutter Ianthe at Portchester. He wrote to his mother:

The gales rather wasted the week-end, as Hanson in whose boat I was, was unwilling to get his sails wet because of the difficulty of getting them dry again at this time of year. But it was good fun what there was of it. We spent the first night under the old castle at Portchester ... a real fairy story castle, built by Richard II and unaltered except very slightly. We went down steps from the corner of the watch tower to get to the mud and our dinghy, and lay there in a lovely sunset with the old castle cut out against the sky as the stars came Out. Quite lovely. Then we got away in the early morning under engine and headsails, and went down to Portsmouth, and through the harbour, and away by Gilkicker Point, which I passed on my way up channel last year, and across to the Wight, and anchored off Seaview Pier to wait for the tide to rise enough to get into Bembridge, when we duly got in ... most interesting tricky little passage between the shoals, which Hanson knew by heart ... I had only to steer and do what I was told, which was a pleasant change for me, after always being responsible. We got into Bembridge, and there we lay.

Nancy went on the mud at the end of October after covering, according to Ransome's diary, 615 miles in thirty passages. He was by then a member of the little sailing community at Pin Mill. The Butt and Oyster was their club. Nowadays Pin Mill is a picturesque tourist trap, but at that

time the Butt and Oyster was the haunt of barge skippers and their mates
and yachtsmen all meeting on equal terms.

Mr Gee was the self-styled Mayor of Pin Mill. He had a little fruit and
vegetable shop, known as the Mayor's parlour, in the cellar underneath
Alma Cottage, where the cottage gable-end fronts on to the lane. He had
a fine chain of office presented to him by cadets from the *Ganges*. The
Mayor had a passion for eels, and Ransome used to exchange eels for fruit
for his supper. He would often fish for eels while he was at work in
Nancy's cabin. He rigged up an arrangement whereby if an eel took his
bait the butt end of the rod in the cockpit knocked on the cabin door and
brought him up on deck to deal with it.

At that time, Miss Powell still
lived at Alma Cottage, where she
had been born in the days when it
was the Alma Inn. Part of the L-
shaped block was occupied by her
brother, Jack, who made sails for
barges in the sail loft next door.
After travelling widely, she returned
in 1918 to run her tearooms and
guest house there until she was
forced by ill health to leave in 1955.
In January 1937 Ransome
presented Miss Powell with copies
of *Swallows and Amazons* and
Winter Holiday to prepare her for

Pin Mill from Alma Cottage

inclusion in the new book. After publication of *We Didn't Mean to Go to
Sea* she enjoyed meeting admirers who asked her about events in
the book. She had to learn how to make omelettes, however, as the
youthful visitors gave her no peace until she did:

> Miss Powell laughed quietly, and put the tray down without waking
> Jim. 'He'll be all right when he's had a bit of food,' she said. 'Many a time
> I've seen him and his uncle asleep the both of them when they've come
> in from sea. I might have known he was coming, with the supper I've got
> for you ... pea soup and a mushroom omelette.
>
> It was what they always asked for if they'd found-time to let me know
> they were coming. They would send me a telegram, 'PEA SOUP AND
> OMELETTE PLEASE', and I would know they were on their way.

Later that month Ransome let out a few secrets about the new book in
a letter to his mother:

The grown-ups in the new book don't really play a very large part. In ninety per cent of the book they are not there at all. In the rest they come in the background in general, except for a few chapters.

Minor grown-ups: Woman who lets lodgings at Pin Mill. Sailmaker at Pin Mill. Boatman ditto. Greengrocer ditto. Bargee. Fisherman ... nurses ... doctor.

Major grown-ups: Mrs Walker. Commander Walker. Jim Brading who has just left Rugby. Dutch Pilot.

But in the bulk of the book there are only the four *Swallows*.

I have got to page 176 in the rough draft.

Very little of Ransome's working notes for *We Didn't Mean to Go to Sea* have survived but I would like to quote this paragraph on seasickness which was omitted from the book:

Different people are seasick different ways. Some are quiet about it. Others, who would like to be quiet, are noisy. With some it comes on slowly, little by little, like a slowly rising storm, until at last it shakes them helplessly to pieces. With others there is a change of colour, a sudden almost surprising feeling that all is not well, a headache, a tightening of the skin across the forehead, and then urgent need to lean out of the boat. Noisy or quiet, the seasick cannot help themselves. It is no good being cross with them.

Pin Mill (from *We didn't Mean to Go to Sea*)

In February Ransome learnt that *Pigeon Post* had been awarded the first Carnegie Medal for the best children's book of the year. He was not over-impressed and vowed that he would be sailing in *Nancy* at the beginning of June and too busy to attend the ceremony in person — in the event, he went ('It was a very fine day and a large round medal'). *We Didn't Mean to Go to Sea* progressed steadily throughout February and March, but Ransome's plans for an early start to the 1937 season received several setbacks.

April 7. *Nancy* was rigged on the mud berth. Every single thing wrong.

April 12. Afloat.

April 13. Work on rigging. They still have not puttied the mast chocks. Jackstay made fast with bobstay rigging screw. Forestay absolutely slack. All pull on topmast.

April 17. Chocks still not puttied. Water pouring in. Carpet soaked. Dick Tizard arrived dead after motor bicycling from Hill Head, Fareham. Took him home to hot bath. Then joined damp ship.

April 18. Rigging. Stuck plasticine round all visible leaks in mast chocks, and fastened new canvas with lashing, tacking down with lead strip on deck. sailed with good wind, main and jib to Kirby Creek, where anchored for night in old place.

Seventy Years on Pin Mill looks much the same

The next day Ransome telephoned for George and Josephine Russell to join as ABs for the return trip, and in an hour they were aboard. He recorded in the log:

Sailed, full sail to Harwich, cooking lunch on the way, took off staysail to ease her for the sake of the cook. Ate. Outside the harbour found a grand wind, reset staysail, promptly emptying table into lee bunk, smashing one willow pattern porridge plate. Dick had presence of mind to grab the beer bottle, but grabbed the wrong end. Went out to Cork Spit buoy against tide. Dark clouds astern. Turned to meet them and presently had a hard squall, followed by rain. She fairly heeled to it and jumped. Roared back to Harwich, finding sunshine and light wind in the harbour, could not lay course. Went about for Felixstowe Dock to take a photograph. Going about to proceed, wind now S but did not want to jibe as very near pierhead, jib carried away from sheets. Got it half down, rehooked them on, and then raced up the river, wind dead aft to Collimer, a broad reach to Pin Mill, found our mooring clear, went on to Potter's Point, downed sails and stowed coming back to mooring under power with all sails and gear dry and stowed before we picked up the mooring buoy. Tea. Sent the ABs ashore. Supper. Called on Keryl with Dick and listened to Harry King inspired by cold rum and water telling stories.

Ransome was delighted by the way in which the teenagers had responded to the rough water. A day or so later, Evgenia joined George and Josephine for a short run down to Shotley, but she complained that it was not worth the effort of making ready and stowing things away afterwards, and anyway *Nancy* was too small for more than two aboard. They motored back to Pin Mill and rushed off to the circus in Ipswich where Ransome laughed more than any of them. 'George and Jos. very good as crew, but must learn to make ropes fast after hauling in,' he noted in the log.

In May, Rouse took a week's holiday in order to crew for Ransome. They decided that if the wind were westerly, they would go to Holland and if it were easterly, they would head down Channel. On the Saturday morning the wind came hard from the north-east, but they decided to at least go out and see how *Nancy* liked it. They left Harwich harbour and found that *Nancy* 'liked it very well'. It took them just 12 hours and 20 minutes to reach Dover from Harwich, and it was while entering the harbour there that they experienced a spot of bother — described in this extract from an account of the voyage which Ransome wrote for the *Cruising Association Bulletin.*

We had a grand sail past Ramsgate's blazing front, and I was considering making a night of it and going right on when I heard a slight rattle forward and found that the rigging screws of the starboard shrouds had all but unscrewed themselves. I put this right as well as I could in the dark, and then, as it was blowing pretty hard and gusty and inclined to rain, decided to go into Dover and wire them properly in daylight. At 10.50 pm we passed through the eastern entrance with Billy ticking over ready to do his job when wanted. We took in sail in the outer harbour, not without a bit of trouble. The jib would not roll up, and the blocks were looking for a chance to box somebody's ears. Then with all sails on deck and Billy going slow, we groped for the Submarine Basin, which neither of us had entered before. I had expected to find it a sardine tin, close packed with submarines instead of sardines, but found it a fine little place with plenty of room, though in the dark and the rain it was hard to see just how much room there was. Rouse went forward to play with the anchor.

I could not see what he was doing and a slight misunderstanding resulted in our being blown back too near the entrance before the anchor went down. He yanked it off the bottom again, and when I put Billy in gear to get back to our chosen spot, the propeller wound up *Queen Marys'* painter and cut her adrift. Luckily she drifted into a patch of light by the entrance, and Billy, in spite of adornments, gave enough steerage way to let me steam round and catch *QM.* with the long boathook. Rouse, meanwhile, was wondering what was happening, as he could no more see what I was doing than I could see what was engaging him. This time he had all ready to let go on the instant, and in a few minutes the anchor was down, *QM.* was on a new painter, the Bogie stove was alight, and supper was well under way. I was an ass not to have hauled the dinghy up short before going into the Submarine Basin when I was fully occupied with lead and tiller.

May 16. Bright, clear, cold day, with gentle NE. wind. We could see the propeller looking like Medusa's hellish mop. A man sailing a pretty little Harrison Butler passed close by and told us where we could put her on the hard to clear it. We debated this. It would have meant the loss of a whole day. We decided to try something else first. Rouse, who is luckily of light displacement, knelt, stripped to the waist in *QM*, tied under *Nancy's* transom. I took my colossal weight out on the bowsprit end to help cock up the stern of the ship. Rouse, plunging his arm to the shoulder, carved away at the tangled rope till he had a free end to pull on. Then he sang out to me to come and turn the engine over to unwind it. A short bit would come away, and I would then resume my place to smoke a pipe in comfort on the bowsprit, while he went to work again with his knife till he had freed another end. Then more unwinding, another scrap of rope removed, and me once more the idle lounger on the bowsprit and he once more the gallant diver. This went on until, with chattering teeth, Rouse announced that the propeller was clear.

I poured neat rum into him and am happy to say that he suffered no ill effects. A solid beef steak pudding luncheon may have helped.

They left at four the following afternoon. It was such a grand wind that they decided to sail all night and all through the next day. Finally, they had their supper at anchor under Porchester Castle. The wind suddenly swung round to the west and they sailed from Portsmouth on Wednesday. Once more they arrived in Dover harbour in time for supper. They reamained in harbour on Friday as it was blowing so hard that Rouse had difficulty in getting ashore in the dinghy. They left Dover about ten the following morning and were just in time for a 'rollicking supper' at the Butt and Oyster. Their cruise showed Ransome yet again what a staunch ship he had. '*Nancy* is a good little boat, considering that she was built as a cruiser not a racer and is so comfortable that a man can spend months on end in her.' Can one detect here a note of gladness that there was no moaning minnie to spoil their voyage?

It was 'an extraordinarily pleasant and lucky little cruise,' Ransome said. 'Harwich to Portsmouth and back between one Saturday and the next. With five nights in port and two at sea, and a whole day in Portsmouth and another in Dover. I daresay it will be a long time before winds and tides are so kind to us again.' He was certainly right in that prophesy!

* * * * *

While Ransome was at work he never allowed Evgenia to read the typescript. However, on June 15th, *We Didn't Mean to Go to Sea* was finished and handed over. Ransome escaped from the 'critic on the hearth' and took *Nancy* to Pyefleet single-handed. He was late getting away from Pin Mill under the staysail alone as the wind was too strong for full mainsail, and he would have had great difficulty in taking in a reef. It was late indeed when he anchored below the Walton Buoy and lit the fire. Next morning brought a moderate north-westerly wind and Ransome decided to try for Brightlingsea. The wind strengthened 'and was rather overpowering which made luncheon rather difficult and wet. So handed staysail. But going like a train'. Brightlingsea looked very crowded so Ransome went into the Pyefleet and anchored just as the rain started. Ransome was up making his cocoa at 5.30 the next morning and under way before 8 with Billy to help and *Nancy* was off Clacton pier by half past ten. He wrote in the log:

Heading NE by E½E. Carried right on past the Outer Ridge buoy, and tacked too soon. I should have carried on to the Platters, had to tack again. Very dark over Harwich, and bad looking cloud. Very hard squalls caught me with full sail up, and I had a bit of a job, but everything held. Got into harbour, worse squalls, and I got forward and handed staysail, getting a proper splash over all while doing so. Rolled up one reef, stopped Billy, and sailed easily up tacking all the way. Walton buoy 2.46. Met a crowd of *Ganges* boats and one of them nearly put me aground. I called to him (he being close to windward of me) asking if he'd go about as I should have to, and he cheerily replied 'Oh not just yet ... I'll keep out of your way.' I knew he couldn't, and had a very narrow squeak. I sounded after getting clear, and saw that I must have been all but touching. Started engine and got in sails in Butterman's Bay, and picked up my moorings at Pin Mill at 4.30, too dead beat to stow. had some tinned herrings and fell asleep. Waked later on, stowed sails, washed decks and so home, to hear the sad news that my book had a good skeleton, but was dead, flat, nowhere amusing, no dialogue, no characters, and not interesting. I asked were there any good spots and was told 'No'. But next day she remembered two paragraphs that were fit to pass. This sounds perhaps worse than it is, or anyhow sounded so to me, dead tired anyhow. Went to bed and slept like a log.

The trip featured in a letter to Miss Atkinson of Jonathan Cape, who looked after the publicity of the *Swallows and Amazons* books:

I've just got back from a rather exhausting experiment, of taking *Nancy* to Brightlingsea and back without anybody else on board. I had a good voyage there, and had no trouble in anchoring etc, and a very pleasant night, but the return voyage yesterday was a beast, head winds the whole way and some beastly squalls when I had too much canvas on her, so that I got into Harwich pretty well done. This is my excuse (jolly good one) for not dealing with things properly today. The experiment worked all right, and in normal weather it would be easy, the only difficulty coming through not having someone to hold on to the tiller while someone else goes forward to deal with the sails — you want to be at both ends of the boat at once. But barring the squalls it was very jolly, and resulted in working out several dodges to make things easier. My reason for going was that my new book was being read by a stern critic and I thought it best to be out of the way. (The resulting criticism was pretty devastating, but will be useful. Tell Howard who will laugh. I am now starting revision, and I hope to send him a slightly less flat, dull and non-amusing version in a month's time.

Ransome had a more appreciative, if somewhat sleepy, audience when he read several chapters to Taqui and Susie Altounyan after they had returned to Broke Farm at the end of a long day aboard *Nancy*.

He was able to get hold of more helpful criticism from his friend Molly Hamilton, who had been full of encouragement during the preparation of *Swallows and Amazons*, when she went for a sail down river to Felixtowe. She had several useful suggestions to make, including the idea that Jim's accident should remain a secret during the North Sea crossings. Ransome settled to his typewriter and began the revision. For a while he was too busy to sail *Nancy*. Then, on July 17th, Evgenia consented to sail with him again and they made for Hamford Water, where they met the Rouse family. *Mermaid* had just come in from a fast passage and Rouse told Ransome that Clive had said, 'Daddy, she's going faster than her fastest!' This exclamation was lent to Roger aboard *Goblin*. They had a happy weekend, the highlight of which was the large eel that Evgenia caught.

In the middle of August Ransome took a break from revision, and Evgenia agreed to join him for a sail to Woodbridge. It was a windless morning, so they motored down to Collimer Point where a slight wind encouraged them to set sail. There was fog at sea, but they were in no hurry, as there would not be enough water over the bar at the mouth of the Deben for some time. When they were off the entrance, Evgenia began to steer while Ransome sounded all the way in. They reached the Ferry at 3.40 and picked up the vacant mooring belonging to a friend at 5 pm. Just before they reached the buoy there was a horrible grinding sound somewhere below the stern. Something was clearly wrong with the propeller shaft, but they decided that enough was enough, and investigation could wait until the next day.

When he went overboard for a look at the shaft, Ransome found the nut on the stern tube was flying around free. Ransome arranged for *Nancy* to be put against the quay for repair the next day, went to Pin Mill by bus and drove back to fetch Evgenia home while he slept aboard. The following day Nunn, the boatbuilder, replaced the nut, added the locknut which had been missing, replaced a chipped place in the rudder and laid down three brass plates in the deck to take the CQR anchor, and charged 16s/6d and 2s/6d for a week's moorings, as Ransome had decided to remain a while.

For the next four days Ransome worked peacefully in *Nancy's* cabin and made real progress with the book, completing 52 pages. On the fifth day, with Evgenia back aboard, they motored only as far as Waldringfield, having been warned that the hard NE wind would make conditions off the bar pretty beastly. Encouraged by the NW wind, they set off the following day, but the hard sluicing tide made steering difficult, although Billy drove them over the bar without trouble. Outside, they set full sail and, as they

did so, an accidental jibe nearly put Ransome overboard. To complete his
chagrin he misjudged the strong tide and failed to pick up his mooring at
Pin Mill at the first attempt.

The jib was flapping. The young man had grabbed the boathook and
was waiting ready to reach down and grab the buoy.
'He'll just do it,' Titty said almost in a whisper.
'Beautifully,' said John.
'Oh,' gasped Titty. 'he can't reach it.'
Perhaps the ebb pouring out of the river was stronger than the skipper
had thought. The wind had dropped. Under jib alone the cutter had been
moving very slowly. Now, with the jib flapping loose she lost her way. Just
as the young man reached down with the boathook she stopped moving.
He made a desperate lunge for the buoy but the boathook was an inch
too short. He tried again and missed it by a foot. Already the tide was
sweeping her back.
'That's done it!'

By the beginning of September the revision was complete and ready
for Evgenia's eyes again. Ransome sent a copy to Wren Howard ('Here it
is, but I am very dissatisfied with parts of it. Still I am prepared to accept
your verdict'). He took *Nancy* off to Kirby Creek and returned the
following day. The diary entry is brief. 'Genia says book does not need
much doing to it at all. So it will get done this year after all.'

Wren Howard sent a telegram of approval and urged him to 'steam
ahead with the pictures!' From the surviving correspondence it is clear
that Howard was unusually influential in the final pruning of the
typescript. On 10th September he wrote:

I do honestly think very well of the book indeed. It gathers pace in a
most satisfactory manner, and works up through crisis to an admirable
conclusion. Dawn and the arrival in Holland are magnificent.
I completely agree with the deletion of the first two and a half pages.
(Ransome had at first linked the narrative to *Pigeon Post* by describing
the *Swallows* train journey from the north.) To start at the foot of p 3 will
make a much better start.
Chapter 14 should certainly come out altogether. It is far better for the
reader to know nothing about Jim until chapter 26. Chapter 15 is
excellent and makes a very necessary break in just the right place.

In spite of this encouragement, Ransome's last word to his publisher
was a dismal, 'I fear a lot of people will say the thing's too tough for babes.'

The plot of *We Didn't Mean to Go to Sea* is simple. While waiting for their father to return from China on leave, the *Swallows* are allowed to sail as a young man's crew aboard his cutter, *Goblin*, for a few days, as long as they remain within the harbour. They all promise. The wind drops and the young man goes ashore in heavy mist for petrol and has an accident. The tide rises. The fog comes down and, when the anchor drags, *Goblin* drifts out of the harbour. The weather worsens and there is no alternative but to sail on — to Holland, where their father makes a pierhead jump from his steamer to bring them home. Readers of Maurice Griffiths's *The Magic of the Swatchways* (1931) would have noticed the resemblance to another North Sea crossing that began in fog and ended in Flushing.

This is not, like *Peter Duck*, just an entertaining tale made up in the cabin of a Norfolk wherry, but a real test of courage, family unity and seamanship.

Susan pushed the chart at John and put her hands to her ears. John was still talking when she was able to listen to him again. 'We can't stop,' he was saying. 'Even if we had no sails, the tide would be taking us somewhere. You saw how it rushed us past those buoys. If it took us on a shoal, we'd be wrecked before we could do anything at all. And if we go on past the lightship we'll be charging into shoals on the other side of it. Remember what Jim said about that man who lost his boat. When in doubt keep clear of shoals. Get out to sea and stay there. If he were on board he'd be doing it now. He'd get outside as soon as he could and wait till he could see before trying to come back. And if we steer a bit south of east ... Do look at the chart and you'll see ...'

'But you don't know where we are now ...'

'Yes I do. We must be getting near the lightship. Listen to it.'

'Beu ... eueueueueueu.'

'But we can't.'

'It's the only thing we can do,' said John.

'But we promised not to go to sea at all ...' Susan moaned and turned her head away. Titty and Roger were both looking at her, and she could not bear to see their questioning faces.

'We didn't do it on purpose,' said John. 'We're at sea now, and we can't get back in the fog. If we tried we'd be bound to wreck the *Goblin* on something. Like trying to get through a narrow door in pitch dark. The door's wide open if we go the other way. You can see it yourself. If we go a bit east of south-east we'll get through. There's nothing for us to hit for miles. It's no good thinking of doing anything else. We've got to do it. South-east and a little bit east ... and we'll be all right. But we've got to do it now or it'll be too late. That lightship's awfully near ...'

'Beu...eueueueueueu.'
The Cork lightship, sending its bleat out into the fog once every fifteen seconds, was like the ticking of an enormous clock telling them they could not put things off for ever.

'We can't keep a promise when it's already broken,' said Titty.

'Is that another buoy?' said John. 'Over there. Do keep a look out. I've got to watch the compass and the sail ...'

'Can I sound the foghorn again?' said Roger.

'No ... Wait half a minute. We've got to make up our minds.'

'Let's do what John says,' said Titty. 'Daddy'd say the same ... You know ... When it's Life and Death all rules go by the board. Of course, it isn't Life and Death yet, but it easily might be if we bumped the *Goblin* on a shoal.'

'How shall we ever get back?' said Susan.

'If we keep her going about south-east till the fog clears, we'll be able to get her back by turning round and coming north-west ... And anyway, when it clears we'll be able to see things ...

'Beu ... eueueueueueueu.'

The lightship bleated again and John's decision was made. There was not a moment to lose.

The book was published in November 1937 and there were three further impressions that month and another in December. The reviewer in *Punch* was right when he said, 'Perhaps the best of all ...'

Wren Howard told him: 'I spent a delicious day with it on Saturday, and am writing to thank you for the pleasure it gave me. I think in many ways it is the best of the lot, and I shall never believe another word you say about your own books.'

As the season drew to a close Ransome managed a few short trips, sometimes taking Evgenia as crew, though she remained adamant that the cabin was too cramped and the galley too small. By the end of the season he had sailed *Nancy* thirty-eight times and covered 878 miles.

In October they hired a 4-berth motor cruiser, the *Royal Star*, for a week's fishing on the Broads. They made for the River Thurne, and on their first day Ransome noted that the score was 16 — 14 in his favour, although Evgenia had caught all the best fish. They fished every day, each making good catches, while Ransome carefully kept a record of the score, until he had to be rushed to hospital for an operation on an umbilical hernia. Blaxland promised a complete recovery and, encouraged by this news, Ransome covered the walls of his hospital room with possible designs for a new boat with a larger galley: 'a boat in which Genia, the best of all sea-cooks, should have a galley she deserves'.

King's Ransome

If old Mr Gee was the Mayor of Pin Mill, then the Kings were certainly its Royal Family. Everything centred round their shed, just above the high water mark where they built their boats. They lived in a cottage alongside the boatshed, a few yards from the Butt and Oyster. Harry King's two sons worked in the business and a few first-class shipwrights, trained by King himself, were regarded as members of the family rather than an employed workforce. As each year passed it was remembered, and referred to by the Kings, as the year of this boat or of that. Mrs King always hung her washing on the foreshore in front of the cottage, and thought nothing of wading out in seaboots to unpeg it.

Soon after their arrival in Levington the Ransomes became friends with the King family. Ransome lent Mrs King all manner of books to read, starting with Trollope's *Barchester Towers* series. After his operation he had a bad time of it and claimed, whenever he had a relapse, that only prompt action by Blaxland could save his life. He returned to Levington at the beginning of January 1938 and, as soon as he could manage it, went across to Pin Mill to see Harry King about a new boat.

Evgenia's desire for space aboard the new boat was to result in a saloon that was very roomy even by the generous standards of the day. Fred Shepherd, the designer, had a reputation for producing small boats with excellent accommodation and seaworthiness. He drew a canoe-sterned yacht of 35 feet overall in length (28 feet on the waterline), with a beam of 10-feet. She had a long straight iron keel and drew 5 feet. She could take the ground when necessary and was ideal for cruising on the East Coast. Ransome was a little in awe of her 50 foot mast, but the rig, although lofty, was easy to handle. The mainsail had an area of less than 350 square feet, so could be handled easily by one person. Shepherd's original design was for a bowsprit, but Ransome decided to go for a stemhead rig and so the two small headsails also presented no difficulty.

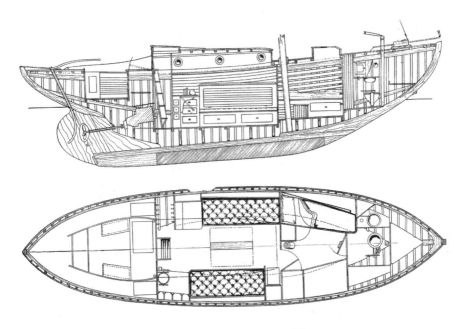

Selina King Accomodation Plan

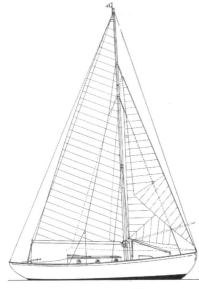

Selina King Sail Plan

Into Evgenia's saloon with its six foot headroom went two large settee berths six feet six inches long, a coal locker and a little stove, an oilskin locker, a chart or writing table, and of course the splendid galley with lots of shelf space. The fresh water tanks, each holding 15 gallons, were placed under the seats in the self-draining cockpit and the two 10 gallon fuel tanks were under the side decks. The bridge deck was hinged to give access to the little engine below. The WC was positioned right forward, the plumbing kept to a minimum by means of a removable washbasin which was emptied down the lavatory. The forecabin contained the third bunk as well as a wardrobe, sail bin and chain locker. The Ransomes decided to dispense with the six-foot pipe cot 'for child' above the forward bunk. A winch was fixed to the mast in order to keep the foredeck clear.

They wanted to call the boat *Molly*, but there was already a boat of that name in Lloyd's Register, and as they did not wish to qualify it in any way, they decided upon Evgenia's second choice, which was *Selina*. When Harry King told Ransome that he had an aunt of that name, Ransome declared 'Then we shall call her *Selina King*.'

On March 8th Ransome went to King's to pay the first instalment. He was greatly encouraged by the sight of *Griffin* which had been moved out of the shed in order to leave room for *Selina* to grow. Harry King was having an afternoon sleep in his cottage when Ransome arrived, but one of the boatbuilders took him across the garden to the old bus overlooking the anchorage. It had been fitted out with a table and chairs, and it reeked of apples that were stored there each winter.

After the visit Ransome wrote: 'I never signed a cheque with more pleasure in my life.'

The following day Parker, the designer's assistant, met Ransome in Ipswich and together they went to King's to see the first stage of the building. Outside the shed, protected from the elements, stood a huge stack of pitch-pine planks long enough to reach from stem to stern without a join. It was never Harry King's practice to join the hull planking if he could avoid it. Parker was there to check that King's were going to build *Selina* as she had been designed. First he climbed up to the loft where he carefully measured the lines chalked on the rough wooden floor before announcing they had been drawn with Mr King's usual accuracy. Then he checked the moulds around which the actual hull would be constructed and found that these too were without fault. Tactfully Mr King had taken his men off (as usually he did at around eleven o'clock) for coffee in Mrs King's kitchen. When they returned, King asked Parker quietly what mistakes he had found.

'Didn't think you would,' he said when Parker reported none. 'Been building them long enough ... nine hundred of them, big and little.'

'And *Selina's* going to be the best of the lot,' Ransome exclaimed.

'Well, they do say that practice makes perfect,' said King. He showed them the oak slabs, with the bark on, showing the shape they had grown, from which her timbers were to be cut. Some of the oak had been growing on the other side of the river long, long ago, when schooners for the fruit trade were being built at lpswich.

After a lunch of chops and beer at the Butt and Oyster, Ransome climbed aboard *Griffin* and sat himself down in the cockpit, which was about the same size as the one planned for *Selina*. He began to imagine himself aboard his new ship. *Griffin's* mast had not been stepped, but the timber from which *Selina's* mast would be cut lay near by, and in his mind's eye he saw its 50 feet towering above him. In the cabin young Norman King was busily working and Ransome took the opportunity to ask him when he thought *Selina* might be ready.

'If nothing stops us, she should be ready by the middle of June,' was Norman's answer.

Ransome remembered the previous ship which had been built for him and how, in the end, he had taken *Racundra* from the builders three months late and still unfinished. Nevertheless, as he sat there, he began to plan her trial run. He would take Rouse, the best mate *Nancy* ever had. Holland? ... No, perhaps somewhere nearer home, within reach of her builder. Just in case. Brightlingsea or Burnham, or up to Lowestoft to test her properly.

Then he thought of *Nancy*. It would be unfair not to have one final cruise in her. No, he would not consider taking *Selina* out until the autumn.

Norman King's prophecy proved optimistic, and for the next two months Ransome made frequent visits to the shed while the men were finishing *Griffin*, and *Selina's* only existence was in the timber that had been set aside for her.

One vital piece of timber bothered Ransome. The design called for a keel almost 3 feet wide and 5 inches deep. The elm length which had been selected was barely wide enough, with the bark showing near the middle. There was also what looked 'suspiciously like a crack' at one end. Ransome described how he felt:

From March till May, I could not walk through the shed without looking sideways at the keel, with that bad place in it amidships, and that other place that might be a crack or might not. I saw her stem piece, a lovely bit of oak, her stern, as good, and the gorgeous massive piece that was to be her deadwood, to take the propeller tube of the little engine that we should use for getting in and out of harbour. Each piece was a pleasure to look at, to touch, and each was to be fastened for life to that keel, from which I had to turn my eyes away.

When at last work started and Harry King began to shape the keel, it became clear that there was indeed a crack that ran deep into the heart of the timber. The search for a replacement might have meant further delay, but the Ipswich sawyers had just taken delivery of some huge elm trunks, which, if sound, would give Ransome just the keel he wanted. It had been arranged that he should visit them to watch the keel being sawn.

When he arrived he found a great trunk being lifted by a crane and loaded on to a cradle so that it could be brought forward to meet the saw. Wedges and grips held it firmly in place. After carefully adjusting the height of the bandsaw, men and boys stripped off the bark with axes and yanked out old nails.

'Those would make a mess of your saw,' said Ransome.

'Means a new saw if it comes up against a nail,' said one of the men.

'You find all sorts of things in trees,' the foreman observed. 'Stones for instance. Someone throws a stone up and it lodges in a fork, and the tree grows up around it, and there it is thirty years later, in the very heart of the tree. We found a pistol once, an old kind of pistol. That had a story behind it I daresay.'

The log met the bandsaw with a hiss and a jet of sawdust and the cradle slowly carried the trunk past the saw. It ran back again and the men prepared to lift the outer plank to reveal the keel piece. As the plank rose they could all see a dark hole of rotten timber in the middle.

'You never can tell with elm until you cut it,' said the foreman. A moment later he began measuring lengths either side of the bad section. 'Coffin lengths,' he explained. Ransome recalled years later in the unpublished part of his *Autobiography*:

Two trees were cut through and condemned before we found the perfect keel. Then there was the iron keel that was to go below it. For that a wooden mould had to be made, and when it was made we were at Cocksedge's foundry, to see the great cauldron of molten iron slowly tipped and the fiery stream poured from its lip. We saw the three-and-a-half-ton iron keel come from Ipswich and, with half the population of Pin Mill, helped to manhandle it into Mr King's shed. Then came the moment when the wooden keel was resting on the iron one, with stem and stem post, both of which we had seen in the raw, sticking up at each end, and the long double row of timbers, so that the boat was like an unclothed skeleton.

The planking rose higher and higher to the cheerful sound of shipwrights at work in the shed. Then came the time when *Selina* was no longer an open shell but began to have decking and cabin coamings.

That Easter the Ransomes hired five *Fairways* and one *Whippet* from the Jack Powles yard at Wroxham for an expedition to the Norfolk Broads. Ransome was admiral and he and Evgenia had one *Fairway*, while George Russell and his cousin Raymond Hubbard had another. (Mrs Russell had put her foot down and kept Josephine at home). The Youngs had two, with three boys in one and the parents and the youngest in the other. The *Whippet* was sailed by Taqui and Titty

Altounyan, while the Arnold Fosters (sailing friends from nearby Nacton) had the fifth *Fairway*.

Each crew was required to make its own skull and crossbones flag to measurements provided by Ransome so that the fleet could be recognised at a distance across the low-lying land. They were all good flags, but none as flamboyant as that which Evgenia made for the flagship. On one of the flags the teeth came partly unstitched and rose and fell in the breeze. The large flags were rather tricky to hoist and several young sailors fell backwards while checking that the flag was flying to their satisfaction.

Raymond Hubbard, who was fifteen years old, had never met Ransome before and knew nothing of sailing. He quickly became a Ransome admirer. With his brown beret on and puffing away at his pipe, Ransome was a marvellous shepherd of his rather novice flock. He helped newcomers to stow their sails, advised reefing when he thought it necessary, and signalled by waving his arms like a windmill if he saw anyone doing something risky. He was always kind and entertaining with his good humour and fund of stories. Evgenia was at her best too, patiently showing George on the first evening how to use a Primus. They thought her rather like a kindly school matron, with her concern for their comfort and cleanliness. Perhaps she inclined to be whistle happy, for whenever she wanted Ransome she blew loudly on her whistle. Ransome reacted so strongly to the blast that they hatched a plot to take his photograph as he jumped to it. George kept a careful log of the cruise.

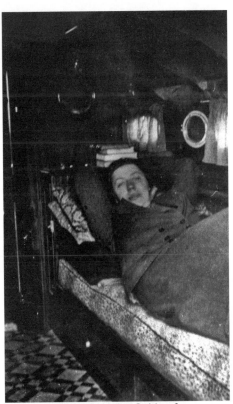

Evgenia in the Cabin of a
Broads Fairway Yacht

We arose at the usual time and had an amusing, but windy time getting away. The Young boys started first but lost their main-sheet O.B. to the accompaniment of yells of laughter from their parents. Then

Ransome towing through the bridges at Potter Heigham
(Brotherton Collection)

Titty and Taqui went off without mishap. Then Mr Ransome nearly fell into the river in the excitement of getting the Arnold Fosters off. The Ransomes got off after a false start and much puffing of the longshore loafers. We just managed to come round in time, missing the bank by a foot. We left the Youngs to put in a reef. We would have been glad of one for the first mile towards Horning, but afterwards we were blanketed by the trees and were very thankful that we were carrying full sail ... We arrived rather late but stowed (the sails) and I rowed Mrs Ransome up to Ludham Bridge where she advised John in his shopping after he had slipped up over some veal. We filled up with water and rowed back. When we returned the whippet post had arrived and I received three letters, each marked by the whippet post-mark. We then received an invitation to supper with the Ransomes that we accepted with alacrity. We stowed and retired below to rest till Mrs Ransome's whistle blew. We had an excellent supper of plum pudding, cold tongue, tomatoes and hot potatoes. The Rum came out of its retirement 'for medicinal purposes only' and was used to light the pudding. We did not get to bed until eleven o'clock ... We spent the night between some hymn-singing girls to starboard and yelling schoolboys to port.

They had their share of headwinds during the week and Raymond did plenty of pulling and quanting. Each night they met at the mooring Ransome had chosen that morning, in time for supper. Ransome noted that the little *Whippet* was so well handled by Taqui and Titty that they were never late. A camp-fire was lit and they all joined in the singing while the girls played penny whistles. Even on the Broads, it was not possible completely to forget about events in Europe. One afternoon, after a visit to the Pleasure Boat Inn, when the whole fleet was strung out in line astern across Hickling Broad, a newly-camouflaged bomber from a nearby airfield roared low over their heads.

George Russell sailing *Coch-y-bonddhu* at Pin Mill

By the summer George and Josephine Russell were wanting a boat of their own, and when they returned from school for the holidays Ransome generously lent them *Coch-y-bonddhu*. If King's were to build them a dinghy, he said, that would only take men off *Selina*. *Cocky* was badly in need of paint and varnish, and before they put her in the water the young Russells sanded and scraped her. They put a coat of bitumastic paint below the waterline, four coats of varnish on her topsides and two coats inside. They kept her for a year or so until George came across an old boat on Lowestoft beach. The young Russells paid £10 for it and restored the boat for themselves. All the same, King's did build a dinghy, for on October 15th Ransome collected a 10-foot dinghy with a brown sail, which he called *Swallow*.

Meanwhile *Nancy* was made ready for another season and although a page or two of Ransome's log are missing, it is possible to piece together the story of his summer afloat. At the beginning of June he took *Nancy* on a 'Whitsuntide' cruise to Burnham with the faithful Rouse as crew. Leaving Pin Mill on Friday evening within minutes of Rouse's arrival, they anchored off Shotley for the night and watched Harwich Regatta before leaving for Walton in late afternoon. They anchored inside Stone Point and went ashore to look for flints. Next morning they took in a couple of reefs and were off the Pye End buoy by 11 o'clock. Sounding carefully through the Medusa Channel they were abeam of the Wallet Spitway Buoy by 3 o'clock when the tide turned against them. With the wind heading them in strong gusts, Ransome found that his hand bearing compass had been left behind and had a hard time of it 'guessing' the bearings from the steering compass. At 7 o'clock they called on Billy and with the help

Looking towards Ransome's favourite anchorage in Kirby Creek)

of the engine, arrived off Burnham shortly after nine and anchored. Next day Ransome went to Cranfield the sailmaker, to see about a suit for *Selina*. After two days at Burnham, and with his compass having arrived safely in the post, they left Burnham only to arrive off the Swin Spitway Buoy at low water. The sight of a motor vessel, a Thames barge and an excursion steamer aground in the Spitway made Ransome decide to 'jill about' while they had tea and wait for more water. When the steamer *Crested Eagle* began to go ahead *Nancy* went through, finding at least seven feet of water, and made for Pyefleet.

At this point in the log there is an empty page, except for a note that they sailed 35 miles. The log for the following day makes it clear that they had reached Orford Haven and left early in that morning. They took the pilot to see them safely over the bar and headed for Lowestoft. *Nancy* passed the Southwold light in the middle of a rain squall, but by careful use of his sextant Ransome was able to calculate that she was 2.4 miles offshore. At 4 o'clock they motored between the Lowestoft pierheads. They found a welcome at the Norfolk and Suffolk Yacht Club, but retired early, and Ransome set his alarm for 3.30 am. He prepared their breakfast before waking Rouse, and they set off an hour later under power to make the most of the tide which set southerly from 6 o'clock. Near the Sizewell buoy they ran into a calm, but Billy kept them going until they were passed Orfordness, when a few puffs from the east gave promise of more to come. Rouse turned in for an hour's sleep at 2.30, but Ransome makes no mention of taking a break himself. They reached Pin Mill at 7.30 pm — 15 hours and 43 miles from Lowestoft. Rouse had one more day of his holiday, so they made for Kirby Creek and returned in time for him to catch a late train from Ipswich. They had been away nine days and had sailed and motored 215 miles. That was the end of Ransome's extended cruising with *Nancy Blackett*, although he visited Kirby Creek a further five times, the River Deben twice and Burnham before summer was over. On August 22nd he took a small boy to the Oval to 'see Hammond make 300 against the Australians'. But when they returned that night, it was Len Hutton who had made the mighty score: 'I expect that boy and I shall remember until we die that we were among those present on that tremendous occasion.'

The Spanish civil war and the aggressive foreign policies of other European powers had convinced Ransome that soon Britain would be drawn into another devastating war, and long before summer was over he had made up his mind that it was idiotic to be building a boat at such a threatening time. On September 13th *Selina* was moved out of King's shed and stood in her cradle awaiting some few finishing touches. Ransome sat in the cockpit, looking across the river and wondering whether war would come before she was launched. He had the idea of writing a book about her building and her eventual passage on the high seas. Although he gave it up before the book was finished, and is said to have lent his notes for it to Uffa Fox, who included an account of *Selina King* in his *Thoughts on Yachts and Yachting*, several interesting chapters survive from Ransome's original text and these are well worth reading, including the following passage.

Selina King outside the shed where she had been built
(Brotherton Collection)

The Launch

A ship launched at Pin Mill does not, at the blowing of a whistle, the pressing of a button and the uttering of polite words by some distinguished person, slide suddenly stern first into the water, to be brought up on to hawsers when already afloat. We have no slipway, no railroad track, no wheeled and moving cradle to be released and glide down into the water by force of gravity. Our foreshore is of gently shelving mud, and the only force that we can use to take her out over the mud is that of human beef and muscle. Between one tide and the next, we have to take our ship out from the hard ground outside the building shed and far enough towards the deep water for the tide to float her when it comes in.

This is the way Mr King does it. He builds up half a cradle on the starboard of the ship, and lists her over till she rests on it, her topsides protected by a mattress. This cradle rests in a shallow wooden trough. A similar shallow trough is under her keel. An anchor, deep sunk in the mud, takes one block of a tackle, the pull of which comes to a windlass anchored by the shed. The tackle is made fast to [the] cradle and the slide under the keel. Mr King's men turn the windlass. Norman pushes. Frank with a lever helps to start her, and after a mulish sticking fast, she moves inch by inch along those two shallow slides. Another pair of shallow troughs are being greased by happy Tommy, and, presently, these are laid beyond the first pair. The ship is hauled on to them and Tommy with his grease pot, greases the first pair which are then taken out and laid beyond the second pair.

Thus, inch by inch, she moves towards the water. The whole operation is most delicate and Mr King likes to be alone at it, with no owners hovering nervously round, expecting every moment to see their ship fall over on her side. I felt pretty sure he would have liked us to be on the other side of the river. He had no choice ... Mrs King had promised to christen the new ship, and, for the reasons already given, she had to do the christening at some moment during the ship's slow progress to meet the tide.

Now below Mr King's shed there is a bit of hard gravel. Below that there is a sort of slip way of boards bedded in the ground. Below that again is the mud ... Obviously Mrs King could not wade out waist deep in the mud to christen her as she met the tide. The slipway is treacherous with slime, and I wanted no accidents to mar the happy day.

(They decided that the ceremony would take place when the ship had reached the outer end of the hard ground.)

Mrs King was very shy and suggested someone else should perform the ceremony.

'I've never done it,' she said. 'I always keep out of the way when there's a launching.'

I said, 'What about Queen Elizabeth?' If Queen Eli can go to Glasgow to launch the *Queen Elizabeth*, Mrs King must make an effort and come out at the right moment to launch *Selina King*.

"Well, I've never done it,' said Mrs King.

'It's quite easy,' said I. 'You smash the bott [sic] and the words, and then you drink her health.'

'But I can't do that!' said Mrs King. 'I can't touch a drop. It's my heart.'

'You needn't drink a lot,' said I. 'But just a sip you take, to bring good luck to the ship.'

'I'll do it,' said Mrs King. 'Not to drink it, but just taste, like Holy Communion.'

That morning I had still been a little afraid lest Mrs King should renege at the last minute, but, with the launch of the *Queen Elizabeth* still in mind, I had come provided with two bottles of (not Empire wine exactly, because I could not get it) Champagne that at least had been bottled in England and a suitable supply of glasses. One bottle was for *Selina*, the other to be reverently sipped as Mrs King suggested, by the launchers. I did not expect that anyone would enjoy it, but I was firmly set on observation of the proprieties. So, now that he had made up his mind to it, was Mr King, and I heard a serious talk between the two of the 'Shall I say "I name you *Selina King* or should it christen you"?'

'You're not baptising her,' said Mr King, 'only naming her.'

'I name you *Selina King*,' said Mrs King quietly to by way of rehearsal. 'And what if I don't break the bottle?' said Mrs King. 'My eyes are not what they were.'

'You won't miss her,' said Mr King. 'I'll see to that and explained to me that he was going to take no chances, he had seen enough of bottles dangling by the neck and swung this way and that until someone had to

Evgenia with Polly — or is it Podge

go and break them on the stem as if they were bludgeons not bottles. His notion was to sling the bottle from both ends, so that it would swing to fairly meet the stem plumb in the middle.

Alas for plans. *Selina* was a big ship to work by hand down the shore to the edge of the slipway. Mr King had watched over every inch of her progress, now adding his weight here, now signalling to the windlass hands to go easy, now carefully adjusting the greased troughs end to end as she moved from one to another. By the time she was resting at the shoreward end of the slipway, and he called a few minutes' rest for all hands, his mind was full of other things than bottles, and instead of making the two ends of his sling fast on either side of the stem, he made both fast to the same spot on the stem head, so that in effect they were no more useful in directing the bottle than if they had been a single string. The moment had come, but there was no Mrs King. I ran into the yard where at Pin Mill we go to get the best water to fill up our tanks. She was not there. I found her in the house, ready with a dozen excuses. She had not on her the clothes suitable for such a ceremony.

'Oh come along Mrs King. You'll break my heart if you don't.'

She relented. 'I must put on a coat to make myself decent.'

'You're never anything else.'

But no, she must have a coat, and presently I was leading Mrs King with a coat on over all, though it was a grand day, down the shore to *Selina*. There hung the bottle. I saw at once that Mr King had not slung it quite as he had meant, but hoped for the best. I got out my camera. There should be on the opposite page to this a beautiful picture of Mrs King naming the ship and the bottle magnificently exploding on that proud bow that was so soon to meet the sea. There is nothing of the sort. And why? Mrs King took the bottle in hands that trembled from anxiety. She released it, while all of us stood round, encouraging. It swung gently past the stem, swung back and dangled. She took it again and again let it go, this time giving it a longer swing. Again it dodged the stem and again dangled. 'Third time's lucky.' Mrs King took the bottle in both hands, determined not to be beat. She forgot Mr King's instructions about naming, and desperate, cried, 'I christen thee *Selina King*', which was about as near baptism as she could get. As she said it, she hurled the bottle blindly at the stem before her. It exploded with a crash, and, from close by where he had been lurking waiting for his moment, Norman dashed out and open mouthed caught the champagne as it dripped, and made me laugh so that I missed the photograph altogether.

But I had other things to do at that moment than play with a camera and, in a very few minutes, Mr King remarked that the tide would not wait for us, and *Selina* once more began her movement to meet it.

The tackles were taken further out, the windlass was manned, Norman and Mr King and Frank nursed her as she moved while Tommy lavished grease on the slides to such an extent that we ran short, though fortunately not until there was no real need of more. She moved slowly down over the planked slipway and came to rest at last with her bows already off the slipway and hanging over the deep trench dug in the mud through which she would at last go out into the river. Yet again the tackles were shifted, this time to the outermost anchor of all, that was to be the weight of the final tug of her launching. There was no more to be done till the tide lifted her, or partly bore her weight before she should make that forward plunge into the trench. Mr King walked round her, had a last look at the cradle, and went off to the midday meal. *Selina*, leaning sideways on her cradle waited there alone. We went aboard *Nancy* to wait for the rising of the tide.

It rose sooner than we expected, and yet another photograph was missed, that of the water first lapping round *Selina's* keel. By the time I got there it was already an inch or two deep all round her. I waited till it would float a dinghy, and paddled out to her in *Nancy's* little pram. She was just the shell of a ship, but still clearly a ship. Already out there in the river, a

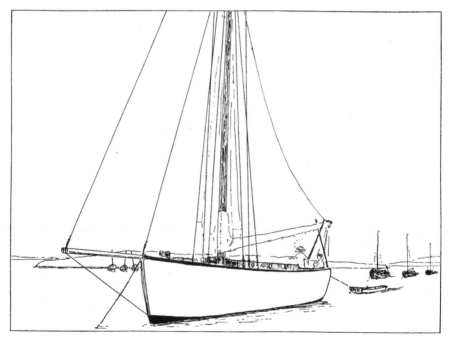

Lapwing (from Secret Water)

mooring had been cleared for her. In an hour, in half an hour, in twenty minutes she would be afloat. Presently Norman and Frank joined me. She was beginning, every so slightly, to lift from the cradle on which she was leaving. We climbed aboard and Frank made fast the warp that would be used to tow her. Norman looked round to the little group far away on shore, waiting by the windlass. The moment had come.

'She'll go with a run,' said Frank, and I crouched on the deck. I never saw the final work at the windlass, when Mr King, as he always does, himself gave the last few turns that sent his new ship afloat. I felt a slight jerk. She was moving. Then a sudden plunge as she went head first down from the slipway into the trench. Bits of the cradle were floating away. Norman was hauling on a rope. I added my weight to his.

'Steady,' called Frank.

He cast off the tackle that had been so to speak the umbilical cord connecting us to the windlass and the shore. The big blue pulling boat had our tow rope, and *Selina King*, still feeling the mud about her keel, moved on. A moment later she was clear of the mud. I took the tiller for the first time, and followed our tug out, past dear old *Nancy*, past *Lapwing* (the Busk family's yacht), to a mooring further from the hard, a mooring that had held a yawl of twice *Selina's* size.

* * * * *

There was little cause for rejoicing in the wider world on September 27th 1938, the eve of *Selina's* launching, when Ransome wrote in his diary the single word 'War'. Two days later Prime Minister Neville Chamberlain flew to Munich for talks with the Reich Fuhrer Adolf Hitler. That evening Ransome gave a dinner at the Butt and Oyster for all King's workmen and his sailing friends, which by all accounts was a jolly affair. The following day saw Chamberlain back, waving a piece of paper to the newsmen as he left the aircraft. 'Peace in Our Time' was what it purported to represent; Ransome confined his diary entry to simply 'Peace'.

It was some time since Ransome had earned his crust with political journalism and, when his mother asked what he thought about the Munich crisis, he wrote with circumspection. Perhaps from his reporting of the upheaval of the revolution in Russia, he had come to learn how useless it was to parade uninformed opinions on the devious business of power politics. 'Just as I think that country best governed in which most people are able to forget they are governed at all,' he once wrote, 'so I think those times are best in which most people need not bother their heads about "the news".' He preferred to joke when asked a question about the colour of his own politics, and once gave the impish reply — 'Fishing.'

All the same, he ventured to tell his mother that 'in spite of all that will be said against him, I think Chamberlain has done extremely well'. He reminded her that both the Czechs and the Poles had gobbled up bits of neighbouring territory, and confirmed that 'Chamberlain seems to me to have done right WHATEVER the outcome. Because, if we do after all have to fight, we shall have the moral support of the whole world' for at least trying to obtain a just and peaceful settlement of European borders first.

When events took a turn for the worst, Ransome started firing off salvoes in all directions and confiding in Dick Stokes, the Labour MP for Ipswich. He regaled his mother with gloomy forecasts of mass unemployment and 'a vast struggle between economic systems'. A few days after war was declared, he wrote: 'The Russians have always said that the next war of this kind would result in world revolution, and they are following out a perfectly consistent policy to that end.' Soon he was finding words of praise for Churchill, berating Foreign Secretary Halifax for one inept move after another and asking: 'How soon shall we call in Lloyd George who alone had the courage to speak out ... 'The blame for miscalculating Stalin's intentions and allowing Hitler to fight on one front instead of two should be laid firmly at Halifax's door, he told his mother, ending his lengthy war homily by recommending Agatha Christie's detective story *The Murder of Roger Ackroyd* and reporting his own reading of *The Three Musketeers* and *The Vicompte de Bragelonne*. 'Old Dumas always blooms afresh.'

Meanwhile, in 1938 there was an Indian summer to enjoy before the clouds of war arrived. The sale of the *Nancy Blackett* was Ransome's one regret, though that soon lifted when he saw how well Reginald Russell cared for her, even calling his house 'Blackett Cottage'. On October 6th he would be able to take *Selina King* to sea at last.

First the high mast had to be stepped, and to accomplish that it had to be towed on its transporter, *Black Jack*, by the shining new yacht upriver to Ipswich, where one of the big cranes would lift it into position.

Dick the engineer dropped down the hatch into the engine room and, after checking the oil levels and the grease caps, gave the engine a turn or two with the cranking handle, allowing a few minutes for it to warm up. 'I looked down at the engine,' Ransome wrote, 'and, but for the spinning shaft and the quiet hum of it, could not have told it was running. There was not a hint of vibration. All the same, *Selina* was alive, and in another moment would be moving under her own power.

It was overcast and raining, yet not as windy as the day before, when they made their way upstream. Ransome was at the tiller, though the ship was not yet his. He felt how easily she steered. 'No test of what she would be like under sail, but still a satisfaction.' They passed the famous Cat

Ransome at broke farm with Podge — or is it Polly

House, where the story goes that a stuffed cat in the window — or its absence — was the signal to smugglers wanting confirmation that the coast was clear. At last they approached the town, with the tall granaries towering above the docks. From a distance Cliff Quay, with its row of huge cranes, looked deserted. The big steamer that had been there the day before was gone, and there was no sign of the harbourmaster. Then Dick the engineer spotted wisps of steam drifting away from a smaller crane than the electric giants and knew that they were ready for them.

Ransome returned the tiller to Frank who took *Selina* almost to the dock gates and swung her round. Someone was signalling from below the crane. Round they came and made fast to a tyre on a tug's quarter and to the quay. Frank jumped down into the dinghy behind and from there scrambled aboard *Black Jack*. A dangling hook dropped lower from the crane as it moved a few yards along the quay. Frank caught it and guided it into position before lifting his hand. Up went the hook until the crane took the weight of the mast off the bows of *Black Jack*. 'Then up, up, and there was the mast that had seemed so huge when we had only man power to use on it, swung up into the air above us as if it had been a match.' The bow rope was slackened and another thrown ashore. Slowly *Selina* was eased in until she rested under the mast as Frank scrambled back aboard.

'Where's that penny, Frank?' Ransome asked him.

'I've got it wrapped in a bit of paper.'

Ransome hurried below, unwrapping it as he made his way through the cabin and carefully laid the shining new 1938 penny, 'head uppermost', in the mast step.

There was a shout from the deck — 'Lower away!' The huge foot of the mast went down through the deck head while Ransome and Norman King guided it towards the mast step. There was a slight jar and Ransome ran up on deck in time to see the wedges being put in round the mast as it dropped below the foredeck.

Once more Ransome took the tiller as the rain began to come down in earnest and he headed *Selina* into driving wind. By the time they had reached Pin Mill again, Dick, the engineer, aboard *Black Jack* was so cold he could hardly make fast to the buoy.

The following morning they set up some temporary backstays. *Selina*, even with the mast in her, floated like a balloon — or so it felt to Ransome who moved, when aboard, with the greatest care. The lead pigs that King had ready were put aboard. She was now steadier, but the upper part of the rudder was clear of the water and it was obvious she was not down to her waterline. Fred Shepherd sent Parker along to look at her the next day. One glance at *Selina* was enough for him to confirm Ransome's suspicion that her trim was right enough but that she needed to be put down bodily into the water. All the lead that King had ordered for *Selina* was aboard, but nearby lay half a ton of lead which Commander Martin had not needed for *Griffin*. Nobody knew where they could contact Commander Martin, so in his absence his spare pigs were put aboard *Selina*. They rowed around the hull and Parker measured the freeboard. After a few small adjustments *Selina* was floating less than an inch below her designed waterline. Parker agreed her trim was perfect.

Back at Broke Farm Evgenia was busy with upholstery and stitching on yards of piping to give the mattresses a professional finish. Frank Adams set up the rigging. Although not quite to their satisfaction, they agreed that it would serve for a trial sail. Ransome carefully greased the mast track as far as he could reach and then they began to slip the sliders on the edge of the sail into the track. When all was in place, Frank began to haul the sail up the mast. It rose smoothly until within a few feet of the masthead, where it stuck. Frank pulled, eased, and pulled again harder.

'Stop!' yelled Ransome. 'Don't try to force it. Let's have it down and take a look at it.'

It was too late. As they lowered the sail they could see the tear and found one of the eyelets had come away. The cause of the trouble appeared to be the third slide from the top that was of a different pattern from the others. It had square corners that Ransome filed away. The sail needed a sailmaker.

I took the sail ashore and to Ipswich, where a procession of four carried it up to the enormous sail loft over Whitmore's shop in the docks, the finest sail loft but one that I have ever seen, the loft where all the barge sails are made and mended, a high airy place, with a polished floor, and huge windows from which you could look down on the docks, and the sailmakers sitting at their work see their own topsails towering past outside. Here the experts looked at the tear in the sail, decided to double the torn place with a patch on each side to give the necessary strength to take a new eyelet. They did this, and cleverly tanned their patch to a colour indistinguishable from the rest of the sail, and charged me the sum of one shilling and fourpence.

The second time the sail was hoisted, it went up without a hitch and Miss Wiles joined them for a sail down river. There was a light wind which at times fell away to nothing and so they were glad to use the engine. There was enough wind for them to see that all was not well with the staysail halyard, although from the deck it was not possible to see exactly what was wrong. The story continues in Ransome's own words:

I weigh so much that no one likes the task of hauling me up the mast, and some who have tried have found it impossible. Miss Wiles, of *Keryl* lying close by, who had herself passed through all the torments of rigging a new ship only last year, volunteered to be hoisted up and check over a number of points of which I had made a list. She climbed, standing on my shoulders, into the bo'sun's chair. She took with her, fastened to the chair, a canvas bucket in which I had put a tin of grease and a screwdriver and a small file. She weighs about twopence halfpenny, a great advantage to a seaman, and I could run her up hand over hand. She had hardly passed the lower cross-trees before she sent down the news of what was wrong with the staysail halyard. Frank had not been able to shackle the halyard block in the proper place and had made it fast where he could.
'Jib halyard's fixed the same way,' said Miss Wiles.
I hoisted away until she was at the masthead.
'Now then, for that track,' I shouted up to her. 'The place where it stuck when we tore the sail is about four feet from the truck.'
'There's a screw not flush,' said Miss Wiles.
I swore gently. I had noticed the screws that were not flush while the mast was ashore, and had been assured that all would be smoothed off. In the hurry of other things this had not been done. At different points, *Keryl's* skipper found other screws not dead flush with the track. With the screwdriver and file she put them right, and, as I lowered her slowly down, she nobly greased the track from head to foot.

The next day brought a hard easterly wind. With the rigging still rather makeshift, Ransome could not resist the opportunity to take *Selina* and try her under sail. While Evgenia took aboard plenty of food for three, Major Busk took a break from laying up his *Lapwing* and joined *Selina* for the day. Frank came aboard at the last minute to substitute stronger stuff for his bits of string and partly, Ransome suspected, because he did not trust them to get *Selina* under way for the first time without help.

The ebb had just started and they decided to leave under staysail alone. Frank took the tiller, Ransome ran up the staysail and Major Busk cast off their mooring. They were off. As soon as they had enough speed, Frank brought her into the wind and they hoisted the mainsail. *Selina* heeled over more than expected, but picked herself up at once.

'You take her now, Sir,' said Frank. 'And drop me near the hard.'

Frank dropped off into his dinghy and they were away.

Selina had a great beat down the Orwell that morning, keeping in the deep-water channel to make the most of the ebb. Major Busk cast off one backstay while Ransome hardened in the other every time they went about. They had reached the Guard buoy when the Cook demanded to know when they were going to stop throwing her about long enough to have lunch. Already Ransome had decided not to risk the makeshift rigging outside the harbour. Instead they took a broad reach up the Stour. So it was that they lunched for the first time aboard *Selina* in brilliant October sunshine, while they drove up against the ebb past Shotley, Harwich piers, the lightships in for repairs and the line of steamers along Parkeston Quay. No cider and smoked salmon sandwiches ever tasted better.

They turned just before Ewarton Ness and sailed long legs and short back to Shotley Spit buoy, passing the bare poles of the unfortunates who had brought their season to an end already as they drove home against the tide. Then, while the Cook steered, they brought down the mainsail, and with impeccable timing Ransome lowered the staysail to come broadside to the ebb, stopping neatly beside their buoy. In two minutes Major Busk had the chain aboard and made all fast. The trial sail was over. It had been an unqualified success. Here is how Ransome took up the story again in the book that he left unfinished.

* * * * *

That night came the news that Commander Martin was bringing *Griffin* back to Pin Mill, that he intended to pick up the lead which he had rejected in the spring and to take it aboard the *Griffin* on her way to Oulton Broad to lay up for the winter. I was a little worried, because, after all, there was the lead stowed in *Selina*, and I had gone to the expense of having the designers down from London to check her trim, and to get her balanced as she should be. However, Mr King had already sent for a new supply of lead to give to *Griffin* when she should come. And, if the worst came to the worst, I could not believe that Martin would insist on lead being taken out of *Selina* when she had been delayed in the spring on his account and was only now at last getting ready to sail, whereas he in *Griffin* had had his season's cruising. Still, I was worried about that lead, and anxiously watched the hard each day to see if it had arrived. Meanwhile I had another go at that rigging.

Frank ruefully admitted the shortness of the topmast shrouds, the shortness of the main halyard, the hopeless leads of jib and staysail halyards, and that the forestay and jibstay were not bolted in their proper places on the mast bands.

One by one these things were all put right. I had not the heart to ask for new forestay and jibstay, both of which were too short. They were lengthened by shackling in three or four links of chain. New topmast shrouds were made, and a new main halyard. Then came the day when, with all these things ready to fit, Frank came aboard to fit them. Already the yard was busy with a new boat, and worse, was in the full throes of laying up the boats whose owners had done with them for the season. Frank came aboard alone, and, with some tremors at the thought of last autumn's operation and all the stitches in my inside, I had to make up my mind to get him to the top of the mast without help. I had good reason not to wait. The night before, just after dusk, a red and green light and a low masthead light had come up the river and moved in towards the shore out of the channel below the hard. It must be *Griffin*, I thought, and sure enough there in the morning lay the *Griffin*. Commander Martin had come back. Mr King had already heard that his lead was to be expected any day, so I met Martin and told him at once that the original pigs of his lead were in *Selina*, and that fresh lead was coming for him.

'If it doesn't come before Friday, I'll make him take the lead out of *Selina*,' said Martin.

'Oh look here,' I said. 'We are only now ready to sail, and you have had your season, and if the lead does not come in time for you to take it with you, I will gladly pay the costs of sending it after you to be delivered aboard at Oulton, where you are going to lay up. It's already the end of October, and you can't do us out of the few days' sailing we may yet have.'

'I wrote to King that I wanted that lead, and if it is not here by Friday he'll have to take it out of you.'

'We'll put to sea,' I laughed, never dreaming at that moment that he meant it.

'I'll paper the ship,' he laughed back.

Well, I had promised my wife that we should at last get to sea on Saturday, sail round to our favourite Hamford Water and let *Selina* spend her first night in a strange anchorage and all that Thursday I spent in getting Frank up and down my fifty-foot mast. The first time was easy, hauling him on the main halyard, which has a whip purchase. But he had to send that halyard down, and then come down himself with the sheave at the masthead, and the next time I had to haul him up with no purchase at all. I knew I ought not, and the pains in my miserable innards made it clearer still. But the job had to be done and there was no one else to do it, and by evening the job was done and if I were in a state of physical collapse I made up for that by mental joy. The ship was rigged at last as she should be. Her trim had been checked by her designer. And when my wife came aboard in the evening, I was able to tell her that we should be ready to sail. We had hoped to sail at Whitsuntide, but to sail in October was better than not sailing at all.

Martin came alongside and invited us aboard the *Griffin* and we spent a pleasant hour or so, admiring all that he had done to her. King had already heard that the lead would be there in the morning, so that there was no shadow on our evening, except that I had very much overstrained my sides.

'We watched you hard at work hauling Frank up the mast,' said Martin. 'I thought you ought not to be doing it, and if you'd only thought of asking I could have sent my hand aboard to help.' I wished he had, but thanked him all same.

Next morning, the Friday, I went ashore, and Tommy the boy, who knew how worried I had been about that lead, met me with an even broader grin than usual, and pointed to a pile of bright new pigs of lead stacked by the shed. It had come and I was glad, glad even that Martin was to have as King pointed out, much better lead than the rather clumsy rough pigs he had rejected in the spring that were now under *Selina's* floorboards. We spent the day getting ready, and in the afternoon prepared to go home to bring our provisions for the first week-end afloat in the new ship.

Mr King and Norman and Frank and Tommy were taking lead out to the *Griffin.* We were in our car, just leaving, Mr King said grimly, 'Commander Martin say this isn't as big a weight of lead as he left.'

'What are you going to do?'

'See what else we've got.'

He found a few more odd pieces and wheeled them down the hard in a wheelbarrow and took them off to the *Griffin.* We were just starting, when some instinct made me wait. I could not believe that Commander Martin, knowing as he did all the details of the long struggle we had had in getting *Selina* ready, would insist upon his pound of lead to the extent of crippling her after all. Yet, he would be within his rights. We waited, sitting in the car.

Suddenly, I saw a boat leave the side of the *Griffin*.

'It's all right. They're coming ashore,' I said, and as I said it, saw the boat stop alongside *Selina*, saw people step aboard. I ran down the hard and took the first dinghy I could reach. My wife had run after me, and insisted on coming too. It was a beast of a dinghy, and I could not shift the rowlocks, and so had to row amidships, with my wife in the stern and the bows cocked up out of the water. It was desperate, horrible rowing against the ebb. It took a long time. The boats had returned to the *Griffin* by the time we reached her.

'We've taken eight pigs,' said Mr King.

Commander Martin saw our faces and went below. He had been absolutely within his rights. He had done nothing he was not justified in doing. We rowed back, passing *Selina* on our way, her rudder once more showing above the water, her trim destroyed. We were back once more where we had been three weeks before. There would be no sailing for us that week-end. In the morning, *Griffin* had gone. By dinner time that day, we learnt, she was at Lowestoft, her sailing finished for the season. Ours was not yet begun, nor likely to begin. For the sake of carrying with him those eight pigs of lead instead of letting me send them after him, when, after all, he had in addition to the ballast that had served him through the season, almost the whole of the comparatively small amount he had rejected, for the sake of those extra eight pigs on a voyage of a few hours, Commander Martin had thought it worth while to stop us sailing altogether.

* * * * *

More ballast was ordered for *Selina* but it was not until November 18th that Ransome could start the log, and from then until Christmas he was aboard most days. Sometimes he slept aboard, and from time to time Evgenia joined him. One afternoon of strong winds and driving rain she had to give up all hope of going ashore, as it was almost impossible to stand on deck, let alone use their dinghy. That day she was marooned aboard.

Sometimes Evgenia arrived for lunch, complete with pheasant or duck, or they patronised Miss Powell's tearooms at Alma Cottage. On one memorable occasion Ransome wrestled with *Pongo*, the cooker, and cooked himself chops, kidneys and beans.

There was plenty to occupy him. The battery needed charging every few days by running the engine for periods of up to ninety minutes at a time. Having spent months watching others at work he was able to take a hand himself at fastening down the floorboards and adding a handle to make the companion hatch easier to slide.

Pin Mill Hard
(unused illustration for *Secret Water*)

At other times he fished, and caught eels, dabs, flounders and whiting. As Evgenia did not care for eels these were often given away. He tried various ways of catching whiting and finally discovered that the secret was to use a small bait and strike hard. The next time he turned up at the Busks for a game of billiards he gave them a present of half a dozen.

On November 19th they took *Selina* out for the first time since her rigging had been put right. Ransome had spent the morning fishing without any success. When Evgenia joined him aboard just after eleven o'clock, they decided to make the most of a good strong, westerly wind and sail down the river. They hoisted the main and staysail and left on the ebb tide at half-past twelve. An hour later they were off Shotley Spit with its row of anchored barges, and they kept on until they turned at the Beach End buoy after only an hour and a quarter's sailing. The wind had dropped a little and they had a long beat up the river, but the sun was shining, *Selina* performed well, and they were alone aboard her for the first time.

A month later they tried unsuccessfully to put *Selina* on a mud berth for the winter. It was a grand day but there was not enough tide and the attempt was abandoned until after Christmas. Yet even when not sailing, Ransome kept a log at the Pin Mill anchorage.

Blowing hard from SSW — 10.30 a.m. — Bar. 28.8. Forecast: Wind southerly, veering westerly, strong to gale. Further Outlook: Wind veering west to north-east, moderating slowly. Gale warning on all coast. *Selina* throwing herself about a good deal. Skinned eel 11.15. Started stewing 12.15., salted chunks in a bit of melted butter in the double cooker, water boiling in a stewpan. Terrific shindy outside. 12.15., Fishing boat IH 123 dragging fore. Pointed it out to Harbour Master Burroughs. Wind lifted sheets of spray off water over our boat. She heels over a good way, but not, I think, as far as the yawl *Boojum* lying to the mooring astern of us. Very glad I am aboard in case anything goes wrong. Overhauled another anchor gear. Mooring chain on buffer spring. 1.15, the eel which had been simmering ate magnificently though the row outside was tremendous. I put away a whole good eel and a banana. Wind still south of west though inclined to veer. Tightened all tyers on the mainsail. Steamship in Butterman's Bay has swung broadside, right across the channel. Another, astern of her, seems to have done the same. Still blowing like stink. Doubt if I could pull ashore now.

4 pm Bar. 28.85. Quantrill's boat obviously dragged on my mooring. Will his anchor slide along and bring him foul when the tide turns? 5 pm Went ashore. Nearly blown off the hard. Took eels to the Mayor and got apples and pears in exchange! Saw Quantrill (the local taxi driver), who came off. His boat had fouled the mooring. He shifted her and came aboard for a glass of rum.

Among the daily entries of the times of high water, the barometric pressure and the number of fish caught, there is one entry that reads 'BBC announcer drunk.'

The year ended with the following: 'Nice sunny day. Came aboard 10.30. Lit fire. All dry and well. She is a grand ship.'

Selina was put on a mud berth early in January and once a week Ransome visited her to air the cabin, light the stove and check that all was well. She stayed on the mud until March 6th when she was put back on her mooring, and the following week he sailed to the Beach End buoy. The log entry for March 31st opens with the usual weather forecast and a note about the reading of the barometer in the cabin. This is followed by Chamberlain's statement: 'War if Hitler touches Poland.' There follows a note about a game of billiards.

All through 1938 Ransome had been looking for a quieter home, and one preferably more convenient to Pin Mill. In the Lake District their home had no neighbours and at Broke Farm there was a noisy child next door, who often drove Ransome to seek peace and quiet afloat. In January 1939 they heard that Harkstead Hall, a pleasant square brick farmhouse, was to let. Pin Mill was only a couple of miles away, beyond the Grange, which was the home of the Busks.

The Ransomes enjoyed their days at Harkstead Hall. There was a good room for Ransome to work in and Evgenia kept herself busy in the garden where the roses were her special pride. These were so plentiful that they used to row through the anchorage distributing bunches to their friends.

On Easter Sunday *Selina* sailed with an unusually large crew aboard when Ransome was joined by George and Josephine Russell and Jill Busk. They went upstream, for once, to have a look at the docks in Ipswich, for the first of which Ransome's own ancestors were partly responsible. There was very little wind and they had a pleasant sail past the Cat House and Woolverstone and Ostrich Creek. A steamer lay alongside Cliff Quay, and Ransome decided to tack right up to the dock gates so that his crew should pass close to the steamer on the way. They saw a barge leave the buoyed deep-water channel, and as it was high water Ransome decided that *Selina* could do the same. A flock of sparrows flew across and perched in the rigging.

'Land birds!' cried the crew. 'We must be near land.'

They were. Jill Busk, then aged fifteen, was at the tiller when there was a long crunch and *Selina* stopped. George was away in the dinghy almost at once with an anchor, but it was no use. The tide was already falling and they were fast.

'Women and children first.'

A delighted George rowed Jill and Josephine ashore and they returned to their homes by bus. George returned to join his skipper but there was little anyone could do. They carefully laid out the anchors well astern, in the hope that they might pull her off at the next high tide. Meanwhile she lay over further and further. Barge after barge, skippered by Ransome's friends, left the lock gates with the tide while Ransome took a little comfort in the sight of the scars of other unfortunates on the Knoll where *Selina* lay almost on her beam ends. At seven in the evening they were able to row ashore, where they met up with the Busks for a meal at the Great White Hart. Afterwards George went home and Ransome spent most of the night in the lock-keeper's hut. George returned at three o'clock in the morning when still they failed to get her off. The outlook was not good with a lower tide each day until the spring tides returned. The lock keeper knew of a first-rate digger, and, with Busk and George to help, they dug a deep trench along her keel towards the channel. The CQR anchor was taken to full length of the chain and dropped in mid-channel. Just before four o'clock they tried to winch off. The anchor began to plough deep into the mud but *Selina* remained fast.

'She won't do it,' said Ransome, and as he spoke *Selina* seemed to slip downhill and she was off. That was the only time Jill Busk sailed with Ransome but she felt he was not at all cross with her for putting them aground. He was not. 'My fault throughout,' he wrote in the log.

A fortnight later they had their final cruise on the Norfolk Broads before war took over their lives. This time Josephine Russell was allowed to crew for her brother, and the Youngs and Arnold Fosters went too, but Taqui Altounyan had returned to Aleppo. The party was joined by two younger girls, Vicky and Susan Reynolds, and their parents. *The Northern River Pirates* had another perfect week sailing the waters above Acle Bridge. The Young brothers remembered the Ransome's favourite mooring spots from the year before, and took great delight in arriving before them, leaving Ransome to find the next best place along the bank. George and Josephine Russell captured the Youngs' mop and ran it to the masthead in triumph! George again carefully kept his log and recorded:

After we got into the Bure (river) we met a whole lot of boats all going the same way and the circus began. James's and our boat dealt with five of them so effectively that they were forced to tie up at the side. One of them rammed us and was so forcibly pushed off by the mate that they promptly went into the bank.

We turned down Fleet Dyke to try to get to South Walsham, but in a very narrow bit with the wind dead ahead a wherry was moored and we could not get past. I tried to row in the dinghy but there was too much wind and I was nearly cut in two for my pains as Josephine could not see me.

At the beginning of September, for the last time he took George and Josephine Russell aboard *Nancy Blackett* to Kirby Creek. Arriving at his favourite anchorage flying a large Jolly Roger, they found *Lapwing* at anchor and the young Busks camping on Horsey Island. Major Busk had made a blank map and they all joined in the exploration of the maze of winding channels and small islands.

Secret Water opens with just such a blank map made by Commander Walker for his family to complete. When the Admiralty cancels his leave and the children are marooned on Horsey (Swallow) Island with a borrowed sailing dinghy, they have to complete the map themselves. They meet a local boy (the Mastodon) who belongs to a secret tribe — the Eels. Soon he is helping the *Swallows* with their exploration and letting out too many secrets about the tribe. Unexpectedly, the *Amazons* appear, and they all become blood brothers and sisters of the Eel tribe. The other absent Eels, who know nothing of this treacherous union, send a message ordering the removal of interlopers. All is peace in the end before Titty, Roger and Bridget have a frightening experience trapped in the middle of the Red Sea — a muddy causeway known as the Wade which links the island to the mainland and is uncovered for only a few hours each day.

Stranded in the Red Sea (from *Secret Water*)

In *Secret Water* Ransome displays his profound under-standing of human nature. Bridget, who is allowed to join her elders at last, is a beautifully observed character:

Bridget thought of last night. She had been in bed long before this, in a real bed, in a room with dark curtains. For the first time in her life she was sleeping, just like the others, in a tent. She wriggled a little. It was not so comfortable as a bed, but the others had always seemed to like it. So would she. She wriggled again. That must be a crease in the rug with the hard groundsheet and the ground underneath. That was better. A faint whiff of burnt reeds drifted in through the open mouth of the tent. A curlew called. Again there was a sudden chatteration of gulls. Yes. They were alone, on an island. And she was old enough to be with them at last. She put out a hand to feel for Susan.

The change of focus was the suggestion of Wren Howard, who had written, 'I have an idea that the next book might perhaps revolve around Roger, presumably Titty and some new characters from Pin Mill. Temporary exclusion of John and Susan would give a new focal point and age-level.' It is not easy to define the special quality of *Secret Water* let alone explain it. To Hugh Brogan, it is the 'quietest of all the *Swallow* books', with a 'stiffly awkward' opening. Christina Hardyment comes closer with her view that it is 'the most elusive ... Perhaps the children are growing up.' Though from start to finish a simple sailing story, it has a subtlety missing from many of Ransome's other books. Nothing is quite what it appears to be in a landscape that is perpetually altering — so much of it revealed and then covered up again by the tide twice a day. Relationships between the characters are tested in a sort of adolescent state of flux. Mystery and suspense are generated less by formulated action than by responses to the watery environment — something Ransome had come to know a good deal about through his voyaging on the East Coast. More than just the exploration takes on the air of a serious practice exercise for the serious business of grown-up life, yet not even John is quite ready to give up the good things of childhood. The fluid situation also gives rise to plenty of humour, not least when Roger, who has adjusted to the ebb and flow of their muddy island life, visits a grocer's shop in the mainland town (Walton) and hears repeated to each customer in turn the same pleasantries as if uttered unconsciously by some clockwork automaton.

Nancy, for once a visitor and somewhat out of her element, has to suppress her natural desire for war in order to support her old allies in their sober map-making. When the absent Eels tell the Mastodon not to have anything to do with the explorers she mis-reads the situation and sees it as the opportunity for war:

'If it was only us,' said Nancy at last, 'we'd go straight for their camp, bang an arrow into the middle of their fire and see what happened.'

Eventually, when she realises that their secret preparations for the Corroboree instead of circumnavigating Peewitland have prevented the map from being completed, she is determined to make amends by plotting with Peggy to creep out of camp to do it at the crack of dawn.

Ransome dedicated *Secret Water* to the Busk family who appeared in the book as missionaries and savage Eels. Their cutter *Lapwing* was faithfully portrayed, though it had a strange effect on the explorer *Swallows* and the piratical *Amazons*.

Nancy and Peggy wondered whether the *Lapwing* was as big as the *Goblin*, and learnt that she was bigger. The explorers were shown all over her, and, with a good deal of squeezing, it was found that only four need have tea on deck if the he-missionary sat on the companion steps to pass up cups of tea and buns when wanted, and the she-missionary sat in the doorway between the saloon and the forecabin, which she said was the best arrangement as she had to keep within reach of the kettle ... The he-missionary showed John round the decks, and Roger bolted out to join him, because, as he explained afterwards, it was too much for him to hear Nancy solemnly talking about gardening.

All through the summer the threat of war hung over them. Feeling that it might be for the last time, people were snatching all the time they could aboard their boats. Ransome sailed *Selina* on short voyages down the Orwell to the Cork light vessel or to the Beach End buoy. Evgenia kept her promise and sailed with him although she claimed that she had lost six inches from her roomy galley, for which she blamed him and the designer. Jill Russell, whose family had bought *Nancy Blackett*, sailed with him and he was most impressed with her as a crew. Miss Wiles and Josephine also joined him when they could. Sometimes Ransome sailed single-handed. He had *Selina* so well balanced that she would sail herself while he corrected the proofs of *Secret Water. Selina* made four short visits to Kirby Creek, with *Swallow* in tow, and once Ransome took her right up to Beaumont Quay. He made the outward passage on a rising tide and had to pole the last 200 yards. By the time he returned the tide had risen sufficiently for him to sail. On another occasion Ransome walked across the Wade in order to buy stores in Kirby Le Soken and returned by a lorry crossing to Horsey Island.

The Ransomes would meet up with the Busks and in *Wizard* and *Swallow* explore the upper waters to Landamere. They learned a novel method for catching worms. Two small boys showed them how to look for one of the small creeklets running off the saltings and build a dam. When the flow had

Map making expedition in *Secret Water.* John Busk in *Wizard*, Mrs Busk and Michael in *Zip*, Gillian Busk in *Jo*

stopped they plunged their arms into the mud below the dam and soon had a good catch. The boys explained that there was a man in Walton who made his living catching worms this way when no one else could.

Their last visit to Kirby Creek in *Selina King* took place less than a fortnight before the outbreak of war, leaving Pin Mill one morning on the last of the flood. With a north-east wind they reached easily down to Felixstowe, where they joined up with Captain (later Rear Admiral) Corson in *Wild Cat*. Corson had been at school with Ransome and was then in command of the *Ganges*, the boys' training establishment at Shotley. His two sons and he were avid readers of Ransome's books and earlier that summer had sailed up to Pin Mill in the hope of meeting him. Corson attached a small tender, which he called *Titmouse*, to his cutter *Wild Cat*. They reefed the mainsail and Corson took Ransome's favourite photograph of *Selina King* from the lee quarter, showing her smoking along. While they were anchored in Kirby Creek, Ransome sailed *Swallow* up to Landamere and into Hamford Water, and Evgenia paid a call on the King and Queen of Horsey Island, the Arctic explorer David Haig-Thomas

Selina King towing *Swallow* (Brotherton collection)

and his wife Nancy. Sometimes they were called 'The Eskimos', a reference to Haig-Thomas's Greenland Exploration.

They had to beat out of Hamford Water the following morning and *Selina* went aground on the spit. A helpful tow from *Wild Cat* took them off the mud in half an hour, without the need of the Mastodon's splatchers. George and Josephine Russell joined them for a pleasant passage to Stone Point a couple of days before war was declared, but already the party was over.

Gradually their friends departed. Busk, who was an authority on tank warfare, had been recalled to the War Office early in the summer of 1939, and they expected London evacuees to descend on them any day, despite the number of naval bases making that part of the east coast vulnerable to attack from the air and the sea. Ransome did not like the thought of leaving *Selina* on a mud berth and preferred to move her to Oulton Broad, where Leo Robinson could keep her under cover in his boatyard. Corson managed to obtain authorisation for Ransome to make a wartime voyage from Harwich to Lowestoft. On it *Selina* was described as a British merchant vessel in ballast. The only condition was that he was forbidden to enter port by night. Although Ransome had been sailing single-handed, he knew that bringing a 12-tonner into a busy port was another matter entirely. Eventually he found an ex-bargeman, called Mo King, to help him. Ransome blacked out the portholes and was so determined to leave (lest his licence be with-drawn) that in spite of the engine's refusal to start they set sail on September 26th.

Ransome had banked on a fair tide that would carry them round Orfordness, but after leaving Harwich with a useless engine their chances of reaching Lowestoft before sunset were small. Instead of clearing Orfordness shortly after high water, they found most of the ebb had already been wasted. Even so, *Selina*, with her big jib topsail pulling well, was going nicely and it would have been delightful sailing except for the sight of masts of sunken ships showing above the waves. It was low water by the time they were off Southwold.

As it happened, the starboard tack carried *Selina* right in to the harbour mouth, where Ransome could clearly see the white water that marked the worst of the shallows. He quickly made a plan of them, just in case. The flood tide was now against them, but Ransome had at last coaxed the engine into life. It ran fitfully, however, and was no real help. It was already growing dark when they sighted Lowestoft and Ransome knew they could never get there before nightfall. *Selina* swung round and ran back for Southwold. Ransome did not stop to reflect that this was where Adlard Coles had brought *Racundra* after acquiring her; he was far too concerned about the tricky entrance to the little harbour that he had always avoided in his coastal voyaging. He recalled his unexpected landfall in an unpublished part of his *Autobiography*.

I had never been into that horrible harbour before, but had read of the misfortunes of others. Still, with that sketch map I had made I thought we might try it, and steered in avoiding as well as I could the places I had marked as shallow. We got in and anchored astern of the lifeboat. The harbour master, who had seen us when we came near the mouth before and had run to the pierhead to warn us to keep off, had gone off to some work. He now wanted to know how we had got in.
'You touched there,' he said.
'We didn't.'
'Well, if you didn't touch there, you must have touched here.'
'We didn't.'
'How many times have you been in before?'
'Never.'
'Well, I'm damned,' said the harbour master.
This was some comfort to us for our failure to reach Lowestoft. That night and all next day it blew a gale. Broken water and a big swell came far up the harbour, or ditch, for it is nothing more, and we were kept busy fending off huge piles torn away from the sides of the harbour entrance. This entrance has been for many years a source of income for the inhabitants of South-wold. It has been repaired again and again, but never so well as not to need to be repaired once more. Nothing could have got out through that entrance next day, with waves breaking over the piers and tearing at the piles.

Conditions were a little better on the 28th and Ransome decided to try for Lowestoft, in spite of the prospect of beating all the way up the coast and the impossibility of returning to Southwold against the tide in the event of failure. *Selina* sailed at 10.45 am at the top of the tide with the wind falling. At 12.45 pm they were still off Southwold Pier, when the tide began to help them. Against the freshening wind they beat to windward for three hours, finally taking a long board out to sea so that the next tack would take them through the Stanford Channel and off the harbour mouth. They nearly came to grief in shooting the piers, but the tide carried them through into the harbour where they found the Royal Navy very much in command.

After showing a young Naval officer their credentials, Ransome was allowed to take *Selina* through to Mudford Lock, where Mo King went home by bus. The next day *Selina* passed into Oulton Broad. Ransome returned to Robinson's yard three weeks later while *Selina* was being laid up under cover, blissfully unaware that he would never be able to sail her again.

Fish out of Water

Shortly after the start of hostilities Ransome offered his services to the Admiralty. When turned down, on grounds of health as well as age, he claimed to have no stomach for the fight and would have nothing to do with the local 'parashots' or Home Guard. Instead he became Cassandra, prophesying doom in letters to his mother:

(26 May 1940) I don't know quite what to think of our turning into a Bolshevic State overnight. Actually we've gone a wee bit further even than the Russians, on paper. But I think you will see that there will not be any of the wholesale shifting of people from one job to another that such a decree might suggest. E.g. I do not suppose they will turn me from earning dollars to making sandbags or anything like that.

(18June) The Position is now a struggle between the whale and the tiger, complicated only by the flock of eagles on each side. A military victory is impossible without an active continental power on our side. There remains the possibility of mutual blockade, England blockading all Europe and being probably blockaded herself.

Though Ransome, once the ace reporter, no longer had his finger on the political pulse, he certainly did not lose his touch as a writer. Between laying-up *Selina King* and the building of *Peter Duck*, Ransome wrote *The Big Six*, *Missee Lee*, *The Picts and The Martyrs*, an unfinished masterpiece called *The River Comes First*, and *Great Northern?* He also began to plan a thirteenth *Swallows and Amazons* book, to which Hugh Brogan, his biographer, gave the title *Coots in the North*. The remarkable range of these stories, written at the rate of one a year, demonstrates that Ransome had several years at the height of his powers remaining.

The Big Six, completed in April 1940, is a brilliant piece of plotting, as even the critical Evgenia recognised immediately. Unable to sail away for the weekend while she read the first draft, Ransome fled to Hampshire where he enjoyed a couple of days trout fishing in the River Meon. He need not have fretted, for Evgenia admitted that 'the framework is better than usual'. Praise indeed!

For several years Margaret Renold had been urging him to write a detective story. He had already planned some incidents for a sequel to *Coot Club*, as he explained to her in a letter in January 1938:

Arthur Ransome (Brotherton Collection)

I have a very gorgeous episode with a pike, and a fisherman and an innkeeper and the *Death and Glories*, which it would be a waste not to work in. I want a cold weather story if possible, because of being able to get some fun out of the cabin those three have built in their old boat, with an old coal stove and a genuine chimney pot on their cabin roof (there is a ghastly episode when they try to smoke eels in the cabin and a fine one when they have a Christmas pudding, and use methylated to get the flames, and subsequently a lot of sugar in the faint hope of it taking the taste away).

Ransome closed his letter with a plea:

Gosh. Margaret. If you can provide the right crime, I'll write you the loveliest detective story there ever was.

The Big Six begins with the three small boys (all boatbuilders' sons) having spent their summer holidays putting a cabin on their old boat, which was similar to the one Ransome refers to in his introduction to E. F. Knight's *The Falcon on the Baltic*:

After more than 70 years in the Swan Inn, Horning Edward Gillard's 21 lb pike is now on display at the Museum of the Broads

There are still ship's lifeboats to be picked up cheaply and, if you are content with good crawling headroom and do not spoil them by some ridiculous superstructure, you can still make reasonable vessels of them, vessels in which you can move from one port to another, sleep and cook aboard, anchor in creeks where you can hear curlews instead of other people's wireless, and at weekends and on holiday live in ecstatic discomfort ... I do not know how many visitors complaining of bumped heads have been silenced by Knight's philosophic remark, 'If one wishes to assume an erect position one can always go on deck.' The number must be very great.

Instead of a crime being committed against members of the Coot Club, Ransome decided, more subtly, that they would be victims of a plot to wreck the club itself. As conservationists forty years ahead of their time, they are natural enemies of George Owden who steals the eggs of rare Broadland birds for extra pocket money. The motive is explained in the first chapter: 'George Owden won't have much of a chance at beardies' eggs next year nor yet at buttles',' said Bill. 'Now we've got her so we can sleep in her, come nesting, we'll be watching all the time.'

The *Death and Glory* is moored at Horning Staithe by the boatsheds. The neighbouring motor cruiser, waiting to be hauled into the shed for the winter, is cast off by George Owden. The Coot Club become the prime suspects, just as he knew they would.

In reality the boatsheds, complete with its dentist's window, gave way to riverside dwellings almost 40 years ago. Otherwise the centre of Horning is much the same as it was in *The Big Six*, thanks to the foresight

Escape from Horning Staithe (from *The Big Six*)

of the Horning Parish Council who bought the land when the malthouses were demolished in the 1920s, and laid out the 'bit of green grass' beside the staithe. Pete's cottage near the Swan has been pulled down and Roy's Stores has new owners. The venerable eelman with whom the Coot Club spent a night near Black Horse Broad was George Parker, who retired just before the Second World War, having spent forty-seven years catching eels. Until recently Horning still had its eelmen who lived in solidly built houses rather than ancient hulks and used more efficient nets.

One night, boats are set adrift all along Horning Reach, and by the following evening almost the entire village is blaming the *Death and Glories*. One of the craft cast off is the racing boat *Shooting Star*, a Yare and Bure One Design that race regularly at Horning. Apart from Mr Farland's *Flash*, almost all the other members of the class are named after butterflies. Ransome had chosen *Grizzled Skipper* as *Flash's* rival in *Coot Club*. At that time there was no such vessel, but in 1938 a boat of that name was registered. The class of more than one hundred is thriving today, and the beautifully maintained craft are still racing at Horning and Wroxham. In recent years the *White Boats*, as they are affectionately known, have been built in glass-fibre, but otherwise they are indistinguishable from the originals first constructed in 1908.

The *Death and Glories* have a brief respite on the upper reaches of the River Thurne, which enabled Ransome to bring in the story of the pike:

'Better wind in, I reckon,' said Joe.

And then, suddenly, the floats dived again, the line pulled taut, the reel screamed and Joe, grabbing the line and rod together as the rod jerked; struck with all his might.

The rod bent nearly double. The top of it slammed down into the water. The line raced out, cutting Joe's fingers.

'He's on,' shouted Joe, getting the point of the rod up. 'He's on. Hi ... Hey! ... Let go with that foghorn, somebody. Go on.Quick ... . Keep at it ... Hey!'

Bill had the cabin door open in a moment, seized the horn, blew and kept on blowing.

'Gee whizz, he is a big 'un,' said Joe, hanging on to the bent rod, and bruising his fingers on the handles of the spinning reel.

After a titanic struggle they land the fish and take it to the nearest inn to be weighed. 'There's one in the Swan,' said Joe. 'This is bigger,' said the fisherman.' The Swan's 21-pound pike no longer hangs above the bar, after the management became afraid that the sight of it might put diners off their meal. Instead the great pike, that had been caught by a twelve-year-old Horning boy Edward Gillard in 1921 has found a home in the Museum of the Broads at Stalham.

Only with the arrival of Dick and Dorothea do the members of Coot Club turn into detectives in order to save themselves. Although Dorothea is inclined to see the turn of events in terms of one of her own Romances, it is she who leads the investigation and presents the detectives' case.

There follow five days (and nights) packed with incident as Ransome builds the compulsive narrative towards the climax in which the rival detectives face each other in front of a lawyer. As Hugh Brogan remarked: 'The plot of *The Big Six* is perhaps Ransome's most ingenious contrivance, and the book ought certainly to figure in any list of detective classics.'

Ransome was hard at work on *The Big Six* while at Pin Mill people were busy fitting-out for the 1940 season as usual. He was relieved to think that *Selina* was safely under cover. His general pessimism about the war did not prevent him joining Major Busk in acquiring enough pitch-pine planking for each to build a yacht after the war had ended. Meanwhile the timber was stored away in Harry King's shed. Ransome had a mooring put down off Shotley so that he could fish from a dinghy, but before he could make use of it that part of the river was put out of bounds. When the call came for the little ships to go to the aid of the half-million troops trapped by the German army on the beaches of Dunkirk, Ransome offered *Selina*. Having only a small auxiliary, fit for entering harbour and little else, the ship was hardly suitable and the Admiralty wisely turned her down. Ransome also approached the Admiralty with a far-fetched suggestion for the defence of small naval craft:

You are probably aware of the simple method of retaliation used by yachtsmen against the drivers of speed-boats who amuse themselves by rushing round and round normally quiet anchorages to the great discomfort of everybody else.

The sailor who can stand this frightfulness no longer, gets out his sailing dinghy and arms himself with a ball of string. He then goes for a sail across the harbour, making fast one end of the string and dropping the ball unostentatiously overboard. The ball unrolls, and the sailor is then towing an immense length of invisible string. The scoundrel in the speed-boat continues his cavorting, rushing about at great speed, and probably showing off by cutting circles round the sailing dinghy. But not for long. The sailor, watching his end of the string (arranged to slip at any serious pull) observes it disappear. Two seconds later the speed-boat changes its tune, and is presently silent, when its horrid owner may be seen anxiously signalling for a tow. While the sailor, looking the other way, returns to his ship to enjoy the peace of the harbour. The speedboat fiend may lose his propeller, and if not will spend the next day or two out of action, and hard at work with a pocket knife.

Very good. Why not apply the same cheap and effective method to aerial attack?

It is obviously impossible to fit small ships with private balloon barrages. But why not let them fly kites?

When the Battle of Britain began, Ransome's letters to his mother took to detailing the local community's attempts to measure up to Hitler:

The parson continues to spout hatred and to tell the villagers he would like the chance of killing as many Germans as possible. The village is, I think, much less bellicose. All it wants to know is how soon is the business going to be over, and is it worth while digging potatoes? They are pretty sick of never having a quiet night, but are inclined to be more contented with their lot after hearing of the bombing of London. It was in Ipswich that our postman had his escape yesterday, and the village is, I think, congratulating itself on being a village.

Our beloved Charlie Burgess, the farm bailiff, invited me to see his dug-out. He has dug a deep pit and sunk a chicken hut in it, putting logs over the top and a lot of earth. It has a bench in it and a chair, and he and his wife and his brother-in-law (Genia's gardener) and his wife all crowd in and play cards by the light of a candle. He is laying down a little cellar in one corner for the beer he brews himself. I suggested planting nasturtiums overhead but Charlie very gravely said that he thought the Germans might see 'em, so he is sowing speargrass instead.

Ransome and the two cats adjusted to the air-raids and disturbed nights, but Evgenia, who worked hard in the garden, had only four nights of unbroken sleep in as many months. They soldiered on at Harkstead Hall throughout the Blitz, despite being told that if the Army or RAF should require the property they would be given twenty-four hours' notice to leave. There was little left, even for Ransome, who always managed to find interest and comfort in little things — unlike Evgenia who was finding life pretty intolerable. It is hardly surprising in those circumstances that Ransome should consider moving back to the Lakes and that eventually Evgenia should agree — although she insisted there was to be no return to Low Ludderburn. Ransome confided to his mother:

And to my great and delighted astonishment Genia says that, given a decent house, water supply, indoor sanitation, etc, she is prepared to go back to the Lakes ... It is very lonely here now that there is no sailing, no visiting yachts, and our local friends departed ... Still, if it does come oft, I shall, for one thing at least, be quite grateful to Mr Hitler. It really would be rather lovely to be back in the hills.

A fortnight later he wrote: 'Your son is once more a lake country landowner.' Their new home was a small modern bungalow called The Heald, midway between Peel Island and Lanehead near the road on the eastern shore of Coniston Water. It cost 'an awful price' but had the great advantage of being known and liked by Evgenia. Seventeen acres of wooded hillside went with the bungalow and half a mile of lake shore, complete with boat-landing. In another letter to his mother he painted a glowing picture:

There is none of that shut in feeling she [Evgenia] didn't like at Lanehead, and the house itself, though tiny, has none of the primitive savagery of Ludderburn. First rate water supply for one thing ... It is a lovely bit of land, half a mile of lake front, and it is a pleasure to think that when we are dead we can let it go to the National Trust if only I can scrape enough to keep it going till then. But I have emptied my purse, stocking, pockets and mattress! Lake frontage in these parts is valued at diamonds an inch.

The Heald had been their home for only a few weeks before Ransome was at work on a new book his publisher was urging from him. Ostensibly

The Heald (line drawing)

a sequel to *Peter Duck*, the story of 'Poor Miss Lee' (as Ransome wanted to call it) represents an achievement of an altogether different kind. Miss Lee, the tiny unquestioned leader of her band of Chinese ruffians, torn between her longing for a career of scholarship and her duty to her father, is a richly complex character. Ransome said that he had based her on Madame Sun Yat Sen, the wife of a leading figure in the Chinese Revolution, whom he met when he visited China in the 1920s. As usual, Ransome made use of the events he had witnessed and people he knew: he had seen the Dragon dance in Hankow and met a host of Chinese 'warlords' and a bird-loving Yangtse River bandit. He was as careful about detail as ever and took endless trouble to see that Miss Lee's Newnham College background was authentic.

The escape from Dragon Town, which occupies the last thirty-five pages of the book, is a triumph of sustained tension, in which the danger of a hair-raising passage on a junk through the gorge at night is somehow more menacing than the threat of the trigger-happy Chinese:

Suddenly they heard Miss Lee talking.
'Better tell John and Nansee to lie down,' she was saying. 'We are coming to the whirlpool ... Will you please shout?'
And Captain Flint roared above the noise of the water that was echoed to and fro between the cliffs overhead, 'Nancy. John. Lie down and hold

fast. Do you hear?'
    Two shouts from forrard, 'Aye-aye, sir,' sounded like the twittering of mice.
    'I keep on the edge of the whirlpool ... if I can,' said Miss Lee. 'You will pull hard when I say. .
    'Aye-aye, sir,' said Captain Flint.
    'Whirlpool!' said Roger.
    'It'll be all right,' said Susan.
    'I wish Nancy was here,' said Peggy.
    The next moment they were in it. They could see nothing, but could hear the enormous swirling of the water. They heard Miss Lee, 'Pull ... Pull now ... Pull.' There was a crash that shook the ship as the mainsail flung across ... A gybe ... Another crash as the mainsail flung back again ... Tremendous flapping. For the first time the feel of wind in their faces ... The *Shining Moon* had been turned right round and was heading upstream.
    There was a thunderous flap as the sail filled again Another gybe ... Another ... And then, with the wind aft, the *Shining Moon* was picking her way downstream below the whirlpool.
    'Thumping good mast,' they heard Captain Flint mutter to himself.

Missee Lee was well received when it was published in November 1941 and went into five more impressions before the end of the year.
    The Ransomes' new life at The Heald was far from easy. It was not apparent until they had moved in, but their new house was more isolated than Low Ludderburn. There were problems with the generator of their home-made electricity and when it failed Ransome had to tackle it himself — 'poor engine!' he wrote. Collecting essential supplies from Coniston village on the other side of the lake was made difficult by petrol rationing, and to economise Ransome took to riding a motor-bike he called 'The Monster'. There was no doubt that they were cut off from people as well as the war during their years at The Heald, and it was a memorable day indeed when Ransome met the Eurasian writer Han Suyin, whose book *Destination Chunking* he had greatly enjoyed.
    In due course the dinghy *Coch-y-bonddhu* joined them in the north and was kept in their little Coniston harbour. Ransome could now fish for perch and trout. While he was at The Heald he suffered two further ruptures and when he was forbidden to row, he taught himself to catch char while under sail. 'The whole difficulty', he explained to his mother, 'is to sail slow enough. Trouble comes when you hook your fish, sixty to eighty yards away, and have to manage sail, rudder, rod, reel and net all at the same time with only two hands and false teeth.' He finally mastered the technique and supped luxuriously from a brace of half-pounders, a

good size for Coniston. In another letter to his mother he described how he provided for his friends:

> I went out one day after five o'clock and found traces of deer in one of my woods, took a good strategic position and waited, filling in the time by working on rough sketches of illustrations [for *The Picts and The Martyrs*] At last I heard a twig break, and presently spotted the white rump patch of a deer, unfortunately not one of the reds but one of the little roes. I had an awful job to get within shot without betraying my sinister presence, but did it in the end and got it through the heart. It didn't move a yard, and then I was very sorry and wished I hadn't fired. However, there it was, and I had an awful time getting the beast down from close under Bethecar to within reach of the road. We ate the kidneys the same night, the liver made yesterday's lunch and Braithwaite came over and skinned it yesterday and cut it up. Sunday dinner for us, for the Gnossies, for Braithwaite and for the farmer who sends my milk.

Braithwaite was the name given to Cook in *The Picts and The Martyrs*. Evgenia loathed the book and told Arthur bluntly that he had 'missed the bus on all counts'. Even after it had been warmly received she made no secret of her disapproval, both of the book and the fact that Ransome had, after five months in which it lay unpublished, ignored her advice and backed his own judgment — and that of his mother and his publisher. In this Evgenia was wrong: wrong in her assessment and wrong to sap Arthur's confidence.

In *Missee Lee* Captain Nancy behaves in an altogether predictable way; in *Picts* we see a much more perceptive portrait of a young woman tempering her boisterous nature with selflessness and concern for others,

Naming *Scarab* (unused drawing for *The Picts and The Martyrs*)

especially her mother. The story is locked into the Lakeland community in a way that none of the other stories are, and Ransome begins to allow his children to grow up in an interesting way — something he might have pursued if Evgenia had been less harsh on the book which, to my mind, is the funniest he ever wrote.

When the Great Aunt unexpectedly decides she must take charge of Beckfoot to look after Nancy and Peggy in their mother's absence, she does not know they already have visitors. There was no way that Nancy could put her off perhaps Dick and Dorothea should go home? Or be hidden away somewhere?

'I don't know what your mother'd say about it,' said Cook.

'Look here,' said Nancy. 'Mother wouldn't want them to go home. She'd planned everything. Only she never thought the G.A. would be here. They're jolly well going to stay. They'll be all right in the Dogs' Home. The G.A. won't know anything about them so there'll be one thing less for her to complain to Mother about. And if we can only manage to be angels for ten whole days she won't have anything to complain about at all. Come on.'

The strangely named Dogs' Home is a hut in the woods close to Beckfoot where the D's live like outlaws, or *Picts*. Just such a hut can be found by a path through Machell Coppice near The Heald. Meanwhile Nancy and Peggy have a dreadful time of it, trying to keep the Great Aunt happy by wearing their best

The Great Aunt steps ashore
(from *The Picts and the The Martyrs*)

The Dogs' Home. The old stone building deep in Machell Coppice is one of the few locations that can be identified with any certainty

frocks and working at holiday tasks, but they do everything to see that the D's have the sort of holiday their mother had planned. The D's are smuggled aboard *Amazon* and taken to Rio so they can collect their new boat, *Scarab*, which was loosely based on *Coch-y-bonddhu*. Before long, half the local community have been caught up in Nancy's plan and are heartily wishing she had never thought of it. To complicate things further, Timothy (Squashy Hat from *Pigeon Post* turned ally), who dares not face the Great Aunt, needs some equipment from Captain Flint's study for his work at the mine:

'It's no good telling me,' said Nancy. 'We'll never find them without you. You'll have to come in and get them for him.'

'But that'll mean explanations, too,' said Dorothea. 'You'll have to say who Dick is.'

'Jibbooms and bobs tays,' exclaimed Nancy. 'There mustn't be any explanations. They always go wrong. The G.A. mustn't know anything about it. We won't even try to take the things until she's in bed and asleep. That's what I meant when I said the difficulty was going to be getting you in. But we've thought it all out. Burglary's the only safe way.'

'Burglary.' Dorothea stared.
Dick took off his spectacles and blinked, short-sighted, at the fire. 'He's got to have those things,' he said.

Ransome was greatly cheered when the Vice-Chancellor of Durham University wrote congratulating him on *The Picts and The Martyrs*. 'He says Vaughan, late Headmaster of Rugby, put him on to the books with *Peter Duck*,' Ransome told his mother. The man had been buying them for young relations but found that he wanted to keep them himself. He had ended up collecting the whole lot and re-read them at intervals. 'Really a very encouraging letter,' Ransome said, 'and God knows I need a bit of encouragement, if, in spite of the local veto, I am to produce any more.' The local veto, of course, was Evgenia's unsparing criticism. But her gloomy prognostications of literary failure were not shared by the reviewers and they are incomprehensible to the millions of Ransome fans throughout the world.

So what, one may ask, is the secret of Ransome's lasting appeal? I believe there is a very simple answer to that question, and it is far more significant than any amount of searching, as critics do, for the influence on him of other writers or for his place in English literature of the last

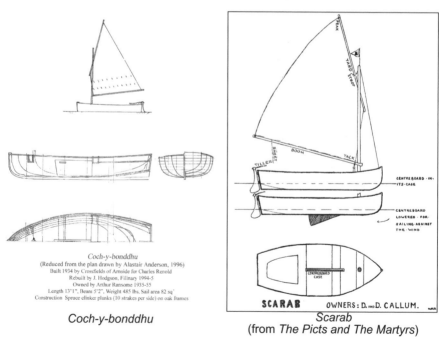

Coch-y-bonddhu
(Reduced from the plan drawn by Alastair Anderson, 1996)
Built 1934 by Crossfields of Arnside for Charles Renold
Rebuilt by J. Hodgson, Fillinary 1994-5
Owned by Arthur Ransome 1935-55
Length 13'1", Beam 5'2", Weight 485 lbs, Sail area 82 sq'
Construction Spruce clinker planks (10 strakes per side) on oak frames

Coch-y-bonddhu

SCARAB   OWNERS: D. ᴀɴᴅ D. CALLUM.

Scarab
(from *The Picts and The Martyrs*)

century or two. In a word, it is enthusiasm. Far more than inventing the 'holiday' genre, more than creating people and places so vividly that generations of readers have asked him 'are they real?' — more even than fulfilling so many wishes and setting his child characters free from caring adults in an idyllic world — far more important than these in the work of Arthur Ransome is his sheer boyish enthusiasm. And this enthusiasm of Ransome's never degenerates into obsession; he never loses his sense of proportion or his sense of humour. Yet when it was deflated, or finally began to wane at an advanced age, so the writing also diminished.

In his early twenties Ransome had become one of London's literati, a devotee of Carlyle and the brilliant essayist William Hazlitt, publishing his own autobiographical essays *Bohemia in London*, at the age of twenty-three, and following that within a short time with *The History of Story-telling* and a critical study of the work of Edgar Allan Poe. He produced some lofty contributions to the *Oxford and Cambridge Review* and prepared notes for a book on Hazlitt. When W. G Collingwood expressed disapproval of Hazlitt because of his quarrel with the poet Wordsworth, and Ransome's publisher declared that he could not sell a book on Hazlitt, Ransome suggested Robert Louis Stevenson instead. Despite the good reviews he was dissatisfied with his work on Poe, whose technique had interested him, and hoped the author of *Treasure Island* would yield another opportunity to examine a true craftsman's skill. It was not to be. With an eye to the fashionable chance, Ransome's publisher suddenly urged him to drop Stevenson for the scandalous possibilities in a study of Oscar Wilde, of whose work Ransome confessed he knew little. His innocent book led to the nightmare of a libel action in the High Court and Ransome escaped into journalism and translating Russian folk tales.

He was altogether too much of an enthusiast to be a good critic. After the turmoil of the war in Russia he turned instead to the essentially peaceful things of outdoor life — sailing, fishing, camping — and enjoyed sharing his experiences with his friends as well as his readers. He did not expect the praise that was showered on him by reviewers of his books, or that his *Swallows and Amazons* stories would sell in their millions throughout the world. Records have been lost and no one knows the exact figure, but in the English language alone it is more than five million copies, and translations have been made into fifteen foreign languages.

A few years ago Bernard Levin began his book *Enthusiasms* with the words: 'We live in a querulous age; more, we live in an age in which it is argued that to be happy is to be frivolous, and expecting to be happy positively childish.' Levin goes on to deplore the shadow cast over the arts — indeed much of life itself — by stony-faced puritans and those cynics who make a political issue of the pursuit of excellence and innocent pleasure. This fear and distrust of joy he finds a strange preoccupation when plainly 'most people are happy most of the time', even in countries 'which are oppressed by tyranny'. It is a theme after Ransome's own heart and echoes something Ransome said in praise of happiness in an essay he wrote in 1953 to celebrate the 300th anniversary of the publication of Izaac Walton's *The Compleat Angler.*

We are an audience in some ways not unlike that for which Walton wrote. We, too, live in times of wars and of ideological struggle, when civilisation, perhaps the world itself, seems threatened with its end, and that calm book of innocent happiness, that pure, limpid prose of his, addressed in days of strife to all who hate contention, is like a lark singing in the blue sky, high over no-mans-land, above the acrid smoke and the thunder of guns.

Ransome and Gillian Busk
beside Coniston Water

The song of the lark is something that everyone can enjoy, whatever their station in life. It knows no social or cultural barriers. That was important to Ransome. 'In the Lake country there are no "lower orders".' He went further in answer to those who accused him of writing about a vanished middle-class world for exclusively English middle-class readers. 'I should be very sorry indeed to think that only children of one particular background can share the fun of open air doings, and the feelings that have been common to all young human beings from the beginning of time.'

Sharing the fun is likewise an experience known throughout the world, even to those most deprived or suffering ill-fortune. For decades readers in places as remote from Ransome's native England as Czechoslovakia, Poland, or even Japan have been taking to his books in their own language. There was a thriving Arthur Ransome society in Japan long before we had one here in Britain.

Such universal power of communication has also led to more than one reader claiming to have learnt how to sail from merely reading *Swallows and Amazons*. And those, like Bernard Levin, who believe that 'enthusiasm itself can be enjoyed at second hand' but who feel daunted by the technique of outdoor country pursuits would do well to get to know Ransome's characters first by meeting them with the D's — themselves townee novices — in *Winter Holiday*. Better still, in my experience of introducing Arthur Ransome to classes of schoolchildren of mixed ability, sex and background, is to hear one or two of the stories read aloud. It is no accident that so many members of the Arthur Ransome Society now in their sixties still vividly recall Uncle Mac's readings on the wireless in BBC Children's Hour. Ransome himself delighted in reading the stories aloud to anyone who would listen. If only we had recordings of those performances.

Eavesdropping on the enthusiast is also Ransome's own view of the proper relationship between the reader and the author. 'Writing is a form of living,' he said in his book *Mainly About Fishing*. 'Readers, overhearing, as it were, an author muttering to himself, share his experiences in so far as they are capable, but being different from him, modify it into an experience of their own.' It does not matter' when or where the mutterer engages in his mutterings, for the reader is transported anywhere at any time, leaving the author free to give his whole attention to what it is that interests him, or her. '*Alice in Wonderland* is a good book not because the story was invented "for" a Miss Liddell,' Ransome wrote, 'but because Lewis Carroll got a great deal of private fun out of writing it for himself.'

... do not suppose that Stevenson wrote *Treasure Island* for anybody but himself. He enjoyed writing it. He enjoyed reading it aloud: to whom? To the boy Lloyd Osbourne? Not a bit of it. Lloyd Osbourne, aged about twelve, Mrs Stevenson, as old as Stevenson, and Stevenson's father and mother, older still, were lucky enough, not so much to hear a story told 'for' them, as to overhear Stevenson telling a story to himself ... A good book is not merely a thing that keeps a child (or a grown-up) amused while reading. It is an experience he shares, something that he himself lives. It calls upon faculties that grow with use and atrophy without it. It is his world and lets him share in other lives, enriches by exercising his own power of imaginative living and so life itself ...

At the centre of Ransome's art, of course, lies his genius as a story-teller. With effortless ease he can arouse your curiosity, engage your sympathy, and without artifice persuade you to hear out his tale to the end — whether he is recounting the wanderings of *Racundra*, gradually unmasking the villians in *The Big Six*, or describing a fisherman talking to the salmon he is chasing downstream, oblivious of all else. This latter episode, from *Rod and Line*, was filmed for television in the late 1970, with Michael Hordern as the fisherman reading Ransome. Later audio and video tapes of Hordern were issued and, although now hard to come by, it is worth any effort or price to have.

A month or two ago I was fortunate in overhearing nearly the whole of the catching of a salmon. I was eating my sandwiches behind a rock when a salmon fisher who did not know I was there came to the head of the pool. There was no one else in sight, and I was startled by hearing him say, not at all below his breath, 'Just by the rock's the place.' He began casting at once and at the second or third cast I heard 'Ha! Looked at it did you? Wondered what museum I'd stolen it from and why I wanted to show it to you? Well, take another look at it. It'll be coming to you in a moment. Now where are you? Hurry up or the gates'll be closed. Last chance of seeing the celebrated Johannes Scotus ... There you are ... .But why not take the beastly thing? Not good enough for you? Rubbish. Now all the wise men say that I ought to offer you a smaller one of the same. But you and I know better. You want to see this one again. And you shall. Now then. Out of the smooth and into the stream. Are you waiting for it or have you gone off to lament your lack of appetite. Ha ... One to be ready. Two to be steady. Three to decide that even if he takes it striking is a mug's game and four to ... tighten ... ra...ther ... FIRMLY.'

(At this point the fisherman came down through the shallows at the head of the pool and Ransome picked up his gaff and took up a position not far away.)

'Yes, my dear,' I heard him say, 'you are perfectly right. That big stone is the place to make for. Get the line round that and we part company. But I lost a relation of yours round that stone and just for that very reason ... steady now ... I am not going to lose you. No, no, my lad. You're on the wrong side. You should have gone on the other side and got the gut on the sharp edge. What? You think you'll settle down there, do you? Tire me out, eh? We'll see about that ... Now then. This way with your head, my friend. Just feel the current on your cheek. So. Out you come. Up-stream? De...lighted. As far as you want to go. Nothing keeping you. There's sixty yards of backing on this reel. Oh. So you don't want to go any further after all. Well, my dear, you'll have to work hard to keep where you are. There's good strong water coming down there. What? dropping already. You might have had the decency to drop this side the stream. You can't think that I'm going to lug you across. Now this little backwater here would be just the place to land you. If you won't see it, I can't make you. But ... look here, if you go much further, you'll have to take a nasty toss into the pool below and I shall have to get down before you. Disobliging brute. Another two yards and there'll be no stopping yourself. Now then, easy, easy ...'

The fisherman slid down over the rocks just in time to keep the line clear as the fish rolled through the fall into the low pool. Few things are more astonishing than the gymnastics of which even an elderly man finds himself capable when he has a good fish at the end of his line. The fisherman went down over those rocks like a boy and, with the fish still on, was moving steadily down the low pool before I had had time to make up my mind to follow him. I had no fish to give wings to my feet and took a minute or two to climb down.

I found the conversation still proceeding, though its tone was much less friendly. 'Tired are you, now? No more tricks of that kind. You've spoilt two pools for me. Couldn't you stick to the ring and fight it out handsomely in one. Turning the best pool of the river into a circus. It'll be a couple of hours before it is worth fishing. No, enough of that. You wouldn't come into that backwater. Try this one. So. Another yard. Another foot. What? Not tired yet? Saw the gaff; did you? Didn't like the look of my face. I shouldn't have thought you had that much run left in you. Coming down again now. Turning over. Keep your head up-stream. Round again. Thank you. Inshore with you. Over it. Now, my beauty ...' The fisherman lifted out his fish, and carried it up the shingle.

There is the mark of a literary craftsman, the born writer conjuring magic from his carefully measured arrangement of words. It completely satisfies, yet makes the reader ask for more.

One of Ransome's young correspondents asked him to write another book exactly like the last, with the same people and the same places and all the same things happening. It is a measure of Ransome's achievement that he never allowed this to happen, for each is a unique creation. Ransome's work had received its first recognition in 1937 when, for *Pigeon Post*, he was awarded the first Carnegie Medal for the outstanding children's book of the year. In 1951 he would become Dr Ransome when the University of Leeds made him a Doctor of Letters for his literary achievements and two years later he would be made a CBE.

* * * * *

Once Ransome had revised *Picts* he took up the idea which had first occurred to him ten years earlier for a story about an old schoolmaster and a fisherman and a boy and a river. The boy was to become the river-keeper of the Beela which runs west of the M6 south of Kendal. The Beela had been Ransome's grandfather's and his father's favourite trout stream, and he himself had come to know it well during the ten years spent at Low Ludderburn. He sketched out the Victorian tale in thirty-one chapters and began the story of Tom 'Staunton'. Tom Stainton was still river-keeper in the 19305 and the book was to be a tribute to the man and to the traditional society in which he lived. He was still toying with the idea in 1938 when he wrote to Margaret Renold: 'I made a good lot of notes a couple of years ago for a story bringing in my respected ancestor, fishing, poaching etc, and your letter made me turn them over once more. The book has to be written some day, but there is one serious snag about it, and that is its retrospective character.'

Evgenia was against *The River Comes First* because it was neither set in the present day nor, in her opinion, about children's adventures so real that readers could dream of having similar ones themselves. She must have forgotten the success of *Peter Duck* and *Missee Lee*! Ransome completed six chapters and stopped. In one chapter, written in the first person, he tells how the boy Tom and his friend Jenny are trapped on an island in the river after a sudden cloudburst makes the river rise in a great spate.

[... Then we saw it. A wall of water, from bank to bank of the river coming down above the ford. A foot high, it may have been, maybe two feet high, but it seemed more than that to me, and it was over the ford and at us before we'd hardly stirred. A wall of water, bubbling at the foot of it, it came roaring down on us. We'd no more time than to get to the high part of the island, and that was none so high, before it was past us and roaring away round the bend below. Where we had been sitting was two feet of water in a moment, and rising fast. I could see it climbing the banks. There was never a sign of the ford, not a ripple of it, just a great sheet of fast water as far up the river as we could see.

I doubt if I could have pushed up to the ford even if I'd started right away, not against that press of water. I knew Jenny couldn't do it, and I knew I couldn't carry her and keep my feet. And still the water kept coming up and coming up. And now there was all manner of drift stuff floating down. I saw a new hurdle go by, and a bucket floating like a boat. And then Jenny's house began to go, first one log and then another and the dead branches we'd used for walls.

'We'll build another, Jenny,' I shouted in her ear, and she said nothing but gripped my hand, and watched the water lipping nearer and the island not half nor a quarter as big as it was. Three or four feet it had risen by then, and the water was pouring through the osiers, and bending them to it and sweeping over them.

It is not clear why Ransome abandoned the book, but Evgenia's opposition and his own ill health and failing confidence must have contributed to its undeserved oblivion. Instead he went back to the *Swallows and Amazons* and wrote the least successful of the series. By the time of *Great Northern?* the four elders are well into their teens, but Ransome did not allow them to develop and so lost the opportunity of adding a further dimension. The plotting is as good as ever, — another exercise in conservation long before the World Wildlife Fund or 'green' issues came into existence or fashion — yet the theme is a mixture of earlier books and the setting is not drawn with the customary warmth and familiarity. But Ransome worked hard on *Great Northern?* and if it

The fishing Lodge at Uig on the Atlantic Coast of Lewis where The Ransomes stayed, and which later appeared as the castle of the Gaels in *Great Northern?*

was, as one reviewer put it, 'workmanlike', that made it no less entertaining to read.

The idea for *Great Northern?* came from his bird-watching friend Myles North, then living in East Africa. A clever piece of detective work by Christina Hardyment tracked down the book's origin — perhaps the most interesting of them all — and she spells out in full the astonishing story of how North managed to revive Ransome's flagging spirits in her book *Arthur Ransome and Captain Flint's Trunk.*

Meanwhile Ransome had been playing for some time with the idea for another story about the *Death and Glories.* In a little notebook containing his drawings, some sketches for his story precede those for *The Picts and The Martyrs.* The three small Norfolk boys, tired of the August crowd of holidaymakers in Horning, decide to stow away aboard a cruiser on its voyage on the back of a lorry to the 'lake in the north', where they hope to find their old friends Dick and Dorothea. 'The Norfolk motor cruiser must thread through the book,' Ransome wrote in a note while wrestling with a plot that refused to come into the open for him. 'John, Nancy etc. scornful because she is a motor boat not a sail ... The *Death and Glories* sticking up for her, remembering *Cachalot* ... Nothing wrong with cruisers so long's they don't moor again a coot's nest ... it's the people in them ...' But what then?

When the story was eventually published in 1988, together with *The River Comes First* and other short stories, *Coots in the North* was introduced affectionately by its discoverer Hugh Brogan, who filled in the gaps from Ransome's handwritten intentions for the rest. 'Thus: Beginning — End — but No Middle or Backbone,' Ransome concluded before he finally abandoned the story in 1949. 'The verdict seems fair,' Brogan wrote. 'But if the plot gave him trouble, the execution did not. So long as he was satisfied with his story, he wrote as well as ever. The opening of *Coots* is especially thrilling and nobody fully knows Joe, Bill and Pete who has not set out with them on their adventure to the north.'

Eventually the *Death and Glories* arrive at the lake, where they are befriended by the owner of the cruiser. He lends them a rowing dinghy so they can reach Dixon's Farm, where they believe Dick and Dorothea are staying. On the lake they see a boat capsize. 'Salvage!' shouts Joe, and they pull alongside the stricken boat. A head, in a bathing cap, surfaces close to the row-boat and Bill makes a grab at it but misses. There is a shout and some violent splashing.

'Shiver my timbers!' said an angry voice. 'What are you playing at? Tearing my hair out by the roots. Hullo! Did I get your nose? Good.'

In his brief notes, Ransome proposed to make use in the book of his newly acquired skill as a char fisherman: 'Fishing under sail. "Why shouldn't we?" asks Nancy, and the houseboat becomes parent ship of a fishing fleet, each small boat hoisting a flag for each fish caught.' And there it was left.

Trust Nancy Blackett to have the last word!

Ducking Under

For Ransome fishing was, of course, one of the delights of being back in the Lakes, but Evgenia found few such pleasures and swore she would leave The Heald as soon as the war had ended. She was as good as her word, and in July 1945 they moved into his publisher Jonathan Cape's London flat while they looked for a new house. Ransome would have liked to buy Rupert Hart-Davis's Highgate house, but Evgenia was very much against the size of the garden, and he confessed to Hart-Davis, 'If I again had landed my missis into a house she did not like, the manufacturing of books for Cape's would have come to a sad end.' They both wanted to return to the East Coast, but Evgenia was very particular and in the end they settled for a town flat in Weymouth Street.

Now that his doctors would no longer permit him to sail *Selina King*, Ransome said he needed a sort of marine bathchair. When Harry King told him that he would be able to build a 'fishing boat' with the timber which had been stored in the shed throughout the war, Ransome decided to sell the ship which, of all his craft, came closest to meeting their requirements. Above all, *Selina* was designed to be sailed single-handed, and as Evgenia observed when it was too late, they could have reduced her rig and sailed her for as long as they did her successors.

He was explicit with the requirements he took to Jack Laurent Giles, who had established himself as one of the country's leading designers of sturdy sea-going vessels and had just re-formed his partnership with Humphrey Barton in Lymington. He asked Giles for a craft that would need the minimum of work to sail and yet provide the maximum comfort for two. He wanted a shallow draught in order to explore the creeks and harbours of the East Coast and still have standing headroom below and sitting headroom above the bunks. He asked for ample lockers and cupboard space, and a tall cupboard for oilskins beside the companion. Barton told Ransome his problem was a most interesting one which he was sure they could solve. He invited the Ransomes to stay with him so that they could look at plans and talk boats.

The first plan was for a 10-ton ketch with a gaff-rigged mainsail and a Bermudan mizzen, 32 feet in length. The cabin coachroof was carried forward of the mainmast, and over the companion there was a doghouse. Below in the saloon there were two settee berths and another in the forecabin.

After consideration, Ransome decided that they had no need of a third bunk. The final design was for a better-looking ketch 28 feet 3 inches long with a draught of 3 feet 6 inches and a beam of 9 feet. The sail plan was arranged for ease of handling — the tall narrow mainsail had an area of only 160 square feet, the staysail 66 square feet and the mizzen 67 square feet. There was also a Genoa, which the Ransomes rarely used. Giles gave the hull the broad rubbing strake following the sheerline which was a feature of his designs. Under the bridge deck was an 8 horsepower Stuart Turner engine, later replaced.

Giles lost no time in preparing the drawings, and from mid-October until Christmas, while the Ransomes were settling into their Weymouth Street flat, more than two dozen letters were exchanged between them. When the first set of drawings were ready Giles wrote:

> You will see from the body plan I have given her a rather motor boaty bow. I hope you will not be afraid of this. It will not worry her sailing a bit, and I think you will agree that it will fit in with the general character of the boat which must perforce be sufficiently '50-50' to justify the rather modest sail plan. The lines generally run in very fairly, and I think King will find that she will go together sweetly and easily.
>
> I have begun to think — Philistine that I am — of the little ship as *Peter Duck*, which is probably very unfair to him, and very naughty of me, but I think that it fits.

Ransome was not happy with the designer's choice of name. 'She will be plain *P.D.*!' he insisted. Having prepared the design, Giles handed Ransome and his problems over to Humphrey Barton. This led to some confusion, as Barton wrote, 'I am working a little in the dark now as I do not know exactly what was agreed upon when you and Giles met last week, nor shall I ever know.'

Peter Duck was built in King's shed alongside Major (now Colonel) Busk's new boat, *Maid Meriel*, also a Laurent Giles design, one of the first post-war *Virtue* 5-tonners. King was able to start the construction on December 6th, and by February 21st *Peter Duck* was planked. When Ransome went to King's to inspect the work so far, he cracked his head

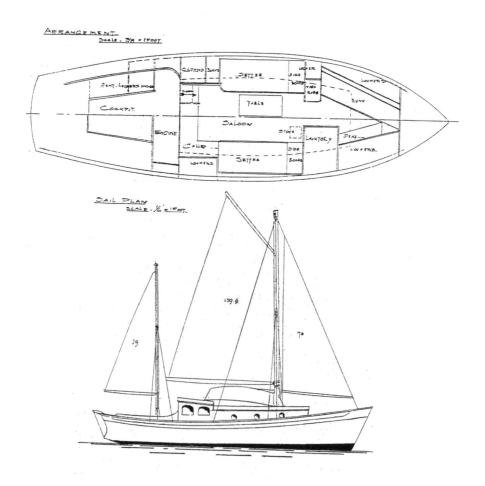

Laurent Giles' sketch for his first version of Ransome's 'Marine Bath Chair'

on the transverse beaming above his bunk by the forward end of the doghouse. He was horrified to discover that, at the aft end of the bunk, there was only 2 feet 6 inches instead of the 3 feet he expected, due to the sheer of the hull. He was angry at Giles's 'mistake', forgetting that the large-scale drawings Giles had given him three months earlier showed clearly that only at the forward end of the bunk was there 3 feet of headroom. He fretted about 'the careless designer' and wished he had never started to build. From then on the story of Ransome and *Peter Duck* would be one of almost constant irritation and mishaps.

There was nothing Harry King could do about it at that stage of the building. He completed the hull, but it was arranged that Stebbings of Burnham-on-Crouch would do the masting and rigging, and they had difficulty in obtaining timber. There was no hope of sailing that season. In any case, Ransome did not go near Pin Mill until August, when he sailed with Busk aboard *Maid Meriel* and noted in his diary that Evgenia was very much against having any sort of boat at all.

They returned to Pin Mill again in September. Although Evgenia could not find a good thing to say about *Peter Duck*, they agreed it was better to have the boat completed. At the beginning of October Ransome tried it out under power with Busk. He had to admit that she had a good modern engine and that the cabin was comfortable and roomy. The following day he sailed again, and the diary entry speaks of the 'enormous fun' they had. Incredibly, within hours he had decided to finish with the sea and bid farewell to Pin Mill. *Peter Duck* was sold to Giles and Barton for £1,200, which just covered his costs.

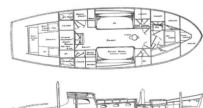
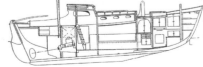

It took Ransome just over a month to change his mind. Whatever their reservations, and with Evgenia's approval, he bought back the boat, losing more than £300 in the process.

Peter Duck was motored round to Stebbings at Burnham-on-Crouch. By the time she was

Peter Duck

completed in April 1947, Ransome had spent more than £2,000. He began his log:

Peter Duck —
('Stop me and buy one,' says Mr. Wall.)
Designed (and named) by Laurent Giles.
Sails (mainsail altered to fit boom) by Gowen.
Masts, spars (Dimensions wrongly given by Giles so that
the main boom does not clear mizzen rigging. L.G. gave
Stebbings the length from mast to end of boom as length
of actual boom) by Stebbings, Burnham on Crouch.
Built by Harry King and Sons.
Winch Afco does not fit chain $^5/_{16}$th. Both supplied by
Barton and Giles.

On April 25th *Peter Duck* was moved to a mooring off the Royal Corinthian Yacht Headquarters in the River Crouch. The engine had been passed by Stuart Turner and the sails bent, so that all was ready for a trial sail. Ransome intended to spend the night aboard and had brought a sleeping bag with him. However, the weather was not yet warm enough, and he had to stay at the White Hart instead.

Busk arrived on board the next morning and they left the mooring under power. After about a minute the engine all but died and they found themselves drifting helplessly through the crowded anchorage. The owner of a 13-ton motor boat called across to say they could secure a line at his mooring, which would hold both vessels. Busk quickly took a warp into the dinghy and made fast to *Amaroo's* stern bollards while Ransome set about tracing the engine trouble. He worked systematically down from the petrol tank and found a stoppage in the carburettor. The obstruction cleared, they motored on down the river for a mile and a half before returning to their own mooring. Not daring to risk hoisting sail until the tide turned, they ate lunch and then left under the staysail. Once clear of the neighbouring vessels they hoisted the mainsail, which was setting very badly, having been cut too long for the boom. Even under this rig *Peter Duck* sailed well and went about without any trouble.

The sound of starting guns let loose a fleet of Saturday afternoon racers from Burnham, and Ransome thought it prudent to keep right out of their way. He switched off the engine, lowered the staysail and made his way slowly up the anchorage. After turning, they found that, under mainsail alone, they could make no headway against the tide. Leaving the mainsail up, they approached their mooring under power, but just as Busk picked up the buoy a sudden gust sent *Peter Duck* off again. Busk dropped

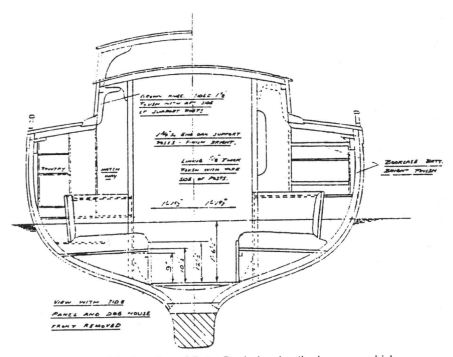

Laurent Giles' section of *Peter Duck* showing the beam on which
Ransome hit his head and the thin cushion

the buoy as if it were a hot brick and they sailed on. After a decent interval, their dignity preserved by a round of the anchorage, they motored back and picked up their mooring without difficulty, and this time without the mainsail.

Cranfield measured the boom next morning and took the mainsail away for alteration while Ransome went off to Pin Mill to collect gear from King's store. He noticed a small dinghy at the yard that he thought might fit on *Peter Duck*'s foredeck. On his return to London he telephoned to ask King's not to sell the dinghy until he had tried her. In the end they decided against having to haul a dinghy on deck and throughout the summer they towed *Swallow*.

A week later Ransome was back and sleeping aboard. The log tells us:

Slipped off bunk and spent hours cursing the careless designer who had made things worse by adding a cushion back. Decided that I must have extension fitted to broaden bunks except at foot where it is impossible.

The question of cushion backs had been raised in the correspondence during the planning. Barton had said that the space behind the backs could still be used for storage and that the cabin's appearance was greatly improved by having upholstered backs — a view shared by subsequent owners. Ransome had requested that the question of seat backs be postponed. His frustration with the boat increased a couple of days later when an engine test showed she would not turn to port in reverse.

The anchorage at Burnham was much too crowded for Ransome's liking, so he left for Pin Mill as soon as he could. But his troubles were far from over. When he set off on May 24th, the dynamo was not working and the winch had jammed. *Maid Meriel* cast off at 3.55 pm and *Peter Duck* followed twenty minutes later under main and staysail. In the light wind Ransome kept his engine ticking over. By the time they had reached the Spitway, *Peter Duck* was ahead, and it became clear that they were going to be very late. Ransome realised that, with no engine to help her, *Maid Meriel* would be swept eastward by the cross tide. So he returned for Busk and towed him through, keeping on the line of the two buoys with Busk taking soundings all the way.

By eleven o'clock Walton Pier was abeam and Ransome made for the entrance to Harwich. He found the mixture of flashing lights ahead confusing. Fortunately the Cliff Foot buoy, which was flashing red every five seconds, gave him a fixed point for which to steer. He lowered the staysail and passed the Cliff Foot just after midnight. Failing to make the winch work, or release the chain, Ransome anchored with the kedge and a long rope not far from Walton buoy at 12.50 am.

After something to eat and a doze he looked out to ensure that all was well and saw a swallow roosting on the lifeline. The swallow remained until after six o'clock, when Ransome found that *Peter Duck* had been dragging her anchor. The boat was drifting very fast as he fought with the anchor chain. At last he managed to free it from the winch and paid out the anchor by hand, whereupon the kedge swept past with the ebb and had to be recovered from astern. They were close to Felixstowe Dock and Ransome must have thought of the similar scene in *We Didn't Mean to Go to Sea*.

What on earth was happening now? He watched the anchor rope leading away from the stem. It tautened till it looked like wire. The tide was pouring past, rippling against *Goblin's* bows. Suddenly the rope slackened, then tautened, then slackened again. The rippling stopped. It was as if the *Goblin* were anchored in still water ... The rippling against the *Goblin's* bows had stopped altogether. Yet the tide must be still pouring out of the harbour. That meant that the *Goblin* must be moving

with it. Yes. The anchor rope was now hanging straight up and down as the chain had hung before. Desperately he began hauling it in.
'Hi! Susan! Come and lend a hand. Quick!'

The rope Ransome had used for the kedge was much shorter than he believed, and he had not noticed this when he paid it out in the dark, tired after the passage.

Maid Meriel had anchored near a barge on the Dovercourt side of the river without incident. When Ransome tried to start the motor, the starter failed. He had to crank it and to haul the anchor by hand — the very thing his doctor had warned him against. *Peter Duck* finally left at 10.50 am and had to head into the last of the ebb before the tide turned and was with them after Collimer Point. The log entry states:

Moored by harbourmaster Burroughs 12.10. V. pleasant to be back and to find I could manage without help, though ruptures are not too kind after all that hauling. Saw old friends, all the Kings, Miss Powell, Holden etc. Busk to lunch. Turtle soup, pie, peaches from USA.

That night it rained and *Peter Duck* seemed to leak everywhere. When he left for London the following morning, Ransome gave instructions to King's that the boat should be painted and all the leaks stopped. He also asked them to see to the winch, which kept jamming.

Ransome returned to Pin Mill a fortnight later to find *Peter Duck* looking very smart in her new paint and varnish but still leaking. All the bedding aboard was wet, except for his sleeping bag. To make matters worse, the winch had not been touched. Ransome decided to do the best he could to dry the bedding and sleep aboard that night in his sleeping bag. It had been arranged that the following day *Peter Duck* and *Maid Meriel* would sail to their old anchorage in Kirby Creek and that Evgenia would stay with Kathleen Busk in the Marine Hotel in Walton and join

The hard at Pin Mill

them each day. It was a beautiful sunny morning and by nine o'clock *Meriel* was ready. With Ransome still doubtful about his engine, Busk suggested that he would wait off Harwich if *Peter Duck's* motor failed. But Ransome told him to go right in, if he found a wind, and to disregard him. Ransome knew his engine: it failed to start, and soon he had a flat battery as well. Now there was no hope of leaving. Ransome telephoned to the engineers and Rampling came out in the afternoon. After a long struggle he managed to remove the faulty magneto and took the battery away for recharging. Stuart Turner promised to put a new magneto on a passenger train at once and Rampling agreed to meet the train at Ipswich.

When Ransome telephoned the Marine Hotel, he learnt that Busk was not yet in sight. Returning to *Peter Duck*, he found *Meriel* back at her mooring. Having reached the Pye End buoy, Busk had not fancied beating up the Twizzle. They consoled themselves with a supper of salmon, cheese cake and tea aboard *Peter Duck*. It wasn't until the following evening that Rampling arrived with the new magneto and freshly charged battery.

Peter Duck was now ready for sea, but the weather was so poor that Ransome spent the next day investigating the problem of his winch. Eventually he decided that there was nothing the matter except that Giles and Barton had supplied the wrong size chain. There was no five-eighths chain to be had in Ipswich — but at least he now knew the cause of his difficulties.

Next morning Busk took *Maid Meriel* to the scrubbing posts in front of the Butt and Oyster alongside the barge *Water Lily* and spent the morning hard at work. Ransome managed to serve a lunch for them of bully beef, green peas and macaroni by juggling two saucepans on the stove. They decided to give up the attempt to reach Walton; 'the wives' would come to Pin Mill the following day.

That evening Ransome had his supper interrupted when Busk came alongside and asked for a hand in moving *Maid Meriel* back to her mooring. Everything was ready, and Burroughs, the harbour master, was bringing his motor boat into position for towing when his engine stopped and the motor boat began to drift off towards Cathouse Point. All Ransome could do was watch and wait while Busk and Burroughs wound up his engine again and again. At last, tired but undefeated, Burroughs abandoned the boat and returned in his dinghy. He took a line to *Cariad*, which was close below *Meriel* on the hard, and they warped *Meriel* alongside. At last the ebb began and they were able to tow *Meriel* downstream to her mooring. It was after 10.30 when Ransome resumed his meal.

The rain began just after midnight. Before long Ransome was putting a waterproof cover over his bunk and a bucket under the worst of the leaks. He returned to bed and hoped for the best.

It was still raining in the morning. With easterly gales forecast, he tried to telephone the hotel but was too late to prevent Evgenia and Kathleen Busk from setting out to join them. All four spent a miserable day huddled below deck out of the unceasing rain, watching for still more leaks. To his surprise, Ransome recalled, Evgenia's dislike of the boat seemed to have lessened.

There was worse to follow. In spite of the work on the engine, when they tried to leave the mooring for a short motor up to the Cat House, the clutch began to give trouble. It was impossible to find neutral, and at one moment the engine was in reverse while the lever was in the forward quadrant! There was nothing they could do but return to the mooring. The log reveals:

> With great skill and beef on Busk's part, we got Burroughs' horrible mooring chain aboard and made fast to the rope attached by a ridiculous knot plus two shackles, two thimbles etc, so it could not pass over the stemhead roller or through the fairlead.

Ransome asked Burroughs to put him on another mooring. The harbourmaster must have known that Ransome was not supposed to do any heavy lifting, but it was a matter of months before he did anything about it, and by that time Ransome had decided to leave Pin Mill.

To add to all the other petty irritations Ransome had to endure that summer, he was unable to use the winch. The chain that Barton had supplied and the winch were not compatible. He tried changing the gypsy wheel on the winch and then the chain itself but without success. The log only records his growing frustration.

A week later Rampling telephoned to say that all was adjusted, and Ransome returned to Pin Mill by train and taxi. He found that Afco had sent the key needed to change the gypsy wheel but no new wheel. Rampling had indeed replaced the gear column but it was now so stiff Ransome could hardly move it, and then it jumped out of gear with such a jar that he feared the engine would leave its seating.

It was farcical, but to Ransome no laughing matter. He wanted a change of scene and was not going to be deterred by mere mechanical failings. He sailed round to the anchorage in Kirby Creek and splashed ashore to the old landing on Horsey Island. After visiting the farm, he sailed round to the Twizzle, where the boatyard found him a mooring that enabled him to leave *Peter Duck* while he returned to London.

A few days later Evgenia agreed to join him, though she would not sleep aboard, and stayed instead at the Marine Hotel while Ransome prepared soup, bread and cheese, biscuits and Ovaltine for himself on

Peter Duck

Peter Duck. He aired the blankets and examined the new gypsy wheel that had arrived at last from Afco. It looked exactly like the one already fitted — and so it was!

Evgenia went aboard next day and cooked lunch and supper. Friends came for tea, but Ransome waited in vain for the Busks to arrive from Pin Mill. At length Evgenia consented to sail with him. When they reached Kirby Creek, Ransome could not make *Peter Duck* go about in the narrow channel and only a mad scramble to start the engine prevented them from going on the mud. But in spite of their problems, they had a pleasant outing and Ransome felt happier about the boat.

When Busk arrived the following day, he thought the ship so handsome that he attempted to photograph her from the dinghy, so that he could show her to the others. Evgenia said the boat looked 'ridiculous', and Ransome did not altogether disagree. 'It is true that she has a long freeboard and her sails are set high (to avoid Giles's doghouse). I propose to lower the mizzen next winter by six inches.'

The following weekend he had the help of his old friend P. G. Rouse, who was at *Ethelinda's* mooring near by. In Hamford Water they were headed by a hard north-westerly wind and sea. Ransome wrote in his log that his boat became unmanageable and would not come into the wind because of the windage of the lowered staysail. It was all very unsatisfactory. Returning to Pin Mill, he arranged for King to put aboard 10 hundredweight of galvanised ballast, which he hoped would improve *Peter Duck's* performance. Although Ransome's log is full of the difficulties he endured with the engine, sails, boom, winch, bunks, leaks and the Pin Mill harbourmaster, his keen interest in the yachting scene is always evident. He recorded the yachts he met while sailing and those that visited the anchorage. He could recognise unfamiliar yachts as having been designed by Dan Webb, T. Harrison Butler, Laurent Giles, David Hillyard, and so on. Encounters with cats were also chronicled. Both Arthur and Evgenia were fond of cats and kept at least one cat throughout most of their married life. There is no record of any of them going to sea. A diary entry speaks of Ransome's remorse after unwittingly reminding the poet John Masefield of his cat which had recently died. 'Letter from Masefield. The little cat of the picture is dead. I know just what he must be feeling, and I wish I had not reminded him — but I did not know.' What a tantalising clue — not the only one leading nowhere! I have been unable to trace any of their letters, and so presumably we shall never know what else the two men found to correspond about.

In the log, 'Met a v. fine tabby Tom by the chemists' would be sandwiched between barometric readings and meals eaten. On one occasion two dozen oysters are put away. Fishing crops up less often at this time than one might suppose. No doubt Ransome was too taken up with the trials of recalcitrant sailing gear, over which he seems unable to take the same philosophic view as he did the frustrations of fishing. He describes a barren day at the river in *Rod and Line* and concludes:

Finally, after fishing till dusk, you set off home. On the way you take a cast, just for luck, in a place where you missed a good one, and get caught up in a tree behind you. You break your cast, strain the middle joint of your rod in taking it to pieces, find that you left the stoppers where you put your rod up, it being now too dark to look for them, tell yourself that after all stoppers do not matter, and in taking off your waders learn that they have been torn by a bramble. In all this I have said nothing about the weather. Suffice it that starting out you have told your wife that it is too good a fishing day to miss.

Even when the ketch was playing up, there was always *Swallow* in which he could explore the creeks and estuaries. But Pin Mill had lost its charm. His young friends had either become victims of the war or moved away. George Russell was killed in battle at El Alamein, John Busk lost his life on *HMS Norfolk* in Scapa Flow, and Haig-Thomas, the King of Horsey

Island, failed to return from the Allied Normandy landings in 1944. Susie Altounyan, who had gone to France to help her aunt run a guest house, was caught and spent the war in a Nazi internment camp. Gillian Busk joined the ATS and became a driver-instructor, afterwards teaching on the South Coast. Those who survived the war found that their East Coast haunts were never the same again. Neither Rouse nor Busk wanted to keep their boats in the old anchorage, and now this beastliness with Burroughs made the Ransomes think seriously of their own future. Before leaving

The Sea Bear (from *Great Northern?*)

for a month's holiday in the Hebrides, Ransome told Burroughs that, unless he had put him on another mooring by the time he returned, he would take away their boat altogether.

The trials and tribulations of post-war boat-owning were forgotten for a while when the Ransomes returned to old haunts on the island of Lewis, which they had visited in search of a setting for *Great Northern?* in 1945. Ransome had taken liberties with the landscape in the book. Stornoway is easily recognised as the harbour from which the *Sea Bear* escaped the grasping egg-collector under cover of night. The country of the Gaels owes much to the area around Uig, their holiday home on the Atlantic seaboard of Lewis, although a possible Scrubbers' Cove may be found north of Stornoway.

Great Northern? had been started three years earlier, in August 1944, and Ransome's diary chronicles its lengthy evolution. Entries such as 'work won't go. I'm too old' and 'this swampy book' appear between accounts of the latest difficulties with *Peter Duck*. Surprisingly, it was

Evgenia who gave him the encouragement he needed to push on to completion. On May 18th 1946 he had written: 'Read all through. Beginning slow. End tame. Mistake in continuing.' A week later, 'G. says go ahead with book.' The following December, after the fourth revision of the first chapter, *Great Northern?* was finished. All Ransome's hard work was rewarded, for when the book was published in October 1947 it was devoured by readers hungry for more adventures and was reprinted four times before the end of the year.

They returned to find that Burroughs had done nothing whatever about their mooring. That was the final straw. They made up their minds to go. After a 'very jolly day' at the Pin Mill Regatta they left for Walton. 'Full sail,' Ransome wrote. 'Tried unsuccessfully to start the engine.' But, *'Peter Duck* sailed like fun, though awkward to manoeuvre and refusing to come about without backing the jib.'

Having spent a couple of nights moored in the Twizzle, they decided to go south and look for a new sailing base. *Peter Duck* motored out against a north-east wind. When they reached the Pye End buoy, they stopped the engine and found the conditions which just suited her. Off Clacton Pier they set the Genoa and considered where to go:

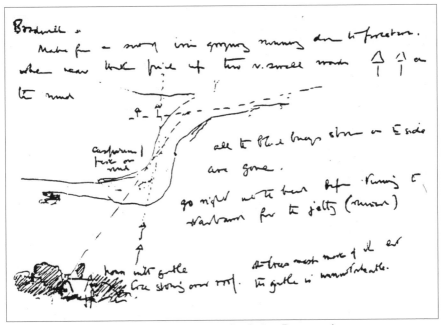

The Marks at Bradwell (by Arthur Ransome)

After sighting steamers in the Blackwater, Bradwell Quay and West Mersea, were tempted to have a nearer look at Mersea. Book says carefully avoid Nass beacon, but there is no beacon, and look for W. Mersea church which is invisible. Mate (promoted from Cook) spotted a racing buoy and after hectic searching of chart and conscience I decided to go in and follow the shore at some distance, hoping to pick up the entrance to the Quarters. Hailed a fishing boat who confirmed position and we downed sails, turned on engine and headed in through a sort of ribbon development of boats. It was like meeting a procession and threading through it.

They stayed for a few days at West Mersea, meeting old sailing friends and house-hunting. They were particularly interested in Bradwell, and one afternoon Ransome was taken to see the marks by the man who put them down, so that he could draw charts of the entrance to the anchorage. Ransome also did some exploring in *Swallow* around the Nass. Once they left the dinghy on the hard at West Mersea for a few minutes and found, on their return, that some lout had smashed his methylated spirits bottle on the seat. There was glass all over the bottom of the boat and Evgenia cut her hand.

Before setting out on the return passage to Pin Mill they were advised to postpone their start as they had left it too late to manage against wind and tide that day. They decided to spend the night at the mouth of the Colne. The next day it was 1.20 pm before they left the mooring opposite the yacht club under power, with the sails all ready for hoisting once they left the creek. When they reached Priory Spit they decided to try and make Pin Mill. Having reached Clacton Pier shortly after three o'clock, they took a board out towards the south-east, and with all sails drawing well and the engine going at half throttle, they had a pretty lively time of it, as *Peter*

Putting on the War Paint (from *Secret Water*)

Duck butted into a head sea. When the engine stopped, as it was bound to do, they found they could not go about. The engine kept starting and stopping for the next hour. It was clear that as long as it kept running they would be able to make it, otherwise they would have a long fight ahead of them. In fits and starts they struggled on until they reached Harwich, where they were helped up the Orwell by the first of the flood. Burroughs had at last cleared a buoy for them and they picked it up at 7.30 pm. The log reveals:

Very pleased with the boat except for her unwillingness to go about. West Mersea in a v. good place for small sailing boats and we propose to winter there, if can get her into shed. Nearer than Lowestoft or Walton and much nicer than Burnham.

They remained in Pin Mill long enough to stock up with stores and left for what was to be their final visit to Hamford Water. In *Secret Water* he had brought that peaceful world of mud and water to life as vividly as any of his settings. Nancy, of course, had seen its possibilities differently.

'It's a grand place for a war,' said Nancy. 'Better than Wild Cat and our river. Surprise attacks from all sides. And savages too.'

Ransome picked up a borrowed mooring in the Twizzle just ahead of another visiting yacht which had been hoping to arrive first. 'Bad, of course to come in against tide in both river and channel,' he wrote, 'but Genia wanted to go somewhere and it was well worth it!'

Next morning they were off at 6.20 am under power, but once in Walton Channel they raised the mainsail and mizzen and set out against a head wind through the Pye Channel. Setting the staysail at Pye End buoy, they beat up to Pin Mill with the engine going, and were moored at ten to nine in time for a much needed breakfast. Later in the day they shifted to new moorings, using the same ground tackle but a much better chain. Their last evening as members of the Pin Mill community was spent aboard *Paracona*, watching the end of the Pin Mill Regatta. The log reports: 'Grand moment when Mr Rampling with fiancee in the bottom of his boat, sailing sideways, brought up against *Paracona's* bowsprit, then drifted past within reach of the Committee's FEET, and received from a yard away the two guns accorded the last to finish.'

The following morning was calm and a beautiful day looked likely. They hurried to leave Pin Mill as soon as possible and were ready shortly after nine o'clock, by which time a light southerly breeze had sprung up. *Peter Duck* slipped away under power. By Collimer Point they met a boat coming up the river whose skipper shouted and made a sign with his arms that neither of them could make out. A short while later, in Shotley Reach, they met a barge whose skipper shouted and made a similar gesture, and again they were puzzled. Thinking that something must be wrong with their boat, they went alongside the barge and asked the skipper what he had said.

'Sorry,' he replied. 'I only said it was a good day.' Then he added, 'She's a nice little ship' — which surprised and pleased them when they were fearing the worst.

Just before Shotley Spit the tide turned, and from there until well beyond the Beach End buoy the Ransomes had to fight both wind and tide. After that they found the wind veering and heading them all the way down the coast. Off Clacton Pier they sighted their Pin Mill friend C. S. Davey sailing *Jenny Wren.* Davey suggested that they both make for Brightlingsea where he had a mooring, and *Peter Duck* could lie alongside. Ransome agreed, and took his ship to the mouth of the Colne, turning so that *Jenny Wren* could lead them in. With wind and tide helping them, they sailed fast up river, but just as Ransome was lowering sails the engine petered out. Evgenia took the tiller and tried to steer under bare poles while Ransome struggled to clear the petrol feed pipe, then the carburettor and filter, and finally the air lock. Helplessly the boat drifted towards some anchored barges. It took several frantic manoeuvres before they got clear and were safely tied up alongside *Jenny Wren.*

That evening Ransome decided to write to *Peter Duck's* designer, Jack Laurent Giles. The rough draft of his letter has survived:

First of all I want to tell you how very pleased I am with many of the qualities of the little ship. She is MUCH faster than I ever expected, and by throwing out the expensive upholstery which artificially narrowed the bunks, we can be perfectly comfortable.

Under sail only, she scurried round from Harwich to the Blackwater between 11.30 am and 4.10 pm. Beating back against head wind I had all sails sheeted hard in, engine running at half throttle and, leaving the Nass outside Mersea at 12.40, I passed Harwich outer buoys at 6.40. This in spite of a number of stoppages of the engine, which brings me to the vital point of this letter.

WITHOUT the engine she would not come about. I had to wear her every time. This of course is serious and I think you would like to say what should be done.

NOTE. She had at first a tendency to lee helm, but that, I think, I have corrected, but to get her to come about without backing the staysail I cannot, and in any sea she won't come about even when the staysail is backed. This (a) makes people stare and (b) is very dangerous in narrow places, besides making it impossible to manoeuvre under sail in an anchorage.

I had hoped to bring her round for you to see and diagnose, but unfortunately I have not yet been able to use the winch for anchoring and I do not like the idea of going at all far depending for anchoring on a light kedge and a bit of string.

When I took the boat away from Burnham, my wife was not with me and it was a little disconcerting on sailing into Harwich at 1 am on a dark night and going forward to anchor, to find that the anchor would go neither up nor down, the chain jamming either way in the gypsy wheel — a danger I had foreseen and pointed out in a memorandum when I agreed that Barton do the buying of winch and chain instead of doing it myself. There was a subsequent difficulty with the Afco people who found it hard to identify the winch and chain as the price charged me does not correspond with theirs.

George and June Jones, who owned *Peter Duck* for nearly thirty years after Ransome, could not understand why it was that he failed to get the boat to go about. They found *Peter Duck* a lovely, sea-kindly craft — a real thoroughbred, at her best in a hard breeze and a seaway. Perhaps Ransome never really liked the boat and soon lost patience when things went wrong with it, June suggested to me. 'He was a nice man, but he could be hasty-tempered.' I am also sure that, sooner or later, if he could not point to a mechanical fault, he would see it as inadequacy on his part. Such things never happened in the boyish dreams which he lived out in his books. Sometimes the real world was too much for him to cope with, and if he could not romanticise them he was apt to pretend that unpleasant situations simply did not exist, a failing that some have seen in his writings on Russia.

George Jones even suggested to Giles that *Peter Duck* would make an admirable 'class' boat, and, with a couple of alterations to the original design, thirty-eight were built. Giles went back to his original conception and carried the coachroof forward of the mainmast and added an extra strake to the hull. They proved very popular craft.

Gregory Palmer, who sailed *Peter Duck* to Russia, told me he saw nothing wrong with the way she handled, despite her shallow draught and ketch rig.

In a good breeze *Peter Duck* makes three to four-and-a-half knots, and will reach five knots with the sheets eased. This performance in *Peter Duck* is only achieved in the best possible conditions; if the wind gets much

Ann and Greg Palmer who took *Peter Duck* to Russia

greater or, even worse dies down to a zephyr, then our performance suffers to a much greater extent than would that of a modern yacht.

We have had no problems in going about with a masthead Genoa but on one occasion with our small staysail found the same difficulty Ransome experienced in going about in a short, choppy sea. We were pleased to find how well-balanced the hull is, for *Peter Duck* will sail herself for quite long periods. With her long shallow keel she doesn't turn by spinning like a deep-keeled or centreboard boat, but sails round onto a new tack in a fairly wide arc using the momentum of her heavy hull to take her through the wind. If the staysail is allowed to flap, the forward momentum is stopped and wind and waves drive the high bow back onto the old tack.

Ransome knew all about long-keeled boats. He described in *The Big Six* how the boatbuilders' sons managed theirs:

The *Death and Glory* sailed all right with a fair wind or on a broad reach but, being an old ship's boat with a long straight keel, one thing she could not do was to spin on her heel and make short tacks. There was nothing for it but to ring up the engines for full steam ahead, which meant that Joe and Bill took to the oars and drove her with flapping sail straight into the wind.

There was a strong south-west head wind blowing when the Ransomes left Brightlingsea for West Mersea. They ignored the advice of their friends who told them it was not the weather for *Peter Duck*. With the ebb under them they motored out to sea and set the mainsail. One minute later the engine stopped. By now Ransome had every reason to feel as much distrust of engines as the ship's namesake who joined the *Swallows* and the *Amazons* on their treasure-hunting adventure in the Caribbean.

'What little donkey?' asked Titty.
'Sailorman's name for the engine,' said Peter Duck.
'Engines and donkeys is all one. One day they'll pull and another day they won't, do what you will with them.'

While Ransome wrestled with the engine once more, *Peter Duck* drifted the wrong side of the buoyed channel. Unable to put her about, he dropped the anchor, which pulled her head round, and was then able to sail the anchor out of the ground and haul it on deck, soaking himself in the process. Evgenia had steered under sail almost to the entrance to Pyefleet before Ransome had the engine working again. They turned and set off and then, yet again, the engine stopped. This time Ransome went about before they lost speed, heading back up river while he resumed his duel with the wretched monster. Eventually Ransome won, and they reached the Bar buoy just after 11 am and ran on close-hauled for the NW Knoll buoy. After that, three or four tacks took them clear of the Bench Head buoy. They were now moving into a very strong head wind and sea. If the engine should fail him again, Ransome decided, he would throw her on the starboard tack and head for Harwich, as it would be idiotic to risk being carried on to the Bench Head or the Colne Bar.

For once the engine did not fail them. They reached the shelter of the Nass and began to look for a grey dinghy promised by Clark and Carter, the West Mersea boatyard. There was no sign of it. As the Fleet Channel at dead low water was too narrow for them to turn, they went right to the end and turned *Peter Duck* by heading towards the mud and going hard a-port with the engine. She touched, swung and as she drifted off they dropped the kedge. Peace at last.

After changing into dry clothes, Ransome had a hard pull in *Swallow*, against the first of the flood, down to Clark and Carter. They were very apologetic, saying that they did not expect the boat to come round against wind and tide. They despatched two hands to help Ransome move *Peter Duck* to a mooring nearer the hard. Afterwards he put them ashore with two shillings and sixpence each. 'Came back to the ship and much enjoyed my tea,' he wrote. 'Agreed with the mate that we ought not to have tried it, but very pleased to have brought it off'

By this time it was well into September and nearing the end of the sailing season. For a week or more they managed a short outing every day, during which they tried Busk's idea of backing the mizzen to help them go about and found that it worked successfully. They also made a circumnavigation in *Swallow* of Peewit Island off Bradwell.

Ransome would have liked to put *Peter Duck* into Clark and Carter's for the winter, but in the shed men were repairing a boat which had dry rot, and Harry King had advised him not to go anywhere near dry rot. He prepared *Peter Duck* for a mud berth and sent to Gowens to make a cockpit cover. The story is told in the log:

Mr. King of Gowens came and measured the cockpit for a cover. He told of his small boy, who as a result of reading my books, decided to sleep in a tent. In the middle of the night they heard him come creeping upstairs and caught the sound of a sob. His mother thought she had better have a look at him and found him indignant. 'Mr. Ransome doesn't know anything about camping ... He never said a word about EARWIGS!!!'

Ransome's days were spent varnishing, caulking, flooding and pumping out the bilge, unbending the sails, taking down the rigging and ferrying sails, bedding upholstery and lights ashore for safekeeping in Clark and Carter's store. 'Bob South and his mate very skilfully, with no other help but my own, lowered and removed both masts, using the main halyard and mizzen halyard to lower the mizzen mast.' These were taken ashore with the wire rigging and screws. Evgenia prepared tea aboard and they would sit planning a new vessel. They wanted no deckhouse next time and a more comfortable cabin with full 6-foot by 2-foot bunks. A stemhead sloop or cutter rig with one mast would do nicely. 'But where nowadays can anyone build?' Ransome wrote. 'Finland? Norway? Have any of them got any seasoned wood? There is none here, though we would rather build here if possible. America? or a Colony?'

Meanwhile, there was the unhappy affair of the Pin Mill mooring to be settled. Ransome paid Burrough's bill despite the inadequate mooring. 'I could not leave or pick up for six weeks and five days. The mooring was put right only in September, a day or two before I left for the last time.' Yet the wretched man had charged him for fifteen and a half weeks.

There was to be no sailing during 1948. In June they moved back to the Lake District, having bought Lowick Hall and the nearby farm, only a couple of miles from the scene of his childhood holidays. They stayed until the autumn of 1950, by which time the estate was really too much for them to manage. It was, after all, Arthur's 67th year. They bought a flat in Hurlingham Court overlooking the Thames at Putney. By then *Peter Duck* had been sold.

Across the Channel

Throughout the summer of 1951 the Ransomes were stuck in a noisy London flat without a boat of any kind. In June Ransome spent a few days with C. S. Davey on board *Jenny Wren*, cruising from Brightlingsea to Pin Mill, but it only served to remind him how much he missed having a little ship of his own. They toured the watering places looking for a sensible and easily handled seagoing vessel. On July 20th Ransome visited Hillyard's riverside boatyard in Littlehampton. His diary records: 'Saw and liked his 6-tonner. Sloop rig but central cockpit, wheel steering. 27ft x 7ft 5ins x 4 ft 3ins.' The entry for the following day was even more encouraging: 'G. [Evgenia] decided the Hillyard would do, though she would have preferred a 10-tonner. I (coward) think that a 10-tonner would be too much for me.' Evgenia had already decided the new boat would be named *Lottie Blossom*.

Well-meaning friends warned them against Hillyard because he was building without a shelf (a longitudinal timber fastened inside the frames underneath the deck). Ransome tackled David Hillyard and his foreman, Tom Jeffers, about their method of building and heard from them that they used a thicker top strake for additional strength, not cheapness. This more than satisfied him: 'We have decided it was good enough for worse seas than we shall put her into on our elderly jaunts.'

Meanwhile, the Ransomes had been trying unsuccessfully to hire a yacht in which they might cruise until George Jones (later to become the long-term owner of *Peter Duck*) agreed to charter his pre-war 5-ton Hillyard sloop *Barnacle Goose*. Ransome took over on September 1st at Waldringfield. During the next ten days they met the Clay family aboard *Firefly* and sailed in company with Rouse in *Ethelinda*. They also paid a visit to Kirby Creek. It was almost like old times. On the return *Barnacle Goose* ran into fog off Harwich, sailing close to the Cork light-vessel without them seeing it. It had happened before in fiction.

The *Goblin* was sailing steadily now, with a gentle, swishing noise, as she drove through the water. John steered, glancing up and down, between the compass and the ghost of the burgee fluttering high overhead. Susan, Titty and Roger tried their best to see into the fog. Every quarter of a minute the Cork lightship moaned its 'Beueueueueueueu ...' And each melancholy bleat sounded a little nearer than the last.

'VERY WET cabin,' was Ransome's verdict on *Barnacle Goose*, but they both enjoyed the experience, although a further month passed and still they had not make up their minds whether to buy. Ransome talked to Hillyard at the Motor Show in Earl's Court: 'Hillyard said I need not decide for a month about the boat. He will keep her so long in case I am not going to be able to sail with my rheumatism etc. Extraordinarily decent of him ...' For more than a week they debated before Ransome returned to Earl's Court to complete the deal.

More than 50 years later, the 1952 specification of a standard Hillyard yacht makes interesting reading:

6-ton AUXILIARY BERMUDAN SLOOP
Length 27 ft 4 in, Beam 7 ft 3 in, Draft 4 ft 3 in
Price fitted with 8 h.p. Stuart Turner Engine and reverse gear — £1325

Keel — Elm or oak
Stem, Sternpost and deadwood — Sided 5 in and moulded as required
Timbers — Oak spaced 6 in centres
Planks — Pine, Larch or Mahogany, carved laid
Decks — Pine, covered with canvas and painted
Deck Fittings — Mahogany
Cabin Fittings — Mahogany and Pine
Cabin Coamings — Mahogany, fitted with port lights
Cabin Top — Pine, covered with canvas and painted
Patent W.C. — Of good make
Cockpit — Fitted in Mahogany
Brass Bilge Pump or Bulkhead
Accommodation — Optional Central or Aft Cockpit
Rig — Bermudan mainsail and foresail with ordinary reefing, cover
    and bag
Spars — Pine of good quality and complete with all running and
    standing gear
Fastenings — All planks fastenings, copper
Ballast — Iron outside, with quantity inside for trimming
Painting and Varnishing of approved colour

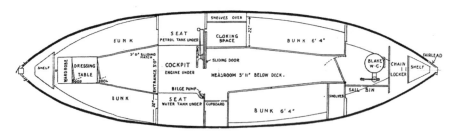

Accomodation plan of David Hillyard's
popular standard centre-cockpit six-tonners

Anchor and 20 fathoms chain
Four matresses — of good quality

The same day he wrote to Lloyds to register her name. Lottie
Blossom was the American film star who kept an alligator in a wicker
basket with which to deter Customs Men from uncovering her
smuggling activities in P. G. Wodehouse's *The Luck of the Bodkins* —
one of their favourite books.

Ransome was wise enough to leave the planning of the internal
arrangements of the cabin and foc's'le to Evgenia something that
subsequent owners have had cause to thank her. *Lottie's* launch was
ruined, however, when Evgenia, stepping aboard, caused the boat to list
savagely and sent the celebration lunch straight into the river. The new
boat was one of David Hillyard's popular canoe-sterned 'standard'
cruisers with tanned sails and a centre cockpit. Between themselves the
Ransomes always referred to the canoe-stern as 'the bustle'.

After the gale force winds and driving snow of a bitterly cold snap that
saw March turn to April, the Ransomes finally set off for their first
passage in *Lottie Blossom* early in the still morning of April 19th 1952.
Due to poor visibility, they saw neither Selsey Bill nor the Isle of Wight.
Indeed for much of the time they could see no land at all. By 9.55 they
were off Itchenor, the engine having taken them all the way. Ransome had
experienced some difficulty with the wheel steering and had left the boat
cutting figures of eight through the water while he tried to ease the
stiffness by thickly greasing the wire on each side of its sheave.

Ransome's first impressions were promising: 'Quite good. Sailed herself,
but, of course does not point high. Comes about admirably. Heaves-to
quite well.' That must have been a such a relief after *Peter Duck*.

The following day Hillyard's sent a man over to their pleasant
anchorage in Itchenor Reach to replace the steering sheave and, when they
were mobile again, Ransome decided to take *Lottie* upstream and into

Birdham Pool. Trusting their Royal Cruising Club chart, which in fact was out of date, they allowed *Lottie* to cut the corner and went aground just outside the lock. With the tide still rising, they could have got off again without much difficulty, but a man from Birdham Shipyard came out and brought *Lottie* into the Pool. Ransome paid his ten shillings for a week's mooring and at low water went to inspect the channel to the lock so that he didn't make the same mistake again.

Their expedition was cut short, however, when Ransome's internal problems threatened to erupt once more. An agonising dash by car got him back to a hospital bed in London where he was obliged to undergo an operation on his prostate gland. Evenia visited *Lottie* at Birdham Pool while Ransome was still convalescing and reported that she liked her as much as ever, but was the end of June before he was well enough to return to Birdham and sleep aboard once more.

Three days later they ventured a mile downstream. The steering was much better but the engine was not pulling properly, so they turned back. 'Everything very disheartening', was Ransome's gloomy entry in the log after he had arranged for it to be inspected the next day. The engineer changed the plugs and, after a thorough engine test, declared their problems at an end. When finally they left the Pool by way of the lock, they were approached, as usual, by the 'Boy Scout' — the name they gave to a lock hand whom they thought much too violent with warps. Ransome was glad to escape from the dangerous fellow.

With a couple of experienced sailors to help, they decided that now, with the season already half gone, they could begin to explore Chichester Harbour. In a 12-knot breeze (about as much as the ship could handle with full sail) they swept down the Chichester Channel and up to Emsworth. With small reservations, particularly over the method of steering, they were delighted with the way *Lottie* behaved. '... inclined to gripe. Rather too much weather helm,' Ransome wrote. But he was also impressed. 'At least this time I know that *Lottie* can sail, and sail well. In fact she is not a 50/50 boat, but 75/75. We thought first 75 per cent motorboat on coming round from Littlehampton, and since yesterday's good sail thought her at least 75 per cent sailing boat.'

Afterwards he had to rest for a week when his insides began to play up, but soon he was back taking *Lottie* out of the Birdham Pool through the lock once again. There was no doubt that he was beginning to feel his age. In less than a year he would be seventy, but he was not the only elderly sailor in the Pool. After evading help from the 'Boy Scout', they shared the lock with *Fiona*, a small motor cruiser 'skippered by a charming elderly dame who gave me a very sweet smile, no doubt telling herself that we were also old enough to know better'.

They returned to their Itchenor Shipyard mooring, fearful with so many yachts milling around that they would have a struggle to reclaim any other mooring once they had left it. From there they explored up Bosham Creek, where they found *Peter Duck* (now painted blue) on a mooring. 'Genia would not look at her, saying she never wanted to see her again or be reminded of the mess she was.' After going as far as they dared in the shallow water, they returned to the mouth of the creek, set the mainsail with the motor still running, went down over the incoming flood to Hayling Island, and there switched off the engine to beat up the Emsworth Channel. They anchored for lunch at I pm. It was an easy sail back to Itchenor in the afternoon, marred only by 'a fearful shemozzle getting into our berth. Berthing at cross-purposes is no good. My fault for not telling him (C.S. Davey who had deserted *Jenny Wren* to crew for them) that we go in stern first ... Never mind. We had a grand day, and Davey said he would like to come again.'

On August 15th they decided on something more adventurous, and left for the Hamble River at seven in the morning, five minutes behind a blue-sailed cutter which turned soon after clearing the harbour entrance. Ransome took *Lottie* two miles out under mainsail before turning into a course of 292° magnetic for the Dolphin. *Lottie* was moving well, not fast but steadily overhauling the cutter. Once past the Hook buoy, they headed into the wind, lowered sail and motored into the Hamble for the first time. The anchorage at Bursledon was very crowded and at length they tied up alongside a green cutter to go ashore. By a pleasing coincidence, the green boat belonged to Dr John Ives whom Ransome had met at West Mersea. Ives returned to find the Ransomes asleep 'like old trees' in the boat that was secured to his own. He told them that his mooring consisted of 100-pound anchors at each end of the chain, and that Ransome was welcome to stay as long as he liked.

A page from Ransome's Deck Log

There followed a period of heavy rain. The bunk and mattress in the after cabin became soaked. Evgenia said she wished Tom Jeffers (Hillyard's foreman) had been sleeping there. On Ransome's bunk a steady drip was falling just where it would be most likely to cause lumbago. When the water boat called alongside, Ransome, always a stickler for doing the correct thing, inquired if he should hoist the flag signal 'F V' when in need of water. No, he was told, people usually hang a bucket in the rigging. While they had the chance they took on not only water but petrol, paraffin and meths as well.

The Hullaballos (from *Coot Club*)

After a week at the cutter's mooring, the Ransomes set off with friends they had made who sailed the 9-ton yawl *Gulnare* for the Beaulieu River, which runs into the New Forest. It was a pleasant still morning, so they motored most of the way, navigating carefully by their 1947 chart from buoy to buoy, while the *Gulnare's* helmsman knew where to cut the corners. They found Black Jack (painted red) without difficulty and rounded the Calshot light-vessel, picking up the Bourne Gap buoy but failing to find the black conical buoy off Stansore Point. Still, they arrived safely at Beaulieu Spit and sailed straight in, only pausing to wait for *Gulnare* before motoring upriver and mooring at Buckler's Hard.

On leaving the pub that evening, Ransome was splashed to the waist when the son of another boatowner upended his dinghy, which was half full of water. For punishment the boy was set to work by his father, a doctor, cleaning up the mess some vandal had made of their yacht's topsides.

Ransome was charmed by the quiet river and its wooded shores. Evgenia picked and cooked some mushrooms, which they ate when the *Gulnare's* crew came aboard the next evening for supper. 'Very late night,' wrote Ransome.

To complete their tour of Solent anchorages the following day they beat across to Yarmouth at the sleepier western end of the Isle of Wight. Failing to understand the harbour master's instructions, they tied up alongside a friendly boat, later moving to a space between two mooring poles.

They went ashore for milk, played with a cat on the sea wall and were back aboard in time to see an RNSA boat with a hefty crew come charging up the narrow lanes under main and large Genoa. It just managed to miss *Lottie* and went crashing into another smaller boat before the crew made fast. The owners of the small boat were aboard, and the offending yacht soon moved off. At closing time, a stream of dinghies with outboard motors sped past and the Ransomes were disturbed by neighbouring hullabaloos until very late. Could they have been any worse than the noisy crowd on the *Margoletta* in *Coot Club?*

A big motor cruiser had turned the corner above the Ferry and was thundering up the river with a huge gramophone open and playing on the roof of the fore-cabin. Two gaudily dressed women were lying beside it, and three men were standing in the well between the cabins. All three were wearing yachting caps. One was steering and the other two were

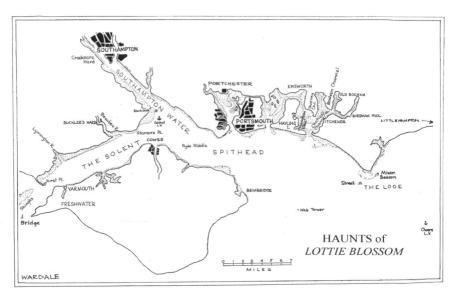

HAUNTS of
LOTTIE BLOSSOM

using binoculars and seemed to be searching the banks as the cruiser came upstream at a tremendous pace.

'They're looking for the *Dreadnought*,' whispered Tom.

The big cruiser roared past them, and from their hiding-place they saw the wash of her swirling along the farther bank and bringing lumps of earth splashing down into the river.

The Ransomes found Yarmouth a charming little town but 'a perfect hell of a harbour' on an August weekend. They breakfasted early next morning, and without waiting to wash or shave were gone by 7.15, heading for Chichester. After motoring on a smooth sea and then enjoying a gentle sail, they arrived back at their old mooring some time after one o'clock. Genia celebrated their escape by making an excellent meal out of odds and ends left over, after which they slept the afternoon away.

An idyllic few days followed in the Emsworth Channel, where they passed a converted lifeboat called *Amethyst*, which Ransome thought exactly like E. F. Knight's *Falcon*. They also explored the Thorney Channel and went round to Bosham, where they picked up a mooring and rowed to the hard by the old mill. There they met an old man who, when he discovered that he was talking to Arthur Ransome, showed them where *Racundra* was lying in the mud. 'Hull looking much the same,' Ransome wrote, 'but she has some sort of silly doghouse. And of course years ago an earlier owner had cut the great beam that carried the bridge deck. Genia would not look at her, but I would have liked to know just what had been done to her.'

On returning to Birdham Pool their minds were made up: they would drive across to Littlehampton and speak to David Hillyard about the possibility of a new *Lottie*. Could the sight of the once magnificent *Racundra* in so dilapidated a state have made Ransome dissatisfied with anything less than he had once owned? Not entirely. For one thing, the small centre cockpit was quite a tight fit for two large folk and for another, they couldn't get used to *Lottie's* wheel steering. On one unforgettable occasion Evgenia had become enveloped by the folds of the lowered mainsail as she stood at the helm. Her violent reaction may be imagined. Besides, he believed that *Lottie* could never be a true single-hander while she had a centre cockpit — an assertion disproved by several of her subsequant owners. Above all, they wanted a really spacious cabin.

Although they had sailed *Lottie* only eleven times and covered fewer than 200 miles, she did, at least, serve to persuade Ransome to build one last time. 'Fools build and wise men buy', he had written thirty years earlier, but he was never to regret this decision to build.

In no time, everything was settled. Hillyard proposed a 6-ton rear cockpit sloop like the one that he was already building for General Gale. He anticipated no difficulty in selling the first *Lottie*.

Evgenia wanted the new boat ready by April 1st the following year, and Hillyard saw no reason why this should not be achieved. Ransome wrote that Hillyard had said the boat would be 'something like *Goblin* and Genia said she would fight tooth and nail, inch by inch, for the accommodation she wanted ... 'The slip of the pen, when Ransome wrote 'Goblin', remains uncorrected, although it had been I5 years since *We Didn't Mean to Go to Sea*. Did he mean to speak of the *Goblin's* real-life model, the *Nancy Blackett*, which Evgenia disdained to go aboard on more than two or three occasions? Several times Ransome tried to get Hillyard to show him the plans for the new boat, but he was told there were no plans for the interior arrangements. Only when the hull was roughly complete would he sit in the boat and work out the best arrangement for bunks and the rest. 'This must be the way he has always worked,' Ransome wrote, 'and a good way too, better than drawing bunks that must in fact poke through the planking'. He would never forget what Laurent Giles had made of *Peter Duck*.

The first *Lottie Blossom* had cost Ransome £1,589, and he gave Hillyard a list of extras that would remain once they had removed the wireless set, typewriter, clock, barometer, hand-bearing compass, Reed's Almanac and *The Luck of the Bodkins* by P. G. Wodehouse.

Basic boat (1952)	£1325
Handrail all round	£30 0s 0d
Afco winch and chain	£21 14s 2d
Track on boom	£3 0s 0d
Turner reefing	£10 0s 0d
Coloured sails - processing	£12 0s 0d
Genoa	£20 0s 0d
CQR anchor instead of fisherman	£4 10s 0d
Accommodation Ladder	£2 15s 0d
Ensign staff and socket	£1 0s 0d
Cockpit cover	£7 0s 0d
Electric light, wiring etc.	£4 10s 0d
Extra for Italian hemp rigging	£8 0s 0d
Registration	£5 0s 0d
Two mushroom vents	£2 5s 0d
Lifebuoy	£4 4s 3d
Extra for Whale pump	£1 10s 0d
Name boards	£2 0s 0d

Mooring ropes	£4 5s 0d
Sundries — Box fitting for batteries, break water, galley fittings, cupboards in Fo'c'sle	£1 0s 0d
Batteries	£13 8s 6d
Paraffin cooker	£11 15s 0d
Grid compass	£1 0s 0d
Total	£1509 16s 5d
Cost of basic boat (1953)	£1375

Kept for use with the new boat were:

Taylor cooker with fiddles	£11 15s 0d
Folding dinghy (unused)	£23 18s 0d
9ft. dinghy with Kapok fender	£42 5s 0d

Hillyard's soon found a buyer for *Lottie Blossom*. On November 10th Ransome accepted an offer of £1,425 from Sir George Mallinson on condition Mallinson change her name, so that the new boat could be called *Lottie Blossom*, not *Lottie Blossom II*.

The previous year Ransome had jotted a not altogether convincing rationale:

A yacht is a pleasure boat, a boat that gives pleasure ... This pleasure is given in so direct and personal a way that we feel discomfort until we can thank the boat for the pleasure she gives, so she must have a name. And this name, whatever it is, gathers to itself associations till it has the magical power of evocation, like the name of some scrubby human being, which for its mother has angelic attributes perhaps perceived by no one else.

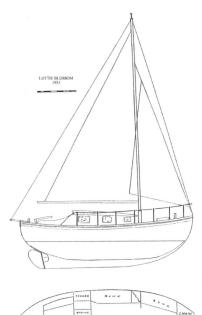

Lottie Blossom

Lottie Blossom's fine airy cabin

This, at least, would explain why Ransome named the sailing dinghy, built for him in Pin Mill after his earlier *Swallow*, which in turn was named after the Collingwood's *Swallow* thirty years earlier.

They spent some time aboard *Bimbi*, General Gale's boat before their own had reached the stage when they could sit in her. Their main cabin would be fully 10 feet long, leaving room for a 6-foot bunk in the fo'c'sle as well as a sail bin and WC. There would be space in the main cabin for a cupboard at the forward end of each bunk and storage for wireless, books, and so on, with possibly a chart table at the after end of one of the bunks. The cabin was going to be as luxurious as they could make it, with the entrance to it by way of steep steps to starboard of the engine.

The hull was coming on well when Ransome discovered that some of the steamed timbers had split. Tom Jeffers promised to replace anything with which they were not satisfied and Joe Robinson, the engineer, found a dynamo, tested it and fitted it in place. Ransome wrote that they ought to be comfortable in their 'colossal' cabin.

Hillyard applied for the boat to be registered and asked Ransome to contact the Ministry's surveyors to arrange a suitable time. When Ransome telephoned the Ministry he was told by a pleasant voice that the measuring would be done by Mr Chorley. Ransome asked if he could be present, whereupon the voice assured him that this would be possible.

'Tell me, Doctor, are you anxious to have this registration done at once?'

'Not in the least,' Ransome replied.

'Well, Doctor, if you had been in a hurry we could have come down to Littlehampton at once, but as a matter of fact we are very busy at the moment, measuring a number of ocean-going ships, so we should be

Lottie Blossom on the slip at LittleHampton

much obliged if you can let us postpone the measurement of your vessel for a fortnight or ten days.'

Ransome was astonished by this courtesy and much enjoyed the vision of little *Lottie* trying to jump the queue of 5,000 to 20,000-tonners!

Mr Chorley measured *Lottie* on February 4th 1953, and Ransome was present as arranged. The interior was, by now, nearly complete. Ransome was very pleased with the cupboards but rather afraid the engine casing would be in the way when Evgenia stood beside the galley. In fact, the engine casing makes a useful seat for anyone cooking. Tom Jeffers had to alter the fo'c'sle arrangements, as there was not room enough for the WC as planned; if centrally placed in the bows it would have obstructed one of the bunks. When Evgenia heard of the change there was an explosion and down they went to Littlehampton the following day.

'Now you go aboard, Tom, and take the worst of it, and when you can do no more, send for me,' said David Hillyard.

David Hillyard and Tom Jeffers were first-rate knockabout comedians, though usually the comedy stopped the moment they were joined by a client neither of them liked. On this occasion, their cunning double act won the day, and Evgenia handsomely acknowledged they were right.

Lottie Blossom's canoe stern that the Ransomes called 'The Bustle'

Now that the first *Lottie* had been re-registered as *Ragged Robin III*, Ransome was able to go ahead with his own registration. The Registrar asked about the name, and heard the story of the smuggler and her alligator.

'Not a very nice lady,' said the Registrar.

Ransome hastened to explain that the name was not chosen out of any particular dislike of Customs Officers.

Evgenia had told Hillyard's the boat was to be a present and must be ready for her birthday on April 11th. Arriving at the yard on that day, they found *Lottie* on the slipway and Tom Jeffers inside busily pumping out. The tide had been high during the night and *Lottie* had floated for the first time. They found five small holes through which water spouted:

> One of the infernal apprentices (a useless young oaf with his eyes for ever on the clock), though warned to be careful about it, had early in the planking process, driven temporary nails clean through ribs and planking, had later removed the nails and never reported that he had driven them through.

Jeffers plugged all the holes and the next day they went for an engine trial. This time there was no launching ceremony; perhaps the holes in the hull put paid to that. A reduction gear had been fitted, and Ransome thought it had more than doubled the power of the engine. Even so, all was not well with the engine; the dynamo failed to perform and petrol leaked out. It took until April 24th to sort out these teething troubles.

The morning of the 24th started badly. The little Stuart Turner engine indulged in a bout of spitting and backfiring and it was some time before it began to behave itself. Eventually they were able to motor out of the river. Once at sea they sailed in all directions under all plain sail and later tried the Genoa. They were both delighted with her performance. Ransome noted how well she held her way, neither griping nor falling off.

Arthur Ransome and Evgenia at David Hillyard's Boatyard, Littlehampton, 1953 (Brotherton Collection)

Lottie was now ready to sail to Itchenor, where Ransome had arranged for a mooring. In their enthusiasm for an early start they rose at 5 am. Again the start was delayed when the engine proved uncooperative. At last Ransome had it running steadily and they left the river. Once outside, *Lottie* began to pitch wildly as the wind met the tide. The mainsail was hoisted without difficulty but the staysail halyard caught in the cross-trees and stuck fast. They tried all the dodges they could think of to free the halyard — wearing ship and going about — all without success. It was a tricky business standing on the bucking foredeck, so, in order to use both hands, Ransome had to lie on the deck, looking (as Evgenia said) like a beetle unkindly turned over, waving its legs, unable to get the right way up. Even this was no use. There was nothing for it but to return to the yard. Once inside the river and in smooth water, Ransome had no difficulty in freeing the halyard, but by then it was too late to try for Chichester.

The following day was squally but the sight of one of Hillyard's little 2½-tonners, *Lena*, setting off for Chichester, made up their minds. After an early lunch they left under power to have a look outside. It was sufficiently encouraging for them to set a course for the Looe Channel, keeping the engine running as they were late in starting. They sighted the Mixon buoy at 2.25 and the Street buoy at three o'clock. By then the visibility was very poor and they overshot the entrance until they saw a ghostly Nab Tower appear out of the haze. They changed course and were cheered by the sight of a boat leaving the entrance. With the tide running heavily and the wind now dead ahead, they lowered sail and motored in. The reduction gear gave much more power than the previous year and they drove over the ebb without difficulty. They overtook *Lena* by the entrance to Bosham Channel and brought up at Itchenor. Just off the Bosham entrance was a 4-ton Hillyard aground and listing heavily. As there was no hope of getting it off for some hours, Ransome rowed across to see that the occupants were all right. He found a very cheerful couple aboard.

'All my fault,' explained the young woman. 'Talking too much!'

Ransome wrote to Colonel Busk with an account of his own folly in a similar situation the following day.

Beating out from Emsworth I carried on a scrap too far and came about and went aground at the same moment. Close on high tide. Indignation aboard as you may imagine. And still more indignation because of my being almost gleeful in putting into operation plans for such occasions. Headsails backed – no result. All sails lowered – no result. Engine in reverse – no result. The Danforth (anchor) taken out in the dinghy and dropped at the end of the warp exactly on the line we had taken the mud. Tugged till it took a grip. Now or never. Whole crew's weight on the rope – no result. Engine reversed and whole crew's weight on the rope. If she don't come now we're done. She did. She moves. Away she comes with the warp being raced in hand over hand. And then that good little Danforth refused to let go and we were swinging around tethered by the tail. Shortened in – full speed ahead – will she? won't she? And away she came towing the Danforth at such speed that it behaved like a kite and the Danforth flukes whirling after, showed like shark fins in a flurry of water. Up sails. Finished with engines, and continued to beat down to Hayling.

A disgraceful affair, but almost worth it for the confidence it has given us (a) in the holding power of the little Danforth on a warp and (b) in the tremendous reserve power of the Stuart with reducing gear.

Genia says she supposes I shall presently be boasting that I put her aground on purpose to test her gear. Of course I shall not. I disgracefully woolgathered and hung on too long. But having put her aground I can't hide the extreme pleasure I had in putting salvage operations into action in double-quick time and finding that they WORKED.

On a passage to Yarmouth on May 11th they met a rough sea in Southampton Water. *Lottie* went charging into it and plenty of water splashed aboard. They considered turning back, but Ransome rightly guessed that the beastliness was due to the wind being against the tide, and that after Calshot Spit they would find a smoother sea. Once round the spit they stopped the engine and a couple of tacks took them off the entrance. They waited for a moment to allow the Lymington Ferry to leave and then went in without difficulty. Waiting to help them moor was the same harbour master who had been there in 1935, when he had brought in *Nancy Blackett* the night the breakwater had been partly destroyed. He was clearly pleased to meet someone with whom to share memories.

The second *Lottie Blossom* with aft steering suited The Ransomes very well (Tony Colwell Collection)

Next morning they explored in the dinghy in the direction of Freshwater. It was an ideal opportunity to try the new outboard motor which Ransome had bought in Littlehampton, and which he kept in the fo'c'sle, much to Evgenia's disgust. The outboard started with a jerk at the twelfth pull and so surprised Ransome that they shot out of the harbour, missing the nearest post by inches. The noise was irksome and they both wished they still had their old *Swallow*. However, Ransome soon mastered the art of steering by the propellor alone. Things went well until they ran out of fuel before reaching Freshwater. Ransome avoided a long pull back to Yarmouth by accepting a tow from a 12-foot sailing dinghy and so returned in time for lunch.

In the afternoon they crossed to the Beaulieu River, and there they stayed until a lull in the weather at sea a few days later persuaded them to say goodbye to their friends and make a dash for Chichester.

Following a week in London, they took *Lottie* back to the Beaulieu River where they had arranged to meet the Tew family for a Coronation Day picnic in Newtown Creek. John and Helen Tew sailed the *Mary Helen*, a 6-ton cutter designed by John Tew and named after his wife, with whom Ransome served for a time on the committee of the Royal Cruising Club. As it happened, a picnic was out of the question on the appointed day, which began cold, squally and wet. Instead they all piled into the saloon of a neighbouring yacht and listened to the Coronation service on the wireless.

On June 5th the Ransomes took *Lottie* up Southampton Water until they reached Cracknore Hard, opposite the New Docks. Here they found *Bimbi*, *Lottie's* sister ship, and Evgenia threw a greeting into the cockpit as they sailed past. It seemed a horrible place after the Beaulieu River, and they turned back immediately and beat out against the wind and tide. Just before they reached Netley, the harbourmaster overtook them to warn of the departure of the liner Coronia. The liner slid past, making hardly a ripple, and disturbed *Lottie* not in the least, unlike the harbourmaster's fussy launch.

Their plan was to take a look at the fleet on June 13th, two days before the big Coronation Review. With occasional showers and light to moderate winds forecast, they drifted away from their mooring at 10.20, but soon started the engine and left the river fifty minutes later. Here they almost turned back due to the engine running very hot. Ransome suspected the boy at the garage had been giving him insufficient oil in the mixture, and as a result the engine had not been having enough lubrication. They did not want to risk it seizing up. Yet, anxious to see something of the ships that seemed to stretch endlessly into the mist, they decided to take a chance. The masts and yards of the Italian schoolship *Amerigo Vespucci*, standing out as a vision from another age, acted like a magnet:

Mr Duck said nothing. He was thinking of the *Thermopylae*, of his own youth, of days gone by. He lifted the telescope again and watched the ship, far, far away on the horizon. Her sails shone now like white sparks in the sunlight, even to Nancy and Captain Flint, who were looking at her with the naked eye.

'Hull down she'll be in an hour,' said Peter Duck at last. 'We'll maybe not see another all the voyage. Rot screw steamers,' he burst out fiercely, 'driving vessels like her off the seas where they belong!'

Passing the aircraft carrier *Perseus*, Ransome was horrified to see the entire flight deck rigged up as a colossal grandstand, complete with red padded seats. Aboard the Turkish *Demirrisar*, seamen were practising for the Review. They had manned the Ship in long lines, then at the blast of 'some sort of Levantine whistle-pipe' they doffed their hats, pressed them to their chests and bowed deeply. Evgenia felt sure the Queen would enjoy this performance.

While they were close-hauled on the return to Buckler's Hard, with the sails drawing nicely and the engine doing its bit, *Lottie* began to overhaul a small ocean racer. The crew aboard the ocean racer assumed that something was wrong with the set of their sails and hauled in the mainsheet, set another headsail and took a pull on their halyards, all the time seeming unable to take their eyes off *Lottie*. In the end Ransome opened the throttle and showed them that he had an engine ticking away. *Lottie's* crew enjoyed the broad but relieved grins aboard the other vessel. They decided against joining the hoards of craft in Spithead for the Coronation Review as they had been allocated a most unpleasant station in Ryde Middle and the forecast promised everybody a soaking on the way back. In the evening, when the other craft returned pretty wet, having failed to reach the official Review area, they were glad they had remained behind.

By the end of June the Ransomes felt ready to sail to Cherbourg. The forecast was for light northerly winds with moderate visibility, except in fog patches. High water was at mid-morning, which enabled them to leave Beaulieu with the ebb. It was almost calm at 11.20 when they cast off and motored out of the river. Once in the Solent they found the wind to be southerly, which obliged them to tack with the ebb to Yarmouth. There they made the decision to go ahead.

The passage passed almost without incident, only one ship crossing their bows before dawn. The wind was so slight that Ransome began to wonder if they would have to be two nights at sea instead of one. He takes up the account in his log:

5.00 Dead calm. Oily sea. Visibility very bad ... The first land we saw was a glimpse of a tall tower, on what seemed at first a point with no land to the west of it, which worried me a good deal as the log showed we had run over 54 miles. Already daylight of course, so no means of identifying the tower. Then sighted what might be a rocky island and began to think we might be to westward of the peninsula and seeing outposts of Alderney. Heavy mist to southward. Carried on and presently realised we had made a perfect landfall, the tower being Cape Levi, the rocky island one of the outer forts of Cherbourg.

8.45. Took in log reading 8.5. Went into Avant Port and found the Y.C. with a crowd of English boats before it and NO buoy to which to tie. I had been told we should tie to a buoy and take a stern warp ashore, and so was not expecting to have to anchor ... Got the anchor over the side with great difficulty, as none of my usual arrangements had been made and I had to twist sideways, and get the C.Q.R. [anchor] through between the stanchions of the pulpit, and persuade the chain to render through the jamming fairlead. Got the anchor down and warps to a buoy ahead of another R.C.C. boat, which turned out to be Lord Stanley of Alderney, with his wife, a very pretty French matelotte with red pompom on top.

All fast 9.45. Customs along at once. No formalities other than declaring our port of departure, Beaulieu which seemed to please them, as we had come from one beau lieu to another.

They went ashore to be greeted by several members of the Royal Cruising Club and others they had met at Beaulieu and elsewhere. A young female sailor they encountered before her single-handed passage in the yawl *Moana*, went back with them aboard *Lottie* for tea, during which Ransome fell asleep three times, just as Jim Brading and John Walker had done in his masterpiece fifteen years before:

And then, altogether unexpectedly, John felt his eyes closing. He opened them and looked all round him. They closed again. His head felt somehow much heavier than usual. He propped it with a hand, with both hands. Nothing would keep it up. Down it went, down, down. Daddy reached out just in time to move John's plate before he dipped his hair in it. John had fallen asleep with his head on the table.

'Skipper's been a long time on the bridge,' said his father quietly.

Lottie remained in the Yacht Harbour for a week while the Ransomes were busy with the social life of the English contingent at the club. They were both tired for the first two days, but afterwards had a busy, and enjoyable time. They preferred Cherbourg to Paris, which they thought too Americanised. Ransome noted down all the arrivals and departures of the English yachts and sometimes permitted himself observations on seamanship.

The forecast for July 7th promised a ridge of high pressure across England, bringing light west to north-west winds. The story of the return crossing is contained in a letter to Colonel Busk:

After leaving Cherbourg on Sunday evening and, thanks to finding something wrong with the engine while coming out from the inner harbour, missed the weather report and forecast which would, I gather, have made us sit tight.

We met John and Helen Tew coming in, not within speaking distance, and saw John Tew making some kind of signal which we think must have been due to having heard the forecast which we missed.

Anyhow we had been long enough in Cherbourg, and so, luckily for us, kept the engine ticking and old *Lottie* forging ahead through the night, with things getting more and more uncomfortable, so that when the beastliness began yesterday morning we were already seeing the loom of St. Catherine's. Finally the engine stopped (foul jets) and after I had cleaned them, losing one in the casing of the flywheel and getting it out with a wire from the pump, we found petrol pouring from the carburettor, and so did the last fifty miles under sail only. We found that when *Lottie* has a wind we think too strong, she has a wind that she thinks is just right. I rolled three turns [reefed] just before six, as she was getting hard to steer and inclined to bury her bows. We had intended going to Chichester, but before we had the Nab abeam it was clear that Chichester Bar would be no place for *Lottie*. I changed course for the forts, and we thought of finding shelter under the island shore from the wind, which up to then had been SW, but it changed, the spiteful brute, and we had our hands full beating through Spithead.

Decided against Portsmouth with no engine to go nosing round with, looking for a place to bring up, so went bucketing on, finding both shores lee shores! Finally decided to seek shelter under the Fawley side of Southampton Water, visibility all but nil in the bad patches. But we picked up the Stourbridge buoy, and the East Bramble, and finally Calshot after a board across from the Lee on Solent side, and here found we could just lay up Southampton Water, which we did, rejoicing in each bit of smooth water, and went right up to the docks where looking for General Gale's boat we spotted a vacant mooring ... Just 90 miles direct from Cherbourg, and *Lottie* proved herself a good little boat, though groaning and squeaking horribly during the worst of the battering. It sounded like wood working on wood, and we think must have been mast strains transmitted through tabernacle and cabin trunk.

They slept. The voyage had lasted nineteen hours. Ransome had been at the helm or struggling with the engine for eighteen of them. It was late afternoon before he rowed ashore only to find the local shops had sold out of bread. On the way back he met a man who told him that one of the ships on the grid had a good cook. Ransome climbed on the grid and up a perpendicular ladder until he could step over the ship's rail and walk towards a man wearing a chef's hat.

'I'm told this ship has a very good cook,' Ransome called.

'Maybe,' the chef said.

Ransome asked him if he had any bread.

'Now if you'd come yesterday I could have given you some, but today I have none to spare.

The man heard how Ransome had been at sea all night, coming from Cherbourg, and that now all the shops were closed, even if he were to go across to Southampton.

'Let's take a look,' the chef said as he disappeared into the galley. He emerged again with a sliced loaf, which he gave to Ransome, who took it back to *Lottie* and was instantly berated for bringing something sliced. He was forgiven when Evgenia heard how he had come by the loaf, and she set to with preparations for their meal 'while trying to hang on to twenty-five pieces of crockery at once in the endless disturbance from motor launches'.

Next day they took *Lottie* to Bursledon, where they left her for a fortnight. On his return, Ransome rowed up to the Jolly Sailor where he found the landlord who on a previous meeting had complained to Ransome of stomach trouble. The man had taken Ransome's advice and stopped using aluminium cooking pans — with almost total success. Ransome had given the same advice to Uffa Fox, who lived his life at breakneck speed, and was suffering and about to undergo surgery. Ransome urged him to throw away his aluminium teapot so he would not need the operation. More to please his friend than anything else, Fox did as he was told and, much to his astonishment, it worked. Fox being Fox, he experimented by reverting to his aluminium teapot, and every time he did so his trouble returned. Finally he disposed of the teapot altogether and, like Ransome, was always very careful how his food was prepared.

Strong winds kept them at Bursledon for a couple of days until the forecast was sufficiently encouraging for them to attempt to reach Buckler's Hard. They left after lunch under mainsail and engine on a strong ebb and were soon at Hamble Point. It was blowing hard still and there were white caps everywhere. After leaving the shelter of Calshot, a lot of water sloshed aboard as they sailed right over to the island shore. A couple of tacks took them to the mouth of the Beaulieu River. That evening the Tews heard about their rough channel crossing when they dined at The Master Builder's.

With the season coming to an end they planned to sail to Littlehampton, but four attempts had to be aborted because of the weather. They gave up and went back to London. A week later they set off on *Lottie's* final voyage of 1953. The engine let them down yet again, in spite of some recent attention by mechanics. Most of the passage was made under sail on that extraordinarily clear day when they could even see the wireless masts on St Catherine's. They motored up the River Arun and tied up at Hillyard's. The season was over. Apart from the constant unreliability of the engine, *Lottie* had proved a splendid boat, and they were both delighted with her comfortable and roomy cabin.

During the Indian summer of 1953 they sailed together twenty-three times, covering over 600 miles. Not since 1937 had Ransome managed so much sailing.

* * * * *

During the winter Tom Jeffers replaced some rusted standing rigging and overhauled and tested the engine. By May 11th 1954 everything was ready for the new season and the Ransomes set out in *Lottie* for Buckler's Hard. Once outside the river, the wind, which was dead ahead, freshened and they gave up after a couple of miles and motored back. By next morning the wind had moderated and they were away early. The engine stopped several times and finally died as they entered the Beaulieu River. Luckily the flood tide had begun and it took them up the river before the wind died completely. Next day they spent renewing acquaintances. They learnt that the Royal Yacht *Britannia* would be coming through the Needles Channel late the following afternoon and both of them wanted to see her, but they had to be away early in order to reach Chichester before dusk.

They set off under sail in the middle of the afternoon, flying the Jolly Roger in honour of two little boys they had just met. *Britannia* passed them at 6 20 pm, but by then it was much too late to try for Chichester. Instead they motored back to Buckler's Hard. Although it was cold and windy for the next few days, they both loved the river and were very much at home there.

On May 11th they made for Chichester under full sail and engine. Just as they reached the entrance the engine stopped, and they had to beat up to Itchenor, finally mooring to No. 5 buoy as their own was taken. A fortnight later, before returning to London, they took *Lottie* back to the Beaulieu River.

Ransome received an encouraging report from his surgeon, who allowed him to continue sailing provided that he made contact at once if anything seemed to be wrong. Cheered by this good news, he went along to the Garrick Club for several games of billiards before returning to Beaulieu to sleep aboard *Lottie* once more.

They were woken by a loud crash close at hand. Evgenia was convinced *Lottie* had been struck by lightning. But the crash was followed by a jar as if something had rammed *Lottie*. Ransome lost no time in going up in his pyjamas to investigate. He could see a large vessel alongside, which turned out to be the 18-ton cutter *Arion*, which had been moored ahead of them.

Ransome held her as well as he could while Evgenia brought up some fenders. *Arion* moved along *Lottie's* side before being brought up suddenly when her chain caught under *Lottie's* stem. Evgenia took the foghorn and together they made all the noise they could. Time and again they sent three shorts and a long (I require assistance) out into the night, but it brought no response. Then Evgenia held *Arion* off while Ransome went below to get into his harness and put on trousers and coat. After more than an hour, all attempts to rouse assistance having failed, and *Arion* lying fairly quietly alongside, Ransome took the dinghy and rowed up to the nearby *Lafiya*. Impatiently he woke Lapthorne, her owner, who agreed to fetch the harbour master while Ransome returned to *Lottie* so that if their mooring carried away there would be some chance of getting the engine started. He was relieved when he heard an engine and in the early morning light made out the harbour master towing *Laftya's* dinghy round the bend.

'Where's *Arion's* hand?' the harbour master demanded, explaining that there should have been someone aboard.

He clambered on to *Arion* and began hauling in her chain. Suddenly it came free. There was nothing but a short length of chain and a few rusted larger links. That was all that had caught *Lottie's* stem. If it had freed itself, nothing could have saved *Arion* from crashing into the boat astern of *Lottie*. Between them, the three men managed to secure *Arion* alongside the posts, after which Ransome returned and examined the scrapes around *Lottie's* stem.

That afternoon Ransome posted a letter to the insurers and arranged for *Lottie* to be put on the slip for any scrapes and damage to be made good. When the skipper of *Arion* finally appeared, he was very appreciative of Ransome's assistance. So he should have been, for *Lottie* was now out of the water for repairs. While he waited, Ransome bought two shillings' worth of ragworms and with them caught fifteen bass at low water, some of which were given to their neighbours.

He was always ready to make the most of any opportunity to fish or watch others fishing. Earlier in the year he had been chided by Joe Robinson, Hillyard's engineer, for almost putting *Lottie* on to the west pier at the mouth of the River Arun at Littlehampton because he was so busy watching a fisherman's wildly jerking rod on the other side of the river.

Ransome attempted to describe the effect on the angler's mind of a rod of any sort in an essay which he included in *Mainly About Fishing*, the last of his books to be published during his lifetime:

No man who has ever travelled with a fishing rod finds himself able to travel happily without one. A rod marks the difference between travel and going to work, though, indeed, a rod in the rack is sometimes enough to make going to work a kind of holiday. It has a magic effect upon its owner, as he sits in the carriage beneath it, conscious of it. The sloth of the imagination is stirred by its mere presence. To have a rod in the rack over your head is to have the fishing faculties on the alert. The landscape swaying past the window is no meaningless phantasmagoria. The rivers are not sleeping beauties but awake and beckoning as on a fishing day. The most imperceptible gradients tell the traveller how he is passing from one watershed to another.

The book also tells the story of his own salmon-fly. In the course of a long correspondence Myles North said that he was able to supply feathers from the Vulterine Guineafowl, a native of Africa where he was living, which Ransome needed for his new fly. After studying the habits of salmon, Ransome had come to the conclusion that they chewed elvers but did not feed on them. He required a lure, therefore, which resembled an elver.

Why on earth should the salmon, unable to eat in fresh water, be sometimes ready to take our flies? 'The salmon does not eat in fresh water,' I was saying sleepily, to myself ... 'His digestion is out of gear ... ' The salmon does not eat ... ' And suddenly I sat up with a start and looked about me. Now the Park Lane Hotel, in 1943, was much used by American officers and men. The lounge was full of them. They were passing by, sitting reading papers, waiting for expected guests, busy with this or that. The salmon does not feed in fresh water. Neither does the American military man feed in the middle of the morning. It was not a meal time. These Americans were not eating. Only a few were talking. But the jaws of every man were going like a machine. Two and two made five at once. I jumped like Archimedes in his bath. A flash of revelation had lit up the whole problem of the salmon and the salmon-fly. In the north, when a new idea hits our hard heads, we are apt to say 'By gum!' 'By gum!' I exclaimed, and indeed gum was the answer. The salmon does not feed in fresh water. No, but HE DOES CHEW GUM.

Later, when Ransome needed more feathers, he sent at SOS to Desmond Kelsall, who as a voluntary game warden, knew very well that the Vulterine Guineafowl was a protected species. However, more feathers were soon on their way to England and no questions were asked about how they were obtained. Kelsall is, after all, an enthusiastic fisherman too.

A good forecast on June 29th sent them scurrying across to Yarmouth, so as to make their planned second cross channel passage shorter. With moderate northerly wind promised, they set out at 10.30, and, once round the Needles, stopped the engine and did the rest of the crossing under sail alone. All was smooth and uneventful. They sighted the flashing red light of Cape Levi at 10.35. An hour later Ransome picked up the Cherbourg light and started the engine to help them across a very strong tide. Before reaching the inner harbour, the engine failed. By this time they had lost all confidence in Hillyard's engineer. They anchored off the entrance and turned in. It was nearly three in the morning.

By the following morning they were secure inside the yacht harbour. They had been moored only a short time when a trawler, anchored near by, began to drag. The chain caught in her propellor which pulled the chain until the trawler's windlass was broken, parts of which flew in the air and landed in the water close to *Lottie*. Helplessly, she drifted down on *Lottie*. Ransome and the one comparatively sober member of the trawler's crew held her until frogmen cleared the propellor and she could be moved to a buoy.

An American warship anchored in the outer harbour, and the Liberty boats making for the shore at speed, upset Evgenia while she was cooking. 'Hell by night as well as by day.' Ashore things were better. They enjoyed oysters one night and tried crab (which they did not know how to eat) another. In Ransome's log is a record of all the comings and goings of English craft, and visits were exchanged with most of them.

One day a 19-ton cutter came in with a young couple and a paid hand. They began to anchor well clear of *Lottie* but the chain jammed and the paid hand wrestled unsuccessfully to free it. Meanwhile, wind and tide were quickly taking her down towards *Lottie*. The first the Ransomes (who were in the cabin) knew of an impending collision was the sight of the large cutter towering over them through the window. They ran up and hurriedly tried to fend off. Ransome called to the paid hand that his anchor had fouled *Lottie's*. The hand, already angry with himself over his battle with the winch, vigorously denied it. Meanwhile the two chains could be felt grating beneath *Lottie*. Ransome insisted that the cutter should go ahead to clear them. The young owner pontificated about his skipper's experience. He had been into Cherbourg hundreds of times, so he put more trust in him than in a stranger. This rudeness left Ransome speechless.

Aboard the stranger's yacht someone managed to get hold of a buoy astern and pulled at it, shaking *Lottie* as they did so. Ransome asked them to slack out their chain so that they could lie quietly, whereupon the paid hand ran to their winch and wound in as hard as he could. There was no more to be said.

Ransome rowed ashore and went straight to the Yacht Club where he spoke to the Gardien. Looking out, the man said that he could see they had now got free of *Lottie*. Back went Ransome with the Gardien to examine the chain. They could see exactly where it had been fouled. *Lottie's* anchor was stuck fast and the Gardien told the guilty boatowner that, if Ransome wanted to shift, he would have to move. The Gardien offered the Ransomes a mooring between two buoys the next morning, so that they would have no further trouble. It was a world away from the peaceful harbours they had visited in the Baltic with *Racundra*.

Night encouter (from *We Didn't Mean to Go to Sea*)

Lottie stayed in Cherbourg for three weeks 'while waiting for good weather for the return. Then, taking advantage of moderating winds, on the evening of July 19th, she cleared the harbour entrance at 5.30 pm, Ransome having settled on a night crossing. Half an hour later the engine stopped. After restarting it Ransome lay down for half an hour while Evgenia took over. *Lottie* drove on through the night, making 5 knots, until shortly after 1.30 am, when Ransome had to alter course to avoid a steamer. He had been here before — at his typewriter!

John's voice rose to a shout.
'But she can't see us. We've got no lights. We've got to get out of the way. Where's the big torch? It's slipped down somewhere. Oh never MIND the pork pie ...'
The steamer was coming straight at them, as Roger had said. There were the masthead lights high in the darkness. Below them were other lights, the shaded lights of the upper decks, the glow of portholes, and the two lights that really mattered, a round green eye and a round red one ... coming nearer and nearer.

Shortly after changing course he caught sight of the loom of St Catherine's. When the engine stopped again they continued under sail alone until it was light enough to see. The engine kept on stopping for the remainder of the voyage. They waited around until they had the flood tide to help them into Chichester Harbour and were on their mooring before mid-day.

Ransome lost no time in reporting the continual and frustrating failure of *Lottie's* engine. He talked to Stuart Turner and was advised to seek help from a Mr Noyce at Itchenor. Noyce inspired confidence from the start. He changed the petrol/oil mixture, added oil to the gear box, and told Ransome that the Rotex dynamo that Hillyard's fitted was made in 1924 and designed to run at 1,000 rpm: it had been running at three times that speed! He offered to fit a new dynamo, pulleys and cut-out. In the end Ransome agreed to let Hillyard's fit a new fast-running dynamo when *Lottie* was back in Littlehampton. But it was all too late in the day. The Ransomes were ready to give up.

Evgenia had been saying for some time that they should sell *Lottie*. A few months earlier, when Arthur had done something silly (the log makes no mention of what), she had left him on board and gone back to London. Ransome wrote in the log: 'G. went to town, cursing my stupidity to the last moment. None the less I miss her very much.' When, on the following day, Evgenia returned, Arthur saw that he had become dependent on her willingness to sail with him. Now, at the age of seventy, he had to agree that she was right.

They made one more visit to their favourite anchorage in the Beaulieu River. On their return to Itchenor they both damaged their hands in a desperate scramble to pick up a mooring after the engine let them down yet again and they were left without steerage way in the crowded channel. Ransome wrote to Busk, who had himself given up the sea, describing the last voyage:

We took *Lottie* from Itchenor to Littlehampton yesterday, for the first time having a third hand aboard. This was because G. had temporarily lost the use of her right hand and I had temporarily lost the use of my left and I thought we had better have at least one pair available ... The very nice chap who supplies water and oil from a float said 'Borrow mine,' holding up two very capable paws, and I did so. He turned up at 7.30 am yesterday, and hoisted sail for me and cast off our mooring. We then had a really delightful passage across the Channel round Selsey, always with time in hand, so that I hove-to for half an hour or so to have slack water through the Looe, and then of course hove-to again off Littlehampton waiting for the water to reach the top of the eastern dickerwork (when there was enough water for us to cross the bar). Everything went like clockwork, and our borrowed complete pair of hands enjoyed himself too, I think. (He had never been through the Looe before or seen Littlehampton except from the shore, and was obviously taking notes for future use ... a delightful chap to have aboard.)

We then saw Hillyard and told him we are winding up. Rather sad now that at long last the engine trouble has been run to earth, but G. has been long decided that we to stop and I suppose we are a bit old.

It was a grand sail yesterday, fresh fair wind, exactly of he strength that *Lottie* best likes. With obvious torrents of rain here, there and everywhere all round, but sunshine for *Lottie*, easily the best sail of the year. So now I swallow the anchor with one gulp and henceforth think exclusively in terms of fishing ...'

Shipwreck, Salvage and Sailing On

POINTS OF THE COMPASS

Fifty-six years have passed since Arthur Ransome parted with *Lottie Blossom*, during which time at least eleven owners have sailed around the harbours of the South and East Coasts. In 1990 I tracked her down to a Surrey garden where her owner, Christopher Barlow, was embarking on some extensive restoration work. Out of the water *Lottie* looked a sturdy and sensible cruiser — typically Hillyard — a little slab-sided perhaps, with rather high topsides and little curve between the garboard and the turn of the bilge, giving her something of the look of a chine boat. In fact, from the early 1960s onwards, some Hillyard cruisers had chine hulls, a development by Dennis Cullingford, who had taken over the business on the death of his uncle.

I climbed aboard and went below and was taken with the light and airy saloon. It had the feel of a real home — no doubt the influence of Evgenia — and looked unaltered since Ransome's day.

Recently, I went aboard *Malina*, one of only four aft-cockpit 6-tonners built by Hillyard in the 1950s, and experienced the same feeling of space in which to move around. A former owner had built a separate toilet compartment in the cabin without compromising on its ample elbow-room, and I felt sure that the tall Evgenia would have approved. I visited *Malina* again while she was out of the water at Birdham Pool, and although more than fifty years old, the hull looked in splendid condition, and I wondered if by any chance *Lottie* was similarly seaworthy.

Lottie Blossom has vanished without trace. Apparently, the Barlow family moved home some years ago and *Lottie* with them. Simon Cullingford, David Hillyard's great-nephew was unable to throw any light on its disappearance, and Hillyard Owners Association members have been unable to trace the missing vessel.

Hillyard's Boatyard remained in the family until February 2009 when it ceased trading — another victim of the recession? There are still a few

Lottie Blossom awaiting restoration in Christoper Barlow's Garden in 1990

of David Hillyard's cruisers on the River Arun and stored in the yard, but the yard itself that once teemed with activity seems to be asleep.

Barlow had acquired *Lottie* in 1983, merely because she was the size and style of cruiser that he wanted, at a price that he felt he could afford. At that time he did not know the identity of its first owner, although he himself had enjoyed the *Swallows and Amazons* books, and had made a point of reading them to his children. The knowledge that *Lottie* was Ransome's final yacht added a great deal to the pleasures of ownership, for Chris Barlow, who dipped into the Ransome archives in order to find out more about *Lottie's* early years.

At first he kept *Lottie* in Mill Rythe off the Emsworth Channel in Chichester Harbour, only a mile upstream from the mooring Ransome borrowed from time to time. They cruised between the Solent ports for four seasons before deciding to move her to his home in order to undertake repairs.

Very little had been changed since *Lottie* had been built. She still steered with the same weather helm, and it remained necessary to reef

the mainsail before she became hard pressed in order to keep her
balanced, although enlarging the jib and taking it to the masthead had
improved her sailing qualities. *Lottie's* construction was conventional
enough for the early post-war years — mahogany planking on oak frames,
copper fastened. All the centre-line and deck fastenings were of mild steel
which had rusted badly and had to be removed. At the time I visited the
vessel, the deck and coachroof needed replacing and new sheer and
garboard strakes, breasthooks and deck beams fitted — nothing that an
experienced shipwright could not handle.

But Chris Barlow made no claims about being an experienced restorer,
however by working carefully and systematically and calling for expert
advice when necessary, he hoped to have her fit for another thirty or forty
years. At that time Barlow was full of plans to retrace *Lottie's* passage to
Cherbourg, using Ransome's log as a guide, when she was seaworthy once
more. One thing that he knew would not have changed was the motor,
the same 8-horsepower Stuart-Turner, well past its best, and just as
unpredictable as it was in Ransome's hands.

* * * * *

If *Lottie Blossom* has been posted missing, what of the other yachts and
dinghies that Ransome had sailed? *Racundra* remained in British waters
under several owners until she came into the hands of J. M. Baldock MP,
who sailed her for the best part of twenty years. Whilst she was under his
ownership I caught a glimpse of the her unmistakeable profile among
more everyday craft at Lymington. In 1976 a confirmed ocean venturer
called Rod Pickering found her in a run-down state in Tangier harbour.
Despite her reduced rig (the mizzen was missing) and lack of centreboard,
Pickering was impressed with her potential. He bought her and embarked
on a lengthy restoration, which included a return to gaff rig. It was his
intention to sail her to England via the West Indies. He planned the sort
of cruise that Ransome and Sehmel had dreamed about almost sixty years
earlier: the sort of cruise she had been designed and built for — a single-
handed wandering across the oceans. In 1978 Rod Pickering embarked
for England, calling at Madeira, the Canaries, the Cape Verde Islands and
the West Indies before foundering on a reef north of Caracas:

Captain Flint spoke.
'She was a good ship,' he said ...

The original *Swallow*, which Ransome featured lovingly in *Swallows and
Amazons*, has disappeared too. I could find no reference in any of his

papers to suggest how or when he disposed of the craft that he described as 'the best little boat that ever was built'. By the time that they left the Lake District in 1935 he had fallen out of love with *Swallow* after suffering an embarrasing defeat when he raced the newly launched *Coch-y-bonddhu* on Windermere and had been beaten by the length of Belle Isle.

"'You'd have caught us in a minute," said Nancy. "New boat. Dry. Clean bottom. She'd run away from us with the wind aft. Jolly good boat."'

Shortly after the publication of *Nancy Blackett* I heard from Roger Fothergill from far off British Virgin

Racundra in Tangier Harbour 1970s

Islands. Fothergill, it turned out, had recently retired there after a lifetime at sea. As a fifteen-years old Westmoreland lad, Roger Fothergill had grown up with the *Swallows and Amazons* books and thought nothing of cycling ten miles each was in order to spend a day on Windermere in his canoe. After one such day in 1935, he learnt from 'Ernie' Walker, the son of George Walker who had looked after the *Swallow* for Ransome, at their boatyard on the Ferry Nab, that the boat was for sale, and Ransome was asking £14. Fothergill's critical eye quickly took in the ballast box amidships and the standing lugsail, and he satisfied himself that it was indeed, the *Swallow*, exactly as described in *Swallows and Amazons*. Once *Swallow* became his property, Fothergill set about improving her performance. The dinghy carried so much weather helm that he felt sure that she would be improved by the addition of a jib. This required a small iron jibboom or bumpkin to be fitted. Next he turned his attention to the keel, which was deepened by a further six inches at the bow, increasing to twelve inches at the stern. The internal pigs of ballast were removed, melted down and cast into a single piece for attachment to the keel.

That done, Roger Fothergill assured me, she made very much less leeway, was better balanced and he felt that he had greatly improved her performance. After sailing for a while on Windermere, Fothergill took *Swallow* to Arnside and cruised among the harbours of the estuary, sleeping under an awning spread over the boom and cooking on a primus. It was the teenager's idea of heaven!

Shortly before the outbreak of World War Two, Fothergill became apprenticed to a shipping firm, and *Swallow* was laid up at Crossfields. What Crossfields thought about the 'improvements'to the boat they had built, is not recorded! Shortly before war was declared, Crossfields sold *Swallow*, for around £12, but by the time I made enquiries, what pre-war records that they may have kept, had long gone.

Every few years, somebody comes forward to claim they own *Swallow*, or that they know where she may be found. Sadly, so far none of these 'imposters' have stood up to the most basic scrutiny.

* * * * *

Mavis, Swallow's 'sister ship' during the summer of 1928, lay snug in her boathouse on Coniston Water for sixty years, waiting for various members of the Altounyan family to take her out from time to time. Four generations were conveyed by her on whatever expedition they required. She has carried fishermen, was trusted not to tip out toddlers on family outings, and ferried passengers across to the village or to Peel Island. In the 1930s she was in the care of Oscar Gnosspelius who went so far as to attach an outboard motor!

Mavis became Roger Altounyan's boat. He was very young when, one evening while fishing alone in her, he caught a pike. He landed it after a struggle, but the most unnerving part of the whole affair was returning to Lanehead with the fish in the boat beside him. After the Second World War he became a physician and for several years helped his father with the hospital in Aleppo. After returning to England, he specialised in asthma (from which he suffered) and developed the Intal treatment and the spin-haler. When he married, *Mavis* carried the newly-weds to their honeymoon on Peel Island.

On his retirement in 1958, Ernest Altounyan returned from Syria to find *Mavis* in a bad state. He decided that the only way to prolong her active life was to sheath the hull in fibreglass. The cure was successful up to a point, and Ernest and Roger Altounyan continued to sail until the end of their lives.

The fragile relationship between Ransome and Altounyan fractured completely when Ransome found that Altounyan had been telling visitors to Lanehead that *Mavis*, with its little brown 'winter' sail, was the original *Swallow!*

In recent years *Mavis* was kept in a boathouse by the stone dock close to the foot of Coniston Water where Ransome, as a child, used to greet the lake on his arrival from Leeds. In 1980, *Mavis* was abducted from the boathouse and was rescued by Taqui Altounyan from the River Crake. After this, Roger Altounyan had a sign made: 'This is a very old boat in peaceful retirement. Please do not disturb her.'

After the death of Roger Altounyan in 1987 the family did not fancy the idea of sending *Mavis* to the bottom of the lake. It was then that Brigit (Altounyan) Sanders and her husband John asked me if I had any ideas for her future. I felt that *Mavis* should be kept where Ransome enthusiasts could visit and suggested the Windermere Steamboat Museum as the ideal final home. The museum already possessed *Esperance* (Captain Flint's houseboat), and all their exhibits are maintained in first-class order and frequently taken out on the lake. It was agreed that the museum be allowed to have *Mavis* on permanent loan, while she remained the property of Roger Altounyan's five children.

At that time it was generally believed that *Mavis* was the 'original' of *Amazon*, even though there was at least one significant difference — *Amazon* was nearly new and varnished, while *Mavis* was painted and of uncertain age. Recently, I heard of the existance of a letter from Ransome in which he says that *Swallow* is a real boat and clearly implies that *Amazon* was fictitious.

Once *Mavis* was ensconced in her new home, Ernest Altounyan's sheathing was removed to reveal a hull in need of extensive restoration. This required funding, and Christina Hardyment's appeal soon drew more than £5,000 in contributions from all over the world. Donations included £1,174 from the Arthur Ransome Club of Japan and £500 from Fison's Pharmaceuticals for whom Roger Altounyan had worked. It was this generous response from so many individuals that brought the Arthur Ransome Society into being.

Among the offers of help was one from an expert restorer, Allan Taylor, to work on the boat itself in a builder's shed in Bowness where I visited *Mavis* shortly after the fibreglass had been stripped away. The little boat was a sorry sight; There was little of the transom to be seen, the keel was rotten, the planking near the stern was in a sorry state and the hull was out of shape. More problems arose when the work started, and it seemed to me that once the restoration was complete, the hull needed to be sheathed in epoxy resin, as I was successfully applying to another dinghy. Allan's Taylor's careful work was not quite finished when the little ship was put on display for the Society's launch in June 1990, in true *Swallows and Amazons* style, to the sound of cannon fire and the raising of a flag. Captain Flint's houseboat was moored to the nearby pier, complete with green parrot (which stoutly refused to utter 'Pieces of eight') and a victim to walk the plank. The jamboree ended with rockets sent high into the night sky. More than two hundred fans had converged on Windermere from as far afield as France, Japan, Canada, the United States, as well as all parts of Britain.

Those who could squeeze into the museum's lecture theatre for the inauguration were welcomed by the Society's President, Brigit Sanders, self-styled 'Ship's Granny', and took part in electing Ransome's one-time neighbour, Dick Kelsall, as the first Secretary. Later, after everyone had gathered in the main exhibition hall, Brigit presented to the Ransome Room of the Abbot Hall Museum a pair of red leather 'Yemini' slippers, similar to those her family had given to Ransome for his birthday in 1929. In the re-naming ceremony young Katy Jennings, representing the latest and youngest generation of Ransome fans, swung the bottle of grog and Brigit declared at the crash of breaking glass, 'I name you *Amazon*. May you inspire with the spirit of adventure all those who visit you.'

It was not until in 1993 that *Mavis-Amazon* took out her first party of Arthur Ransome Society members. Those who sailed her soon agreed with Richard Pierce's assessment, and wisely decided never to sail if there was a chance of encountering broken water. In 1997 it was finally agreed that the regular 'taking up', and subsequent drying out in the Steamboat Museum exhibition hall should end, and *Mavis-Amazon* should remain indoors. Since the Windermere Steamboat Museum closed, she has found a new and appropriate home in The Ruskin Museum in Coniston, just across the water from the boatshed in which she spent so many years. Hopefully, it will not be too long before the Altounyan's *Mavis-Amazon* will be cheek by jowl with Donald Campbell's salvaged *Bluebird*.

* * * * *

Coch-y-bonddhu's tanned sail was a familiar sight on Coniston Water during the war years, but when the Ransomes moved south again she was laid up. Even after they returned to London in 1950, Ransome hesitated to part with the dinghy he had owned for fifteen years. Yet finally, in the mid-1950s, *Cocky* was acquired by John Barnes, the Head of a school at Arnside, from Shepherd's of Windermere. He was under the impression she was the *Swallow* and bought the little boat for his twelve-year-old son Edward to sail. *Swallow* — as they continued to call her — was also used for school sailing lessons.

The Barnes family has another link with Ransome, for Edward's sister, Helen Caldwell, lives at Low Ludderburn. Barnes told me that they found *Cocky-Swallow* was rather heavily built for her size — exactly what the young Russells had found when they had the use of her. Eventually, when

John Barnes retired and Edward left home, the dinghy was sold. The little boat moved north to Scotland and was bought by Jeff Parker-Eaton who kept her at Henderson's Boatyard in Mallaig.

In early 1992, the Arthur Ransome Society Scottish Regional Chairman, Dr Chris Birt visited the yard and discovered that *Cocky* had been sold to a hotel beside a loch to enable guests to fish. Having spent many happy hours afloat while he fished from *Cocky*, even managing to fish for char under sail, Ransome would have been delighted! Mr Henderson sent Dr Birt to a couple living at Glenfinnan. It turned out that they knew *Cocky* well, and at one time had tried to buy her. They directed Dr Birt to the hotel beside Loch Sunart where they thought she was still to be found. Shortly afterwards, Dr Birt telephoned me from the hotel to confirm the boat's identity, running between phone and boat to check details. I was as thrilled as Chris Birt to be able to make a positive identification for once.

Cocky was by that time in a very poor state, having lain under a tree for many years, although the mast and sail had been stored under cover and were in a much better condition. The owners of the Kilcamb Lodge Hotel, Gordon and Peter Blakeway donated *Cocky* to the Arthur Ransome Society.

Newly restored *Coch-y-bonddhu* on Loch Sunart 1996

Coch-y-bonddhu alondside the quay at the Bristol Festival of the Sea, 1996

Having sought expert advice on the feasibility of a complete restoration, the Scottish Region launched an appeal for £4,000. Three years later with the restoration complete, Josephine Russell travelled north to Strontian in Argyll to perform the relaunching ceremony, and be reunited with the boat that she had last sailed more than 50 years earlier on the River Orwell. The hull that had looked so sad three years previously, now gleamed a golden-brown under layers of new varnish. During that time, much had been accomplished at John Hodgson's boatyard in Fianary at Mull Sound: a new transom and stern post had been fitted, and she had been completely re-timbered with good Lake District oak, before being sheathed in epoxy. Her new red sail had been made by Jeckalls of Wroxham. Many Ransome enthusiasts had gathered for the occasion, and *Cocky* made six trips across the loch so that everyone could have a sail.

Cocky spent some years based at the Windermere Steamboat Museum, where from time to time she left the exhibition hall to sail on the lake. She took part in the Bristol Festival of the Sea in 1996 and at the recent Arthur Ransome exhibition at the National Maritime Museum in Falmouth. The Nancy Blackett Trust arranged for *Cocky* to travel south on three occasions, in order to take part in The Old Gaffers Association's annual *Swallows and Amazons* race around Horsey Island.

With the closure of the Steamboat Museum, *Cocky* has found a temporary home at St Anne's School in Windermere in the Dining Hall. She was in the hall for a considerable time without being soaked in the water to 'take up'. Unfortunately when she was launched at Pin Mill this summer *Cocky* sank,apparently having opened up in the centrally heated school in the manner of all wooden boats that spend too long in warm dry conditions, in spite of the epoxy sheathing.

* * * * *

Reginald Russell sailed *Nancy Blackett* until 1952 when she passed to Francis Knight and his wife who kept her in the Walton Backwaters, but visited Holland several times during the five years that she was in his possession. Another Ransome enthusiast, Commander MacIntyre was her next owner, and he and his young family had a lot of fun during one holiday when they re-enacted the story of *Secret Water*. When he was posted to Bonn in 1960, *Nancy* changed hands again. Her new skipper was George Batters who kept her at Scarborough for five years before parting with her to William Bentley.

By 1988 the *Nancy Blackett* lay mid-way along the east pier of Scarborough outer harbour. She had lain there for years, slowly disintegrating, as old wooden boats do, and continually rubbing against the side of the pier as she rose and fell with the tide. In the great storm of October 1987 a car which had been parked on the pier above was swept off and fell on her. It was the final indignity.

That spring, the Scarborough Harbour Committee received a report from the harbour master, Captain Arthur Miller that the pleasure boat *Nancy Blackett* had deteriorated to such an extent that she constituted a hazard to other vessels. Captain Miller told the committee that for some time he had been concerned about her condition, and although she had once been taken out for repairs, these had not been sufficient. Something had to be done urgently.

The harbour authorities had been at loggerheads with William Bentley, Nancy's owner, over non-payment of harbour dues for some time, and things had deteriated to such an extent that messages had to be passed

Nancy Blackett rotting away beside the harbour wall at Scarborough

to Bentley via a neighbour. Bentley claimed he had been withholding payment as he held the authorities responsible for Nancy's condition, blaming their neglect of the pier wall for the holing of the hull.

For the previous ten years *Nancy* had rarely left her berth, and then only for short trips, it was almost as if her owner had lost interest. Captain Miller thought the hull could still be taken away in one piece, and so the committee authorised *Nancy's* removal while they pursued her future with the Arthur Ransome Society. There did not seem to be much future left, for, unknown to them, no such society existed to take an interest in her at that time. The only other suggestion forthcoming was to place what remained of the boat on the town's Marine Drive where one of the councillors thought she could be planted out with spring annuals.

Of course it was an unthinkable humiliation. No one familiar with the adventures of the *Swallows and Amazons* would have dared — or wished — to consign a vessel bearing the name of their undisputed leader, Captain Nancy Blackett, terror of the seas, ending her days as a municipal flowerpot. Had the feminist writer Sara Maitland known of such ignominy, she would no doubt have led a ferocious uprising among the legions who, for more than fifty years, have seen in Nancy their most cherished dreams fulfilled. In February 1990 Maitland acknowledged her own debt to Arthur Ransome in an article in the *Independent Magazine* He had done her 'the magnificent favour', she wrote, of conjuring up 'by some inexplicable alchemy' her one and only 'hero', a childhood role model 'who transcended the restriction of femininity without succumbing to the lure of male-identification'. Nancy was a 'hero who had all the characteristics necessary for the job; who lived between the countries of the material and the imaginary and helped me to live in both'.

There is simply no question: it is Nancy who survives, intrepid, indefatigable, only her equally formidable Great Aunt Maria daring to use her real name, Ruth, while the rest of the community lives in dread of her exploits. Even her doctor is bound to admit, 'Nancy doesn't grow safer with age.' Nor, it would seem, did the sea-going cutter that Ransome named after her — and there are no marks for guessing that rescue was at hand.

Unknown to the committee, a former Scarborough man knew of *Nancy's* plight and was planning to restore the yacht to its former glory. Down the coast in Pin Mill, in the Butt and Oyster Inn where they still remembered Arthur Ransome, there had been talk of bringing his favourite little ship home. The landlord, Dick Mainwaring, assured me that it was no mere rumour. The rescue operation was the brain-child of Michael Rines, who by the first of several strange coincidences that linked him to *Nancy Blackett*, lived on the other side of the river no further than a good arrow's flight from Broke Farm, Ransome's home during the years he had owned the *Nancy Blackett.*

Rines, it turned out when I made contact with him, had known and admired the cutter for twenty years. He knew nothing of her history and was not influenced at that time by Ransome's storytelling; indeed he not read any of his books. He had merely thought of Nancy as the most handsome little craft to ply the waters of his childhood home in the north and had been surprised to find how celebrated she was after he had moved to the Stour and Orwell estuary. Some years before he had seen Bentley aboard and ventured to ask him if he could be parted from *Nancy* for a price, but Bentley had assured him that she was not for sale.

It was quite by chance that Rines mentioned the little ship to his secretary, Clico MacIntyre, whose father had once owned the boat, to learn that as a child she had sailed in her on the North Sea and to the Baltic. Here was another of those compelling coincidences that sought to link Rines with Ransome and the fate of *Nancy Blackett.* Rines told me that when he had last seen *Nancy* she was in a very poor state. All her hatches were missing and she was completely open to the weather and lying on her side in the middle of the harbour. The boat was more or less stripped out inside, he said.

With that our first telephone conversation came to at abrupt end. It was not a faulty line, nor due to haste on my part. A swallow, almost symbolically, had flown into the room where Michael Rines was speaking! In due course, Rines decided to make a more formal approach to Bentley, saying that, should he ever be prepared to sell, he would love to bring *Nancy* back to Pin Mill and her old haunts. In reply Eunice Bentley wrote him that her husband had been unwell and that after a series of mishaps was unable now to cope with the boat. He had turned down many enquiries over the years but was impressed by the letter from Rines. He would be willing to discuss details. Negotiation of the purchase was not without its sticking points. *Nancy* was not going to be relinquished on a nod. The price, Rines insisted, had to take into account the likely cost of restoration. He approached Scarborough Marine Engineers for some rough figures and was quoted between £3,000 and £4,000. Encouraged by this, Rines had *Nancy* lifted out of the water at his own expense for an examination. When the silt had been hosed out, it became clear that the dilapidation was more extensive than had been suspected. The most serious damage had occurred when someone had released the lines holding her against the pier and she had fallen over, breaking more than twenty ribs and three frames, the repair of which would be a difficult and time-consuming business. The estimate rose to more than £7000.

By this time Rines had become a Ransome enthusiast and, after reading *We Didn't Mean to Go to Sea,* he was fired by the idea of recreating the *Goblin's* historic voyage to Holland with a child crew. He told Bentley that the new costing was a terrible blow but he was sure a way could be found to save the stricken yacht. Finally, in June 1988, it was agreed that he would buy her for £3,000. Should the cost of repairs prove to be less than the estimate (that Bentley disputed), then Bentley would receive the difference.

Nancy had been in Bentley's possession far longer than any of her previous owners. He saw no reason why she should be thought of as Arthur Ransome's old boat; Ransome had owned her for a mere three of her fifty-odd years. She had remained Bentley's for a good twenty years longer. He had became impatient with people who were interested only in that brief period in her life, and had even sent away an elderly cleric with a flea in his ear for enquiring if she was Ransome's old boat.

Nancy was moved to Fox's yard in Ipswich where she stood in a metal cradle. Her new skipper managed to find a local shipwright, Stan Ball, who spent that winter working on the stricken vessel. Stan, a seventy-year-old veteran of Dunkirk, was an expert on wooden hulls, and he removed all the interior woodwork and replaced one-eighth of the pitch-pine planking, twenty-six ribs, four frames and part of the transom. He also renewed a good deal of the deck planking.

I first met Mike Rines on my second visit to see the work in progress, and when he showed me the ship's papers. I noticed that he was the ninth owner. He had already begun a collection of photographs of the vessel at various stages of her career to assist with the restoration. He also showed me what appeared to be a small tea towel. It was a chart of the Walton Backwaters, like that in the *Cruising Association Handbook,* which he had found when the cabin was stripped of all the woodwork, and was old enough to been used by Ransome himself on his visits to the peaceful ,Kirby Creek at the time when he was using the region as a setting for *Secret Water.* The resemblance to Ransome's maps in the book is almost uncanny. I saw that the 'Blackett' nameboard was missing from the transom and the one bearing the name 'Nancy' was not original so, as a small contribution to her restoration, I carved a new pair like those that I believed she carried in Ransome's day. The skipper told me he hoped to have *Nancy* ready for the East Coast Boat Show in Ipswich the following May, though before then the task facing him was formidable, and he was still trying to attract sponsorship to help defray some of the considerable cost. Help was forthcoming: Fox's allowed *Nancy* to stand in their yard without charge and gave discount on materials bought from their

Nancy Blackett at Fox's Marina, Ipswich — Winter 1988

chandlery. International Paints made no charge for their provision and Black and Decker gave whatever power tools were required. Thornycroft (makers) and ARS Marine (distributors) waived their profit on a new 20 horsepower 3-cylinder engine. *Nancy* might have been saved from the Scarborough knackers but that was only the beginning of a tremendous effort to secure her future.

To mark *Nancy's* appearance at the East Coast Boat Show in May, Mike Rines organised a celebration dinner at the Butt and Oyster in Pin Mill. On the opening day, *Nancy* looked magnificent: her brightwork sparkled and the shining white topsides and red anti-fouling might have been on a new boat. I found it hard to remember how old and neglected she had looked six months earlier. On board, Stan Ball showed how he was piecing together all the internal woodwork like a three-dimensional jigsaw puzzle.

I found the special guests — Taqui Stephens, Susie and Brigit Sanders — at Alma Cottage where they were staying at the invitation of Ron and Hetty Watts. It had been arranged that these 'originals' should lodge just as their fictional selves had in *We Didn't Mean to Go to Sea*: 'Last they had slept for the first time at Alma Cottage, and morning had waked for the first time to look out through Miss Powell's climbing roses at this happy place where almost everybody wore sea-boots, and land, in comparison with water, seemed hardly to matter at all.' The three sisters had been given VIP treatment earlier in the day at the opening of the Show and then had been taken on a tour down river to visit Ransome's old home.

The dining room at the Butt and Oyster, with its paintings, its model barges, and the river lapping at the windows overlooking the hard, was a perfect setting for such a gathering. Our host had managed to bring together most of those still alive who had sailed with Ransome and knew from experience of his love of life afloat. Others, like myself had come to know Pin Mill first through his writings. I felt sure that Ransome would have approved of our celebration, for he had thrown a party in that same room fifty years earlier; to mark the launch of *Selina King, Nancy Blackett's* replacement.

During the meal I was fascinated to hear Taqui Altounyan swapping Ransome anecdotes with Josephine Russell. Taqui remembered Ransome had long ago watched her first attempts at learning to sail on Coniston Water.

'He was very particular that we should sail in a proper manner,' she told me, 'and didn't like to see us trailing our hands in the water. Anything like that he called 'behaving like a tripper'.

The *Nancy Blackett* may have looked nearly finished, but there was still much more to be done than was apparent. The first problem was to remove the keel and draw the corroded keel bolts. The next major job was the removal of the propellor shaft tube and bearing, and building new mountings for the new diesel engine.

Completely fitting out the interior took an enormous amount of work. The cockpit had to be almost entirely rebuilt. In all this, Rines relied heavily on *We Didn't Mean to Go to Sea*, going to endless lengths to ensure that everything was exactly as Ransome had it. There is a vintage two-burner paraffin stove and an old white sink in the galley. The new engine was fitted slightly further forward, so that there was no room for the cupboard shown beneath the cooker in Ransome's drawing. Otherwise everything was made as authentic as possible. An old compass has been mounted inside the bulkhead, and in the cabin are the blue mattresses and red cushions, enamel teapot and jugs and red plastic cups and saucers, just as there are in the story. The original paraffin cabin lights, clock and barometer were all refitted. The atmosphere within was strongly evocative of the 1930s — a tribute to the care Rines has put into an enterprise that has gone much further than mere restoration.

The actual colour of the sails provided a real headache: *We Didn't Mean to Go to Sea* mentions red and crimson sails, yet in his letter to Taqui Altounyan Ransome speaks of having the sails tanned. Eventually it was decided to have Nancy's new sails tanned, after they had been made. The rigging has been based on Ransome's drawings and contemporary photographs using traditional galvanised wire with splices and modern synthetic running rigging that looks exactly like the old stuff. The mainsail was set on hoops up to the cross-trees — though it would be very difficult now to climb to the cross-trees as John did.

The original navigation lights were re-fitted but, because these did not comply with current collision regulations, modern lights sat unobtrusively beside them. Other required lights had also been fitted, as well as a VHF transmitter and an echo sounder, but these can easily be dismounted for exhibition purposes.

In May 1990, having spent some £35,000, Mike Rines finally took *Nancy* to sea, with the wind gusting to Force 6 or more. She behaved beautifully, pointing much higher into the wind than anticipated. Soon *Nancy Blackett* was sailing to her old haunts in Hamford Water, and down to Brightlingsea, where she was given a real hammering and proved to be so well balanced that her skipper could let go of the tiller and allow the ship to sail herself

It was enough to make anybody happy, just to be afloat and sailing, to see the green shores racing past, to see the bubbling wake slipping away astern, to see all the sails drawing, to hear now and then a gentle,

low thrumming in the shrouds, to see the sunlight sparkle in the spray
thrown out to leeward by the bows of the little schooner.
'I wish this was going on for ever,' said Titty.

His mammoth work of restoration complete, Mike Rines only sailed
Nancy for a season, and he never managed that North Sea crossing with
a crew of children. His other notable trip was to take *Nancy* to Snape
sailing backwards part of the way! Anchored overnight at Orford and
finding the wind too strong to attempt to cross the bar, but not wanting
to remain where he was, Rines decided to take *Nancy* up river instead.
After Aldburgh, the channel is narrow and winding and it is not always
easy to spot the marks. Half a mile from Snape, *Nancy* went aground. Her
skipper soon had her afloat again, but the wind spun her round as she
came off. Without room to turn, Rines tried to make his way upstream
stern first. *Nancy's*
transom stern made the
exercise a tricky one and
she went aground again.
Again the wind spun her
round, but this time she
was heading for Snape,
and the trip was
completed without
further incident.

By the time that
Harbour Marine Services
of Southwold showed
the *Nancy Blackett* at
the 1992 International
Wooden Boat Show at
The National Maritime
Museum at Greenwhich,
she had changed hand
once mores. Her new
owner, Colin Winter had
continued with the
restoration work, and
that same year he lent
her to some enthusiasts
in the Arthur Ransome
Society to race against
Peter Duck.

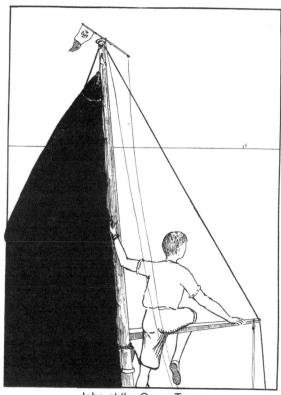

John at the Cross-Trees
(from *We Didnt Mean to Go to Sea*)

In 1996 *Nancy* was for sale again. And once again one man's inspired vision was to have far-reaching consequences. Peter Willis, an Arthur Ransome Society member, launched an appeal to buy the vessel. The 'Mayday' appeal was successful beyond all expectations, and a year later £30,000 had been raised through contributions from all parts of the world, and the following June the *Nancy Blackett* was under new ownership when she appeared at the Sail Ipswich festival. The original steering committee became the Nancy Blackett Trust and they quickly achieved charitable status. As Peter Willis wrote at the time, buying *Nancy* was only the 'beginning of the great adventure'.

Maintaining and operating the *Nancy Blackett* was to prove an enormous undertaking, but there is nothing like a common objective to bind a group of enthusiasts together, and the story of the NBT is one of steady achievement. The following year *Nancy* made her first appearance at the Portsmount International Festival of the Sea when it was estimated that more than 800 visitors went aboard. In 1999 *Nancy* and *Cocky* were

Nancy Blackett at the Wooden Boat Show held at
the National Maritime Museum 1992

reunited for the 'Old Gaffers' race in the Walton Backwaters. That year saw the death of the Trust's Patron, Brigit Sanders. In 2000 the solo global circumnavigator, Dame Ellen MacArthur who had been inspired to take up sailing by reading the *Swallows and Amazons* books, became the new Patron.

I was very pleased to join the dinner guests at the Butt and Oyster in 2001 when we well and truly celebrated *Nancy's* 70th birthday. Later in the year *Nancy*

Dame Ellen Macarthur, Patron of the Nancy Blackett Trust in *Nancy's* cabin

Nancy Blackett at Flushing 2002

was at Portsmouth once more for another International Festival of the Sea. In 2002 *Nancy* returned to Flushing and the trip was repeated the following year with a child crew (and a couple of grown-ups).

The land, seen through the portholes, was coming nearer, no longer a wavy yellow line along the edge of the sea, but a real land, houses, spires, a beach, and windmills. The motion of the *Goblin* was getting easier. Roger and Titty knelt on the bunks to look out, but it was hard to thump the floor while kneeling on a bunk, and harder still to play the penny whistle.

'It's Holland all right,' said Roger ...

In 2004 a couple of dozen youngster from Thetford Grammar School were taken on short trips, and these school trips have increased in the years that followed. *Nancy* has continued to be based on the East Coast, and once again, has become a familiar sight in the Walton Backwaters. In 2005 *Nancy* was at the International Festival of the Sea once more, to mark the bicenttenery of Trafalgar and then she took part in the Fleet Review in the Solent. In 2008 *Nancy* sailed west for the Swallows and Amazons exhibition in Falmouth and last year joined the first London Classic boat rally at St Katherine's Dock.

* * * * *

Selina King came through the war unscathed, safe in her shed at Oulton Broad, but Ransome's doctor thought she would be too much for him to handle. Reluctantly he agreed.

On February 20th 1946 Ransome visited *Selina King* and found that the keel and garboards had dried out. A month later *Selina* was sold for rather less than she was worth.

Ransome put the boat on the market at £1,800, £700 below the figure suggested by his broker Maurice Barton. When Peter Davies offered £1,600 Barton advised Ransome not to accept less than the asking price. Ransome, however, was anxious to complete the deal so that *Great Northern?* could have his undivided attention, and accepted the offer.

Davies did not keep *Selina* long, although she remained on the East Coast for several more years before moving to the South of England. In 1962, a taxi driver called Hal White was living in Southampton in East Bermuda. He had a number of regular customers and to these he would rattle away about the boats he would like to own and the voyages that he wished he could make. A couple visiting the area hired White several times, and at the end of one visit asked him how much he thought he would need to buy the boat of his dreams. White did not know, but he scoured the columns in the yachting magazines and he saw *Selina King* advertised for sale. It was simply a case of love at first sight. He showed his friends the photograph of *Selina* and before returning to the airport they loaned him the money and told him to go and to buy his dream ship, and casually remarked, 'Just pay us back when you get around to it.'

Selina King was still on the South Coast of England, but White crossed the Atlantic to complete the deal with *Selina King's* owner, Commander Blewett. The asking price was more than double that which Ransome had accepted 16 years earlier. White was still perilously short of funds, and on arrival had difficulty in paying the delivery crew. Eventually he sold the cab and began to charter *Selina King* on a full time basis and for the next nine years he cruised among Bermudian waters and across to the USA. During that time *Selina* weathered two hurricanes and had gained the reputation of being a fast little boat. Eventually, White found he needed a larger yacht to sail the Caribbean and he regretfully parted with her. The next part of her career is shrouded in mystery. There has been a suggestion that she was engaged in drug smuggling, but White assured me that the small quantity of grass found aboard on one occasion, really was for the personal use of the owner.

By the age of 70 White felt the time had come to find a smaller craft and in the mid-1990s his thoughts once more turned to *Selina King*. White had heard, as I had done, that the vessel was somewhere on the Eastern Seaboard of the USA. Eventually, by dint of hard work and a little luck, he heard a rumour that she had been seen in Coconut Grove, Miaimi.

When White finally traced the owner he found that *Selina* had just been sold. White still persisted in his hunt, and then a mate of his located the hull and tried to warn him off, saying that vessel was now a liability, The hull leaked so badly that only regular pumping kept her afloat. It was a familiar story of the effects of neglect of a wooden boat, *Selina* had not been touched for several years. The mast was broken, much of the inside woodwork was rotten and the hull was slowly coming apart.

Encouraged by his wife, Ruth, White was not put off by the tale of doom and gloom, or the enormity of the task ahead, and he flew to Florida and bought the yacht for the second time. Her owner had fallen in love with the yacht and was happy to part with her once that he had been convinced that White had the means and the desire to restore *Selina King*. I heard from White from time to time as he set about his great restoration project, in order to realise his dream of returning to Bermuda which he duly accomplished in 1998.

Then, early in 2008, came the news that White was looking to part with *Selina King* once more. Enthusiasts were agreed that it

Captain White

SELINA KING

36ft. Sailing Cutter

Sailed the Atlantic from England

CRUISE THROUGH
THE ISLANDS
Yes! Bring the Kids!

Live-aboard accommodations for four

Swim — Picnic. Sailing Instructions for the asking name it we try and do it.

1 to 8 people	Over 8
Half day £8-17s. or $25	£1-1-3 or $3.00
Full day £15-19s. or $45	extra per person

Reservations call Hal White: Home 1-5559 after 6 p.m. or 1-3093 during day.

Selina King ready to sail once more 1998

would be fitting if she could finish her days in home waters. There was talk of the NBT operating the vessel alongside *Nancy Blackett*. The question of an Atlantic crossing by an old yacht in doubtful condition, to say nothing of the additional burden of operation and maintainance might well prove to be one challange too many, and the NBT wisely gave up the idea. Eventually Hal White sold her to a Canadian, Monty Lamontagne, in October 2008. Monty, a shipwright, currently lives in Bermuda and planned to do so for about three years, after which he intends to take *Selina King* through the Panama Canal and up to Vancouver Island.

* * * * *

Yet another *Swallow* turned up one evening in the autumn of 1989 when Brigit Sanders phoned me with news of a man who claimed that his friend owned *Swallow*.

'Are you interested in looking into it?' she asked me. I most certainly was, and the following weekend I called on Nick Imber at his home in Letchworth. There, upside-down on the lawn, was a 10-foot white-painted clinker dinghy.

'She was bought by my father from Clark and Carter at West Mersea in the early 1950s for twenty-five pounds,' Imber told me. 'At that time she still had Ransome's oars with the letters A. R. inscribed with copper tacks.'

It was quite clear that this was not the original *Swallow*, but the dinghy Harry King had built for Ransome in 1938. I was later able to confirm the identification by means of a photograph of *Selina King* towing *Swallow*.

As we turned the boat over it was evident she had been damaged at some time and was now very frail. I was told how she had been pinched between a pair of lock gates on the River Lea seven years earlier. Since then it had not been possible to keep the hull watertight, and for several years she had been laid up in the garden. Nick Imber had learned to sail in her, and he in turn had taught his wife and daughter Clare. The Imbers used *Swallow* as a tender to their 29-foot barge yacht *Nan*, which they kept on the East Coast. When the original dagger plate case began to leak, they replaced it with a metal one. Apart from painting the dinghy when the varnish became unattractive, the Imbers kept the little boat just as it had been when belonging to Ransome.

I took measurements and photographs so that if the worst were to happen, at least *Swallow* could sail on in model form. I said that should the time come when they felt there was nothing to be done except build a funeral pyre, I should love the opportunity to try to save the hull. After consulting his father, Nick told me that the family would be very pleased to let me have her. The handing over took place in May 1990 at a Ransome Rally in Pin Mill organised by *Yachting Monthly* to celebrate the sixtieth anniversary of the publication of *Swallows and Amazons*.

Swallow was set up on the hard and Sam King (Harry King's son) was able to identify her as one that he had built by the double knees and the moulding on the inwale. Meanwhile *Nancy Blackett* and *Peter Duck* were sailing in company and their tanned sails matched *Swallow's*, forming a visual link between the three vessels. Three generations of the Imber family had come to see *Swallow* off, and we carefully carried her on to my trailer.

Once the little boat was safely installed in my garage it was possible to examine the hull. The keel was hogged. In fact it had broken at both ends of the slot for the dagger plate. The transom was rotten and would need replacing. Much of the planking was sound, but the sheer strakes had gone and the planks at the turn of the bilge had cracked and pulled apart in the accident with the lock gates.

I was confident that I could repair the hull so that *Swallow* appeared sound, but feared that if I attempted to restore her by traditional methods to a condition in which she could sail again, there would not be very much of the original timber left.

I sought advice from various restorers and boatbuilders, and although helpful, they were far from being in agreement. Eventually, I decided to complete as much of the repair as possible using copper nails and roves

Swallow on display at the National Maritime Museum, Greenwich 1992

and fastening with eposxy resin where it was not. In this way, I hoped I could keep much of the original timber and still have a hull sound enough to take part in Arthur Ransome Society events.

I removed the rusty old dagger plate case and as much internal woodwork as possible. The three pieces of the keel came away easily enough and I made a new oak keel which I scarfed on to the undamaged deadwood. The stern knee had to be refastened and glued in place before I was able to remove the transom and use it as a pattern for a mahogany replacement. The sound planks were refastened to the transom using epoxy as the plank ends were not in good condition. With the damaged plank removed from the port side I put a mould into the hull so that I could pull the planking back into shape when I put in the new one and fitted new sheer strakes. I made a new wooden dagger board case and, finally, I replaced some of the timbers with new elm ones, immersed in hot water and bent round a former before fitting. Then I began the laborious task of removing the paint in order that the resin would be applied to bare wood, before I set about putting three coats of epoxy resin to the exterior and two to the interior.

Ted Alexander takes *Swallow* for her first sail after restoration

I had been at work for almost a year at the time of the first AGM of the Arthur Ransome Society's first AGM. The boat appeared sound, but still unfinished when we pulled up outside Alma Cottage for the relaunch. On the long journey from the south I wondered what the members would think if she were to sink in full view of the assembled gathering on shore. Having arrived, I pushed such thoughts aside, and putting two young members from the Society aboard, allowed *Swallow* to float off at the end of a long painter. Suddenly, I felt everyone relax and I became aware of the clicking of cameras. I was only sorry that Sam King had not lived to join the celebration.

In the weeks that followed, the work went on. The sail had survived, but was no longer fit for use. It carried the barely decipherable name of Jeckells of Wroxham. I sent the sail to them to make a copy, but it turned out that there was no need, as they still had its measurements on file from 1938!

Before the end of the summer we launched *Swallow* at Bosham in Chichester Harbour. Ted Alexander and a young Ransome Society member, Edward Purser, took the newly restored dinghy for her first sail. As soon as it could be arranged, the Imbers were invited to Frensham Pond to see the restoration and to sail *Swallow* themselves once more.

The following year *Swallow* joined the *Nancy Blackett* at the International Wooden Boat Show at the National Maritime Museum in Greenwhich, and in 1997 she was moored alongside *Coch-y-bonddhu* at the International Festival of the Sea at Bristol. In 2008 she was reunited with *Cocky* at Falmouth for the special Ransome display at the National Maritime Museum.

In recent years *Swallow* has been sailed by Paul Crisp, who has taken her back to old haunts in Hamford Water and sailed her on the Thames. Her litle tanned sail has become a familiar sight around Salcome harbour each August, for the family holiday.

* * * * *

Peter Duck was bought from Ransome by Philip Hayleman, an agricultural engineer, for £1,692. When, after a couple of years, he parted with her in 1951, she was acquired by Dr O'Brien of Great Ormond Street Hospital, who kept her until 1957. She passed to George and June Jones, who had lent Ransome *Barnacle Goose* when he was considering buying *Lottie Blossom*. George Jones was a marine artist who owned the East Coast Yacht Agency and his family kept *Peter Duck* for twenty-five years until after his death.

At the time they first started sailing they took their young children and found the doghouse ideal for them in bad weather. After taking *Peter Duck* to Holland, they sailed her up the River Thames to St Catherine's Dock, where the operators on Tower Bridge thought they wanted to pass under and raised the bridge for them.

Ransome's desk was gone, so the Joneses fitted a quarter berth on the port side. They thought it a very pleasant cabin, with its 'cathedral crossing' under the tabernacle, in which they hung a lamp.

Peter Duck at Nylands Yacht Club, Riga

In 1960 there was still a demand for easily-handled and comfortable wooden yachts and so the *Peter Duck* class came into being. Laurent Giles made one or two modifications to the original design, including raising the topsides to give extra headroom in the cabin (something that Ransome would have thoroughly approved). In all, 39 members of the class were constructed by the Wroxham firm of Porter and Haylett during the following ten years, by which time the demand for wooden boats was drying up.

In 1984 Richard Payne bought *Peter Duck*. He kept her for three years until Greg and Ann Palmer took her over late in 1987.

I visited *Peter Duck* when she was on a mud berth at Woodbridge at the end of the 1990 season. Ann Palmer showed me the replacement bunk cushions which had fluted covers to match the originals that she had made. The cushion backs that had been fitted in 1946 were considerably thicker than Laurent Giles's drawing, and we sympathised with Ransome sleeping on the narrow and slippery bunks. Greg Palmer has replaced them with wooden boards which can do duty as bunk-boards if required. In this way the bunks have been made a comfortable width. We wondered why Ransome had not had the backs removed himself. I sat in the middle of the bunk with some care (being 3 inches taller than Ransome, I had

Peter Duck in Helsinki Harbour 1970s

expected trouble with the beams) but found I could sit between them without difficulty. The doghouse, giving standing headroom at the galley, is a convenient feature of the saloon which, as I expected, is very well arranged and pleasant. *Peter Duck* was in first-class condition and looked very smart with her pale green topsides and dark green bulwarks.

In 1990 *Peter Duck* had sailed more than 500 miles exploring Ransome's old haunts from her base at Woodbridge. The Palmer's favourite anchorage was Kirby Creek where, Greg told me, he liked nothing better than sitting in the cockpit at that peaceful spot, listening to the birds and knowing Arthur Ransome had enjoyed it too.

The following year Greg Palmer and his son Ned made their epic voyage round Britain. In 1993 *Peter Duck* sailed to the Baltic visiting Ransome's old ports of call — Riga, Runö, Werder through the Nukke Channel to Baltic Port (now Paldiski), Lehepe Bay, Reval (now Tallin) and finally to Helsinki and returned via the Frisian Islands.

In 1994 *Peter Duck* defeated *Nancy Blackett* in their race from Pin Mill down river to Shotley Spit and up the Stour and back. Later that year, when the Palmers joined the *Shtandart* project in St Petersburg, *Peter Duck* crossed the Baltic once more and entered Russia. The *Shtandart* was the 1703 frigate of Peter the Great, and Palmer threw himself into the reconstruction with great enthusiasm until his untimely death in 1997.

The following year *Peter Duck* returned to England in time to take part in the International Festival of the Sea at Portsmouth. By this time, four harsh Baltic winters had seriously damaged the hull, and only regular pumping was keeping her afloat. She was laid up at Woodbridge where she was visited by Ned and Julia Jones, who had loved her as children growing up. Julia and her partner, Francis Wheen were unable to resist the appeal of *Peter Duck* and they bought her from Ann Palmer in 1999. Today, she is a family boat once more, and their children have become the third generation of the Jones family to come to love 'the dear old Duck'.

✷ ✷ ✷ ✷ ✷

Sir Paul Mallinson only sailed *Ragged Robin III* (ex *Lottie Blossom*) for a year or two. When Anthony Rushworth-Lund bought the yacht he found her in 'beautiful condition' and concluded that she had been not been taken out a great deal. In his book *By Way of the Golden Isles*, Rushworth-Lund tells the story of his family's trip through the inland waterways of France to Marseilles and across the Mediterranean to Corsica. After five years cruising in the Mediterranean, *Ragged Robin* returned home, having survived a mistral in the Mediterranean, and being forced to run for shelter from strong winds in the Bay of Biscay.

Ragged Robin III at Southwold

Ragged Robin with Bowsprit as she is today

Surprisingly, Rushworth-Lund makes no mention of Ransome in the book that was published in 1963, and shortly afterwards they parted with *Ragged Robin* in favour of a much larger yacht — a 14-ton *Gauntlet*.

Other owners have been Ransome enthusiasts. Peter St John Howe's love of sailing was, like so many others, inspired by Ransome. He thoroughly tested Ransome's conclusion that the boat was not a single-hander when he sailed 1,000 miles between September 1991 and July 1992 — a feat of which he felt Ransome would thoroughly have approved.

Ragged Robin's current owners, the retired professor of

neuroscience, Ted Evans and his wife, Diana are likewise Ransome fans, and have retraced all Ransome's voyages made aboard the two *Lotties*, as well as following in *Goblin's* wake to Holland and Secret Water. They have owned *Ragged Robin* for eight years, since buying her from Tim Boagey, a sailmaker, who was living aboard at Brightlingsea in Essex. She is still in beautiful condition and her skipper claims to have improved her performance by adding a bowsprit and converting to cutter rig. Ransome might have done the same, had they kept the yacht, for he certainly toyed with the idea and drew a rough sketch of the sail plan.

Ransome's sketch of *Lottie Blossom* rigged as a cutter with a bowsprit

To my eyes, there is something a little incongruous about *Ragged Robin's* appearance these days, with her modern navigational aids and fold-away spray hood and cockpit cover contrasting with the vessel's classic canoe-sterned wooden hull.

* * * * *

When Ransome parted with *Lottie Blossom* in 1954 he had no intention of slipping straight into docile dotage. The following summer they rented a cottage in the Lake District and continued to do so each year until eventually they settled into their final home between Windermere and Coniston overlooking the secluded Rusland valley. Ransome was, after all, a simple countryman who loved books, and was as much at home in the company of river keepers and charcoal burners in the Lake country or the bargemen of East Anglia as he was with his writer and artist cronies at the Garrick Club.

He had already completed more than fifty thousand words of rough draft for the *Autobiography*, which was to occupy him for several years more. Publication was by no means certain and would not, in any event, take place until after his death. 'I may well be forgotten altogether, in which case I should certainly not like to reach from my grave to pluck at people's skirts as they pass.' While working on the *Autobiography* Ransome was also being 'godfather and nanny' to Rupert Hart-Davis's publishing venture, the Mariners Library. He wrote introductions to six of the reprinted classic sailing books and recommended the publication of others. In his appraisal of the Victorian pioneer of solo small-boat cruising — a stockbroker by the name of R. T. McMullen who liked to display his engagingly eccentric views on all manner of subjects while modestly recounting his almost reverential encounters with the art of seamanship — Arthur Ransome perhaps came closest to speaking his own mind.

In his writings, for the first time, yachting ceased to be a sort of social ceremony dependent largely on the presence of spectators, but an affair between man and nature, a series of trials in which the prize to be attained is that a man shall stand well with himself. No winning guns or spectators' smiles matter in the least. In these contests a man is his own judge, and, in secret at least, a strict one.

Bibliography

Works consulted or quoted in this book:

Ted Alexander & Tatiana Verizhnikova, *Ransome in Russia*.
    Portchester Publishing, 2003.
Taqui Altounyan, *Chimes from a Wooden Bell*. I. B. Tauris, 1990.
Taqui Altounyan, *In Aleppo Once*. John Murray, 1969.
John Balchin, *The David Hillyard Story*, John Balchin, 2004.
Hugh Brogan, *The Life of Arthur Ransome*. Jonathan Cape, 1984.
K. Adlard Coles, *Close Hauled*. Seeley, Service & Co., 1926.
K. Adlard Coles, *Creeks and Harbours of the Solent*. Edward
    Arnold, 1933.
K. Adlard Coles, *Sailing Years*. Coles. Granada, 1981.
W.G. Collingwood, *The Lake Counties*. Dent, 1902. (Revised
    edition 1932.)
Francis B. Cooke, *Weekend Yachting*. Edward Arnold, 1933.
Gavin Davies, *'The Peter Duck Class'*, The Boatman, October 1995.
John Dawson, *'Swallows and Amazons'*, Lancashire Life,
    September 1978.
E.A. Ellis, *The Broads*. Collins, 1965.
Uffa Fox, *Thoughts on Yachts and Yachting*. Peter Davies, 1938.
Uffa Fox, *More Joys of Living*. Nautical Publishing, 1972.
Wayne G. Hammond, *Arthur Ransome: A Bibliography*. St Paul's
    Bibliographies, 2000.
H.J. Hanson, *The Cruising Association Handbook*. The Cruising
    Association, 1928.
Richard Hare, *'Ransome's Lottie'*, Classic Boat, October 2004.
Christina Hardyment, *Arthur Ransome and Captain Flint's Trunk*.
    Jonathan Cape, 1984. (Revised and enlarged edition, Francis
    Lincoln Ltd, 2006.)
David and Joan Hay, *East Anglia from the Sea*. Stamford, 1972.
Eric Hiscock, *Cruising Under Sail*. Oxford University Press, 1950.
Eric Holland, *Coniston Copper Mines: A Field Guide*. Cicerone
    Press, 1981.
Eric Holland, *Coniston Copper*. Cicerone Press, 1986.
Peter Hunt, *Approaching Arthur Ransome*. Jonathan Cape, 1992.
John Irving, *Rivers and Creeks of the Thames Estuary*. Captain O.M.
    Watts, 1933.
Rosemary Jones, *'The Story of Selina'*, The Bermudian, June 1997.

E.F. Knight, *Sailing. Bell*, 1889.
E.F. Knight, *The Falcon on the Baltic. With an Introduction by Arthur Ransome.* Rupert Hart-Davis, 195I.
E.F. Knight, *Small-boat Sailing.* John Murray, 1901.
Bernard Levin, *Enthusiasms.* Jonathan Cape, 1983.
R.T. McMullen, *Down Channel. With an Introduction by Arthur Ransome.* Rupert Hart-Davis, 1949.
Sara Maitland, *'My Hero'*, Independent Magazine. February 18th 1989.
Pauline Marshall, *Where it all Began.* Published privately, 1991
Diana Matthews, *Lake Festivals on Windermere.* Windermere Nautical Trust, 1982.
Malcolm Muggeridge, *'A Writer's Ransome'*, Observer Magazine, January 29th 1984.
W.M. Nixon, *'Memorable Racundra'*, Yachting World. April 1982.
George H. Pattinson, *The Great Age of Steam on Windermere.* Windermere Nautical Trust, 1981.
Arthur Ransome, *Pond and Stream.* A. Treherne, 1906.
Arthur Ransome, *Bohemia in London.* Chapman & Hall, 1907
Arthur Ransome, *A History of Story-telling.* T.C. & E.C Jack, 1909.
Arthur Ransome, *Edgar Allan Poe, a critical study.* Martin Secker, 1912.
Arthur Ransome, *Oscar Wilde, a critical study.* Martin Secker, 1912.
Arthur Ransome, *Old Peter's Russian Tales.* T.C. & E.C. Jack, 1916.
Arthur Ransome, *Six Weeks in Russia.* Allen and Unwin, 1919.
Arthur Ransome, *The Soldier and Death.* J.G.Wilson, 1920. Included in *The War of the Birds and the Beasts.* Jonathan Cape, 1984.
Arthur Ransome, *Racundra's First Cruise.* Allan and Unwin, 1923. (Reissued with an Introduction by C. Northcote Parkinson, Century paperback, 1980.)
Arthur Ransome, *Rod and Line.* Jonathan Cape, 1929. (Reisued Oxford University Press paperback, 1980.)
Arthur Ransome, *Swallows and Amazons.* Jonathan Cape, 1930. (Reissued with illustrations by Clifford Webb, Jonathan Cape, 1930.) (Reissued with illustrations by the author, 1938.)
Arthur Ransome, *Swallowdale.* With illustrations by Clifford Webb. Jonathan Cape, 1931. (Reissued with illustrations by the author, 1936.)
Arthur Ransome, *Peter Duck.* Jonathan Cape, 1932.
Arthur Ransome, *Winter Holiday.* Jonathan Cape, 1933.
Arthur Ransome, *Coot Club*, Jonathan Cape, 1934.
Arthur Ransome, *Pigeon Post.* Jonathan Cape, 1936.
Arthur Ransome, *We Didn't Mean to Go to Sea.* Jonathan Cape, 1937
Arthur Ransome, *Secret Water.* Jonathan Cape, 1940.

Arthur Ransome, *The Big Six.* Jonathan Cape, 1940.
Arthur Ransome, *Missee Lee.* Jonathan Cape, 1941.
Arthur Ransome, *The Picts and The Martyrs.* Jonathan Cape, 1943.
Arthur Ransome, *Great Northern?* Jonathan Cape, 1947.
Arthur Ransome, *Mainly About Fishing.* A. & C. Black, 1959.
Arthur Ransome, *The Autobiography of Arthur Ransome.* Edited
   and with Prologue and Epilogue by Rupert Hart-Davis. Jonathan
   Cape, 1976.
Arthur Ransome, *Coots in the North.* Edited and with Introduction by
   Hugh Brogan. Jonathan Cape, 1988.
Arthur Ransome, *Signalling From Mars: The Letters of Arthur
   Ransome.* Edited and introduced by Hugh Brogan. Jonathan
   Cape, 1997.
Arthur Ransome, *Racundra's Third Cruise (Racundra Goes Inland).*
   Fernhurst Books, 2002.
Arthur Ransome, *unpublished sailing logs, diaries, letters, manuscripts,
   drawings and sketchbooks.* The Brotherton Library, University
   of Leeds.
Arthur Ransome, *unpublished draft for his Autobiography,
   manuscripts and sketchbooks.* Abbot Hall Museum and Art Gallery,
   Kendal.
Michael Rines, 'The Life of Nancy Blackett', Classic Boat, May 1991.
Anthony Rushworth-Lund, *By Way of the Golden Isles.* Chapman &
   Hall, 1963.
Hugh Shelley, *Arthur Ransome.* A Bodley Head Monograph. Bodley
   Head, 1960.
Jeremy Swift, *Arthur Ransome on Fishing.* Jonathan Cape, 1994.
Erling Tambs, *The Cruise of the Teddy. With an Introduction by Arthur
   Ransome.* Jonathan Cape, 1933. (Reissued Grafton paperback,
   1989.)
Alfred Wainwright, *The Southern Falls.* Westmorland Gazette, 1960.
Peter Willis, 'Peter Duck after Ransome', Classic Boat, June 2007.
P. G. Wodehouse, *The Luck of the Bodkins.* Herbert Jenkins, 1935.

Norfolk Broads Holidays Afloat. Blakes (Norfolk Broads Holidays) Ltd,
   1947.

Acknowledgements

In the preparation of the text in 1990 I was able to draw I freely on published and unpublished Ransome material and I was most grateful to Arthur Ransome's literary executors, Sir Rupert Hart-Davis and John Bell, for allowing this. Without their generosity my book could not have been written. I was also pleased to acknowledge my debt to Hugh Brogan and Christina Hardyment, who between them did so much to revive interest in Arthur Ransome.

I owe a great debt to Tony Colwell, my editor at Jonathan Cape, who contributed so much enthusiastic support and expert advice throughout the enterprise, and who urged me at some time in the future, to do a revision.

All the sailing logs are stored in the Brotherton Library at the University of Leeds. Here they hold a huge collection of Ransome's letters, written over a period of almost seventy years, including over three hundred to his mother. On the shelves are rows of the thick blue diaries used by Ransome and Evgenia. These stand alongside numerous notebooks, sketchbooks and drafts for all manner of his writings. The builders' plans for *Racundra*, *Selina King*, and *Peter Duck* have survived, and in a large drawer I found about three hundred packets of tiny photographs and negatives, all carefully indexed. The cataloguing of the material has been the work of Ann Farr, whose knowledge and help was invaluable in that as in previous undertakings. John Berry assisted me in sorting through this vast body of material and transcribed copious diary entries for me.

In the Abbot Hall Museum of Lakeland Life and Industry, Kendal, there was a room resembling Ransome's study, containing all manner of books, pictures and artifacts donated by Evgenia. The museum also holds sketchbooks and type-scripts, including some pages of unpublished autobiography. My thanks were due to Vicky Slowe, then the Director, her predecessor, Mary Birkett, and the museum staff for their help in making this collection available to me.

Abbot Hall is also the headquarters of the Arthur Ransome Society and all membership enquiries should be directed there. The Society is 'devoted to the celebration of the life, promotion of the works and diffusion of the ideas of Arthur Ransome'.

Diana Matthews and the staff of Windermere Steamboat Museum were always helpful and I am particularly grateful for their readiness to allow me access to *Mavis* in the early stages of restoration.

I was very appreciative of the help of those who knew Ransome before the Second World War and passed on memories of events which happened as many as sixty years earlier. Reminiscences of *Swallow* and *Amazon* were shared by Taqui Stephens, Susie Villard and Brigit Sanders (all formerly Altounyan), Roger Altounyan, Tadeus Altounyan, John Sanders, and John Berry.

Josephine Russell recalled the days when she and her brother used to crew for Ransome on *Nancy Blackett* and *Selina King*. She gave me photographs taken at that time and lent me her brother George's log, which he kept of two Broadland holidays in company with the Ransomes and the Northern River Pirates. Gillian Beevor (formerly Busk) told me about her father's friendship with Ransome and the origin of *Secret Water*, and Clive Rouse kindly transcribed parts of his father's log where it mentioned Ransome. Jim Clay recalled the time *Firefly* raced *Nancy Blackett* to the Walton Backwaters — and won. Dick and Desmond Kelsall remembered the days when they lived at Barkbooth in the Lake District across the valley from Ransome's home. To all of these I offer my continued thanks, for my book would have been the poorer without their willingness and patience.

All the past and present owners of Ransome's craft were also most helpful: Paget Bowyer, Eunice and Bill Bentley and Michael Rines of *Nancy Blackett*, June Jones, Ann and Greg Palmer of *Peter Duck*, Christopher Barlow of *Lottie Blossom*, John and Edward Barnes of *Coch-y-bonddhu* and 'Bim' and Nick Imber of *Swallow II*.

I was grateful to my researchers in Scarborough, Gwyneth, Derek and Katy Jennings, for their help with 'Salvage' and Captain Arthur Miller for letting me use his photograph of *Nancy Blackett*. I am pleased also to be able to acknowledge the assistance of Dennis Bird, Helen Caldwell, David Carter, Jack Coote, Dennis Cullingford, Sam King, Tony Osler, Richard Rouse, George Southgate, Ron Watts and Raymond Wheatley-Hubbard.

The enthusiasm and interest of Lin Strange at all stages of the preparation helped me through the difficult times. I owed a special debt to the Ross family who became Ransomites almost overnight: Jonathan and Iain helped in the restoration of *Swallow* and their mother Susan offered to make sense of my confusing manuscript and turn it into a properly typed copy, while her husband Richard let himself in for reading the proofs.

In preparing this revision, I am grateful to Arthur Ransome's present literary executor, Christina Hardyment for smiling on the project and for inviting me to dip into the late Tony Colwell's archive.

Ted Evans, the skipper of *Ragged Robin III* (ex *Lottie Blossom*) was most helpful and enthusiastic. Mike Rines, the saviour of the *Nancy Blackett* and Hal White the rescuer of *Selina King*, helped me to bring up to date the story of the craft that had once belonged to Arthur Ransome.

Finally, my warmest thanks to Peter Willis, Chairman of the Nancy Blackett Trust for generously contributing a new foreword, thereby giving this new edition a fitting send-off.